SOUTH AFRICA AND NUCLEAR PROLIFERATION

South Africa and Nuclear Proliferation

South Africa's Nuclear Capabilities and Intentions in the Context of International Non-Proliferation Policies

J. D. L. Moore

St. Martin's Press   New York

First published in the United States of America in 1987

Printed in Great Britain

ISBN 0–312–74698–9

Library of Congress Cataloging-in-Publication Data
Moore, J.D.L. (John Davey Lewis)
South Africa and Nuclear proliferation.
Bibliography: p.
Includes index.
1. Nuclear weapons — South Africa.   2. South
Africa — Military policy.   I. Title.
U264.M66   1987   335.8′25119′0968   86–17693
ISBN 0–312–74698–9

Filmsetting by Vantage Photosetting Co. Ltd
Eastleigh and London

Contents

U
264
.M66
1987

Contents

List of Tables and Figures

Preface

This book examines South Africa's nuclear capabilities and intentions in the context of international non-proliferation policies aimed at preventing the spread of nuclear weapons to more countries. From a brief survey of the human, financial and material resources required to produce a nuclear weapon it is seen that the production of such a weapon is well within South Africa's capabilities. A tentative assessment is made of the number of weapons South Africa could have produced. The means by which South Africa has acquired her nuclear capability and the incentives (and disincentives) the country may have for developing nuclear weapons are discussed.

Although South Africa is arguably one of the nations most isolated and shunned by the international community, Western non-proliferation policies do not seem to have been applied any more rigorously to that country than to other potential 'nth' nuclear weapon states. The book concludes by looking at why this may be so, a major factor being the considerable bargaining strength possessed by South Africa by virtue of being one of the world's major producers of natural uranium and now a producer of enriched uranium. Western non-proliferation policy-makers may have been more concerned to obtain a cooperative attitude on the part of South Africa in her exports of nuclear technology and materials, principally uranium, than with the possible development of a South African nuclear weapon for which there would seem to be little or no military requirement. South Africa's tactic may thus be to use uncertainty about her uranium export policy and possible possession of nuclear weapons as a political or diplomatic bargaining card in order to maintain close relations with, and extract political, economic and strategic concessions from, the West.

This book is a revised version of a thesis submitted for a Master's degree in the Department of Science and Technology Policy of the University of Manchester. I would like to thank Roger Williams and Philip Gummett of that department for originally sparking my interest in the subject. Thanks are also due to Philip Gummett for his wise critical comments on the draft copy of the thesis and to the Science Research Council and the Social Science Research Council for jointly funding me on the Master's course. I am very grateful to Professor Spence of Leicester University for being kind enough to read the thesis and encourage its publication. I would also like to express my gratitude to

Anne Akeroyd, Christopher Hill, Lan White and Harry Wilson, all of York University's Centre for Southern African Studies, for their help, patience and tolerance whilst this work was being completed. Thanks are due to Liz and Patience for the typing. Of course, responsibility for the content of the book is mine alone. Finally I would like to acknowledge the loving support provided by my family, especially my young sons, Jonathan and Richard, to whom this book is dedicated.

J.D.L.M.
York, January 1986

List of Abbreviations and Units

AEB	(South African) Atomic Energy Board
ANC	African National Congress (of South Africa)
CANDU	Canadian deuterium uranium reactor
CDA	Combined Development Agency
CIA	(United States) Central Intelligence Agency
Frelimo	Frente de Libertação de Moçambique
HEU	High-enriched uranium
IAEA	International Atomic Energy Agency
IISS	International Institute for Strategic Studies
INFCE	International Nuclear Fuel Cycle Evaluation
LEU	Low-enriched uranium
LWR	Light water reactor
MNR	Mozambique National Resistance
MPLA	Movimento Popular de Libertação de Angola
MW(e)	Megawatts of electrical power
MW(th)	Megawatts of thermal power
NNPA	(United States) Nuclear Non-Proliferation Act (of 1978)
NNWS	Non-Nuclear Weapon State
NPT	Non-Proliferation Treaty
NSG	Nuclear Suppliers Group
NWFZ	Nuclear Weapon-Free Zone
NWS	Nuclear Weapon State
OAU	Organisation of African Unity
PAC	Pan Africanist Congress (of South Africa)
PNE	Peaceful nuclear explosion
PWR	Pressurised water reactor
SADCC	Southern African Development Coordination Conference
SADF	South African Defence Force
SIPRI	Stockholm International Peace Research Institute
STEAG	Steinkohlen Elektrizitäts A.G. (of Essen, West Germany)
SWAPO	South West African People's Organisation
SWU/a	Separative work units per annum
tU/a	Tonnes of contained uranium per annum
UCOR	Uranium Enrichment Corporation (of South Africa)
UNITA	União Nacional para a Independência Total de Angola

Introduction

Following the acquisition of nuclear weapons by the five permanent members of the UN Security Council, early studies, in the 1960s, on the prospects for the further proliferation of nuclear weapons to 'nth' countries focused on the industrialised countries of the northern hemisphere.[1] These were then considered the only nations capable of developing nuclear weapons; and, following the agreement of the text of the Non-Proliferation Treaty in 1968, the superpowers concentrated their non-proliferation diplomacy on obtaining the signature of the treaty by these states.

However, during the 1970s, with the global spread of nuclear technology (and industrial and scientific capability in general), it came to be realised that 'nth' countries, with both the capability *and* the incentive for developing nuclear weapons, were not likely to be OECD or Comecon member states (most of whom in any case may have felt protected by a nuclear 'umbrella' security guarantee provided by one or other of the superpowers), but the industrialising and increasingly powerful nations of the 'South', such as India, Pakistan, Israel, Argentina, Brazil and South Africa.

This book is about the last-named country: the Republic of South Africa. The book examines both how that country acquired her nuclear technology and weapons capability and the incentives (and disincentives) her rulers may have for developing nuclear weapons. It reviews the measures adopted by the leading world powers to discourage or prevent such acquisition of nuclear weapons and the effect these non-proliferation policies have had on South Africa. It may be reasonably argued that, because of the racial discrimination enshrined in her laws and constitution, South Africa is the most isolated and shunned nation in the international community. She constantly faces expulsion from meetings of the United Nations and its agencies for example. Yet, at least until very recently, Western non-proliferation policies have not been applied any more strongly to South Africa (which, despite strong opposition, remains a member of the International Atomic Energy Agency, a UN agency) than to the other nations mentioned above. Indeed the reverse may be the case. This book concludes by looking at why this may be so.

For those unfamiliar with the subject, the financial, technological and material resources required to construct a nuclear weapon are outlined in Chapter 1. For countries which already possess or can readily acquire these resources, 'delivery' of a nuclear weapon (whether by missile or aircraft) on to a nearby Third World country should not pose much of a problem. (Delivery systems available to South Africa, should that country wish to deploy nuclear weapons, are discussed in Chapter 7.) Only the fission weapon (the 'A' bomb) is considered in Chapter 1 as it is universally accepted, and has been historically proved in the case of the five current nuclear weapon states, that development of a fission weapon is a prerequisite for subsequent development of the far more sophisticated and devastating thermonuclear or fusion weapon (the 'H' bomb).

Chapter 2 recounts the evolution of the international non-proliferation regime aimed at preventing or deterring further nations from acquiring nuclear weapons. In subsequent chapters South Africa's nuclear plans and capabilities are then seen in the context of the effects of this evolving regime. In Chapter 2 the nuclear weapon capabilities and intentions of other industrialising countries are also briefly discussed in the same context. This discussion facilitates an understanding of both subsequent non-proliferation policies designed to curb the 'second wave' of nuclear proliferation and South Africa's nuclear posture. For example, *Israel*, like South Africa, sees herself facing a hostile world: it is widely believed that, like South Africa, Israel may already secretly possess several 'bombs in the basement'. Indeed there have been rumours of cooperation concerning nuclear weapon development between Israel and South Africa (see Chapter 7). *India* is considered by many analysts to be the first country to have developed a nuclear weapons capability in the second wave of nuclear proliferation. India's explosion of a nuclear device in 1974 raised the question of what constitutes a peaceful nuclear explosion as distinct from a weapon test. Subsequent non-proliferation policies have been framed largely as a result of the concern in the capitals of the northern hemisphere following India's explosion.

As explained in Chapter 1, one of the most sensitive technologies in the nuclear fuel cycle, possession of which enables a nation to produce weapons-grade fissile material, is enrichment technology. Like South Africa, *Pakistan* has obtained components for an enrichment plant in a covert way. The centrifuge enrichment technology used by Pakistan differs from the aerodynamic technology used by South Africa; but *Brazil* is being openly assisted by West Germany in the development of aerodynamic enrichment technology, and it is widely believed that South Africa acquired the same technology from West Germany and then further developed it to suit her requirements. When the West

German–Brazilian deal was announced in 1975, concern was expressed in the United States that Brazil might also adapt this technology and then claim that it had been developed indigenously. She might then construct an enrichment plant which would not be subject to international controls. South Africa has shown how this might be done. *Argentina's* motives for constructing an enrichment plant which is claimed to use the diffusion process are also briefly discussed in Chapter 2. The various enrichment technologies, in particular aerodynamic technology, are briefly described and compared in the Appendix.

Also for those unfamiliar with the subject, and to provide a background for the rest of the book, South Africa's international situation and the government's policy responses are introduced in Chapter 3. The chapter focuses on foreign relations and South Africa's international isolation. Internal politics and apartheid policies are therefore not discussed in detail. This means that the collective psychology of the white population in general, and Afrikaners in particular, the so-called 'laager mentality' – a determination to stand up to what is perceived as an almost overwhelming communist-backed 'total onslaught' from the north – is not analysed in depth, although one could argue that such an analysis would throw light on the military, prestige and psychological motives for South Africa's nuclear programme (discussed in Chapter 8). It could also help explain the fact that, except for a small group based in Cape Town opposed to the nearby Koeberg nuclear power station, there is no significant environmental movement in South Africa.

Nevertheless, whilst the 'laager mentality' remains very real, it may be less significant than it was prior to the late 1970s. Since then, ideological divisions have grown, within Afrikanerdom and the white population in general, over the nation's future internal political order. The government's need both to prevent these divisions from further widening and to maintain links with the West may help explain the contrast between its increasingly reformist rhetoric and its lack of significant progress in (a) dismantling apartheid (so far as the majority black population see it), (b) allowing a UN-sponsored transition to independence for Namibia, or (c), for that matter, signing the Non-Proliferation Treaty (see Chapters 6, 8 and 9). Both the black majority population and the international community therefore remain sceptical and unable to put much trust in the government's declarations of good intentions concerning these matters.

However, notwithstanding increasing internal divisions over apartheid, there remains a general consensus within the white population concerning foreign and defence policy. In fact, there is little discussion of foreign affairs in general and nuclear proliferation issues in particular by white South Africans. Despite having the semblance of a free press, South Africans have little knowledge of nuclear matters, which are regarded as state secrets and best left to the government. Thus government leaders and top officials have been able to wrap South Africa's nuclear endeavour in a cloak of secrecy. This may help elucidate an important conclusion of Chapter 8: that one of the aims of this small group of South Africa's leaders has been, by means of hints, rumours and the like, quietly to use South Africa's nuclear weapons option and her capacity for the export of nuclear technology and material, principally uranium, as a diplomatic bargaining counter to maintain her close relations with the West.

Having thus set the scene by describing (a) how a fission bomb is made (in Chapter 1), (b) American-led international efforts to prevent more countries from making one (Chapter 2) and (c) South Africa's inter-national situation and her economic, foreign and defence policy responses (Chapter 3), the remainder of the book is devoted to (i) an account of the development of South Africa's nuclear programme (Chapters 4 and 5), (ii) an analysis of how South Africa has acquired a nuclear weapons capability (Chapters 5 and 7), (iii) evidence that South Africa already possesses nuclear weapons (Chapter 6), (iv) South Africa's motives for acquiring her nuclear weapons capability (Chapter 8) and (v) the interaction of South Africa's nuclear capabilities and intentions with American-led Western foreign and non-proliferation policies (Chapter 9). Although the lead has been taken by the United States, there is now a convergence in the non-proliferation policies of the major Western nations (as noted in Chapter 2). In the latter part of Chapter 9, references to recent Western foreign and non-proliferation policies concerning the South African situation are thus largely to American policies and vice versa. The Appendix provides a data base for Chapters 2, 5 and 7.

Two books have been published which describe the development of South Africa's nuclear capability. They are written from totally different perspectives. Newby-Fraser's *Chain Reaction*[2] is the official history of the South African Atomic Energy Board. Unfortunately it adds little to the information already available in the scientific and trade press and elsewhere. The other book, *The Nuclear Axis*, by Červenka and Rogers,[3] is based largely on information revealed in documents stolen by the ANC from the South African embassy in Bonn in 1975. These documents are cited, without their authenticity being questioned, in the

1978 publication of the West German government's Press and Information Office,[4] which officially denies the allegations, made by Červenka and Rogers and elsewhere, of official government assistance in transferring enrichment technology from West Germany to South Africa. Indeed the West German government publication, *Fact v. Fiction*, denies that there was such a transfer of technology. (These allegations and denials are discussed in Chapter 5 and an assessment made of their validity.) However, Červenka and Rogers go further in alleging that the purpose of the officially-sanctioned transfer of technology may have been to enable *West Germany* to obtain nuclear weapons with South Africa's help. Considerable doubt has been cast on these allegations.[5] Červenka and Rogers offer only circumstantial evidence of visits in the early 1970s by West German generals to Pelindaba where South Africa was developing her enrichment technology. One such visit was by General Rall, the West German representative on the NATO Military Council, in 1974.[6] Immediately following the revelations in the stolen documents, General Rall was forced to retire from the West German armed forces. In any case, Červenka and Rogers are not cited in Chapter 5 or elsewhere in this book unless there is corroborating evidence from another source or they are in turn quoting a reliable source. Luckily there are other sources of factual information concerning South Africa's nuclear programme.[7] These include the scientific and trade press and a well-balanced report prepared for the UN Secretary-General in 1981.[8]

There seems to be less contention in the discussion of South Africa's nuclear intentions than in the discussion of her capabilities. The various sources are detailed in the notes to Chapter 8 and the bibliography at the end of the book, the papers by Cassuto, Betts, Bustin and Spence being particularly worthy of mention here.

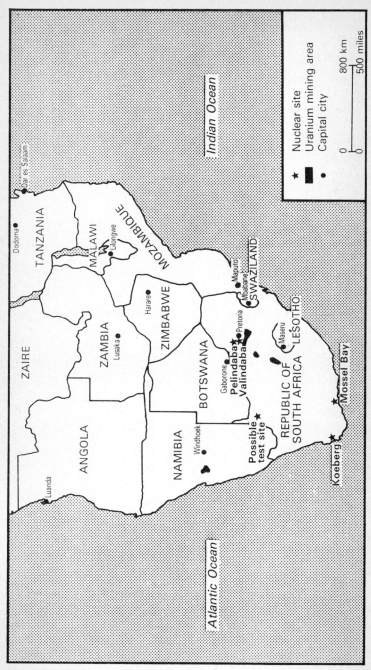

Nuclear sites in South Africa

1 The Technology of Nuclear Weapons

FISSILE MATERIAL AND THE THERMAL REACTOR FUEL CYCLE

To manufacture a nuclear weapon, the main requirement is to obtain a sufficient quantity of *fissionable* or *fissile* material.[1] A fissile element is one whose nucleus is capable of rupture into two lighter fragments, thus forming nuclei of lighter elements, together with free neutrons. These free neutrons may strike other nuclei causing further fission and so on in a *chain reaction*. The minimum amount of material necessary to sustain a chain reaction is called the *critical mass* of the substance. Smaller amounts of fissile material will not sustain a chain reaction since too large a fraction of the free neutrons escape through the surface and are unavailable to cause fission in other nuclei. The critical mass can be reduced, however, if the fissile material is compacted to make it more dense, or if it is surrounded by a shell of metallic material such as beryllium (Be) to reflect neutrons which would otherwise escape. If there is enough fissile material, packed closely together for long enough, and if the chain reaction is out of control, the result is a nuclear explosion: an 'atomic bomb', the explosive yield of which is equivalent to that of 20 kilotons of TNT. Alternatively, the power from a controlled chain reaction in a nuclear reactor can be used to generate electricity.

The fissile material could be uranium-233 (U233), uranium-235 (U235) or plutonium-239 (Pu239). Table 1.1 shows the critical masses for pure U233, U235 and Pu239 metals. For the purposes of safeguarding nuclear installations, the International Atomic Energy Agency (IAEA) defines a 'significant quantity' as being the amount of fissile material 'for which the possibility of manufacturing a nuclear device cannot be excluded'.[2] The 'threshold amount' is defined by the IAEA as the minimum amount of the 90 per cent pure metal from which such a device could be made. For the 90 per cent pure metal then, the significant quantity is the same as the threshold amount. The threshold amounts for uranium-233, uranium-235 and plutonium-239 are also shown in Table 1.1. Under the Non-Proliferation Treaty, any quantity of fissile material greater than these amounts outside the nuclear weapon states would be expected to be under IAEA safeguards.[3] In practice, manufacturing a weapon with these amounts of material would require considerable sophistication, and a country manufacturing a weapon for the first time could be expected to use greater quantities.

Table 1.1   Material Masses needed for a Nuclear Explosive Device

| | Mass of pure metal (kg) | | |
| | Critical mass[a] | | Threshold |
Metal	Without reflector	With Be reflector	amount[b]
U233	17.0	4.5	8.0
U235	50.0	15.0	25.0
Pu239	15.0	4.0	8.0

Sources: [a] Gunter Hildenbrand, 'Nuclear Energy, Nuclear Exports and the Non-proliferation of Nuclear Weapons', *AIF Conference on International Commerce and Safeguards for Civil Power*, March 1977.
[b] 'The Present Status of IAEA Safeguards on Nuclear Fuel Cycle Facilities', *IAEA Bulletin*, August 1980.

It should be noted that, although nuclear weapons are generally made from the metal forms of uranium-235 or plutonium-239, they can also be made from some of their compounds, in particular their oxides. However this would raise the critical mass of the fissile material by approximately half as much again. Moreover, weapons made from compounds would not perform as well. Compared with other problems encountered in bomb preparation, reduction of the metal compound to the pure metal should be relatively easy.

Of the three fissile metal isotopes named, the only naturally-occurring material is the U235 isotope of uranium.[4] This occurs as 0.7 per cent of natural uranium, the remaining 99.3 per cent of which is uranium-238 (U238) which is not fissile. To obtain a greater concentration of the U235 fissile isotope, natural uranium must be *enriched*. Uranium enrichment is a difficult and expensive technology which is discussed in the Appendix.

Uranium-233 and plutonium-239 are not naturally-occurring isotopes. Both have to be obtained from the neutron bombardment of a 'fertile' material, thorium-232 (Th232) or uranium-238 (U238) respectively, in a nuclear reactor. There is no evidence that U233 has ever been used in nuclear weapons and the U233/Th232 fuel cycle has not yet been commercially developed anywhere. Plutonium-239 is obtained from reprocessing spent fuel from a reactor fuelled with natural or enriched uranium (see Figure 1.1). All reactors currently being used to generate electricity are thermal reactors, that is reactors in which the neutrons move at thermal speeds. (Fast breeder reactors (FBRs), in which the neutrons move much faster, are still in the development stage in a few countries such as France and the United Kingdom.) For weapons purposes a large power reactor is not needed to produce sufficient quantity of Pu239 for a nuclear explosive device. A small reactor similar to those used for research purposes, together with a laboratory-scale facility with a 'hot cell' to separate the plutonium, would suffice. Indeed all five nuclear weapon states obtained their weapons-grade material from plants dedicated to this military purpose rather than from civil power plants. However, for the sake of simplicity, Figure 1.1 shows only the fuel cycle for thermal power reactors. Except for minor details, the fuel cycle for research reactors is substantially the same.

Natural uranium fuel is used in some power reactors: notably the Canadian-built CANDU reactor, which uses a heavy water moderator to slow down fast neutrons[5] (see 'Natural Uranium Fuel Cycle' (2) in Figure 1.1). In fact, in general, the nuclear weapon states have obtained plutonium-239 for their weapons programmes from dedicated natural uranium-fuelled research reactors, moderated by heavy water or very pure graphite.

However, most *power* reactors are fuelled by slightly enriched or low-enriched uranium (LEU), in which the concentration of the uranium-235 isotope in natural uranium is increased from 0.7 per cent to between 2 and 4 per cent before fabrication into the fuel elements and insertion into the reactor (see 'Enriched Uranium Fuel Cycle' (1) in Figure 1.1). Apart from the Advanced Gas-cooled Reactor (AGR), developed in Britain but not used elsewhere (and therefore not shown in Figure 1.1), which uses a graphite moderator, these LEU-fuelled reactors are nearly all light water reactors (LWRs), the water being used both as a coolant and a moderator. There are two main types of LWR: the pressurised water reactor (PWR) and the boiling water reactor (BWR). Although originally of American design, light water reactors are now also built by overseas corporations, notably the French Framatome and the West German Kraftwerk Union (KWU) corporations.

As can be seen from Figure 1.1, the two 'sensitive' technologies, giving access to weapons-grade material, are *enrichment* and *reprocessing*. Weapons-grade material can be diverted from the fuel cycle after either the enrichment or the reprocessing stages.

As mentioned, *enrichment* involves raising the concentration of U235

4

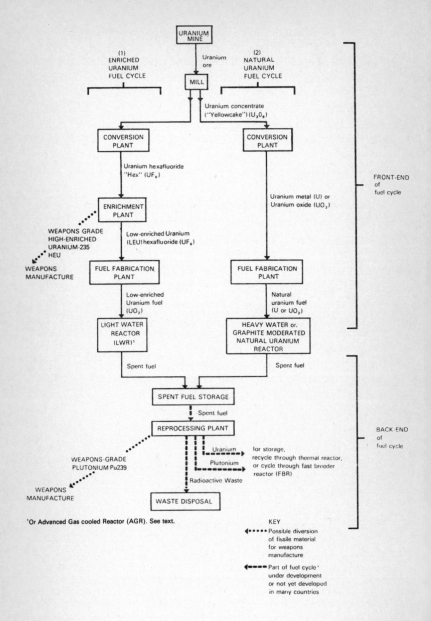

Figure 1.1   Thermal reactor fuel cycles

in the uranium. This is a *physical* change which requires the expenditure of considerable amounts of energy, as most enrichment techniques rely on the small differences in mass of the U235 and U238 isotopes. Theoretically, uranium-235 weapons can be produced from 10 per cent enriched uranium (i.e. 10 per cent U235, 90 per cent U238). In practice, however, enrichment to 50 per cent or more is required, and even then the critical mass would be more than three times that of pure U235 (see Table 1.2). For the core material in their weapons, it is assumed that nuclear weapon states use uranium enriched to at least 90 per cent. Therefore it should be noted that, whereas most power reactors require uranium enriched only to 2–4 per cent U235 (LEU), 90 per cent enriched uranium is usually required for weapons purposes. This high-enriched uranium (HEU) is therefore also known as *weapons-grade* uranium.

Table 1.2   Critical Masses for Enriched Uranium

Concentration of U235 isotope (enrichment) per cent	Total mass of uranium kg	
	Without reflector	*With Be reflector*
100	50	15
90	54	17
80	66	20
70	82	28
60	105	37
50	na	50
40	na	75
20	na	250

na = not available.

Sources: Gunter Hildenbrand, 'Nuclear Energy, Nuclear Exports, and the Non-proliferation of Nuclear Weapons', *AIF Conference on International Commerce and Safeguards for Civil Nuclear Power*, March 1977; J. Rotblat, 'Controlling Weapons-grade Fissile Material', *Bulletin of the Atomic Scientists*, June 1977; Gene I. Rochlin, 'The Development and Deployment of Nuclear Weapons Systems in a Proliferating World', in John Kerry King (ed.), *International Political Effects of the Spread of Nuclear Weapons* (Washington DC: US Government Printing Office, 1979).

Fuel *reprocessing* requires the extraction of Pu239 from the spent fuel from reactors. Spent fuel contains other chemicals such as fission products and uranium. Reprocessing is thus a *chemical* process which is cheaper and requires less technological sophistication (engineering skills, etc.) than enrichment. Reprocessing is, however, not without its dangers, as it involves contact with highly toxic and radioactive waste.

The five nuclear weapon states (NWS) – the United States, the Soviet Union, Britain, France and China – have all developed both U235 and Pu239 weapons. So all these countries possess both enrichment and reprocessing plants. Outside the five nuclear weapon states, the only unsafeguarded enrichment plant is the South African plant at Valindaba, and the only unsafeguarded reprocessing plants are assumed to be in Israel and India, although it is believed that construction of both enrichment and reprocessing plants without safeguards in both Pakistan and Argentina is nearing completion or has already been completed (see Table 2.1 below).

BOMB ASSEMBLY

There are two types of bomb assembly: the gun method and the implosion technique. In the gun method, which can only be used for U235 weapons, the fissile material is formed into two hemispheres, the faces of which are milled in a toothlike fashion to make the area of contact as large as possible. The hemispheres are held at each end of a cylinder. When the gun mechanism is triggered, the hemispheres are brought together, as if down the barrel of a gun, to form a single sphere well above the critical mass. A U235 gun assembly may be attractive to nations determined to develop nuclear weapons, but which lack the pool of scientists and engineers and the computer facilities needed to do the hydrodynamic studies required for the design of reliable implosion-type charges.[6]

The implosion device is somewhat more complex but can be made more efficient than the gun device. It requires a spherical assembly consisting of a core of fissile material below critical mass, surrounded by a material that acts as both a tamper and a reflector. The tamper is in turn surrounded by a high explosive. When detonated, the explosive sets up an implosion, or ingoing shock wave, which increases the density of the fissile material by a factor of about two, thereby making the previously subcritical assembly supercritical.

Plutonium-239 and the implosion principle were used for the first American nuclear test at Alamagordo in New Mexico during the Second World War, and for the second atomic bomb dropped on Japan, at

Nagasaki. The Hiroshima bomb, the first military use of a nuclear weapon, used uranium-235 in a gun assembly. Since then, all other nuclear weapon states except China, but including India (and possibly Israel), have developed Pu239 explosives before U235 explosives. Too much significance should not be attached to this fact, but reasons for it include the smaller amount of fissile material required for a plutonium weapon and, if a natural uranium-fuelled reactor is used to obtain the Pu239, the non-requirement to develop a sophisticated and expensive enrichment technology. However high-enriched U235 is normally used to 'trigger' hydrogen (fusion) bombs, and partly for this reason, the Soviet Union, Britain, France and, as previously mentioned, the United States all proceeded to develop U235 weapons, having already developed Pu239 explosives.

RESOURCES REQUIRED

As far as the cost of a weapons programme is concerned, a detailed report prepared for the United States Arms Control and Disarmament Agency stated that, *provided a country has access to a sufficient quantity of fissile material*, reworking this to the metal, designing the weapon and constructing the weapon could each cost around US$200 000 (1976 figures).[7] Weapons-testing would cost less than US$250 000, but with modern computer simulation techniques, a weapons test would not actually be required. It will be recalled that there was no weapons test on the Hiroshima bomb, the first use of a uranium-235 explosive device.[8]

So a bomb could be built for well under US$1 million (1976 figures). Designing the weapon would take a year or so, but of course this could have been done before the fissile material was available. Indeed, the weapon could have been prepared to such an extent that the assembly and the insertion of the fissile material could be undertaken in a matter of weeks or even days.

Obtaining the required fissile material would be much more lengthy, difficult and expensive. Assuming access to natural uranium concentrate ('yellowcake') and a plant for converting this to uranium hexafluoride, an enrichment plant of the gas centrifuge type (see Figure 1.1 and Appendix), dedicated to producing sufficient quantities of weapons-grade uranium-235 would cost over US$100 million (1976 figures) and take several years to build.[9] A dedicated reprocessing plant would cost less: around US$50 million (again 1976 figures, the money to be spent over several years),[10] but the proliferating nation would need to have obtained spent fuel from a reactor for which a graphite or heavy water moderator would also have to be obtained. Diverting fissile material from commercial-scale fuel cycle facilities would be far more expensive and difficult, especially if international safeguards had to be evaded; but presumably part of the cost would be borne by the energy budget of the country concerned. In any case, as stated, all five nuclear weapon states, as well as those other countries mentioned in the next chapter that are thought to have developed nuclear explosive devices, have used dedicated programmes.

Summing up, a report for the International Institute for Strategic Studies has concluded that the requirements for any organisation to make a nucler weapon are:

(1) an understanding of the nuclear theory involved in fission;
(2) data on the physical and chemical properties of the basic materials in a nuclear weapon;
(3) technical facilities to fabricate a weapon and to test implosion or gun devices and other components;
(4) availability of fissile material;
(5) the will to allocate the necessary resources to develop a weapon.

The report's assessment of different countries' abilities to meet these requirements was as follows:

> In the early 1950s each one of these steps represented a major hurdle for all but a few nations with a high level of technical sophistication. Now, however, the first three requirements are met in almost every country with a significant industrial capability, for the open technical literature, much of it stemming from nuclear reactor technology, contains a wealth of material which was very hard to come by twenty years ago . . . The problem of fabricating a nuclear device is even simpler if the purpose is only to demonstrate nuclear capability and no premium is placed on such military requirements as low weight and deliverability.[11]

A Stockholm International Peace Research Institute (SIPRI) study came to a similar conclusion, stating that the country would need laboratory and workshop facilities to make the various items for the assembly mechanism, and perhaps field facilities for testing the high explosive (but not nuclear) charges; but the country concerned could easily conceal these activities.[12]

Countries trying to develop nuclear weapons may find the need for skilled manpower their greatest constraint. Hopkins, in another SIPRI study, found that, whilst all the so-called near-nuclear weapon states or 'nth' countries (including South Africa) had the requirements for designing a simple fission device that would give a yield in the kiloton range,

> the engineering design and fabrication, on the other hand, require a much wider range of expertise and a considerably larger commitment of technical and financial resources. First of all they require high explosive development and the associated hydrodynamic research. The engineering design also requires detonator development, material studies, critical assembly work, mechanical design and, finally, actual fabrication. While information on all of these subjects is available in the open literature and most industrial nations have research in these areas or in closely related fields, it should be stressed that nuclear weapon development requires a higher degree of competence in physics, chemistry and nuclear, mechanical and chemical engineering, plus more highly skilled technicians, machinists and health physicists than are required in most other industries.[13]

With the global slowdown of civil nuclear power programmes, there may now however be something of a 'grey market' in nuclear engineers and technicians from the West, who would be willing to sell their expertise to near-nuclear weapon states in return for secure highly-paid jobs.[14]

Before concluding, it should again be emphasised that by far the most difficult task facing any 'nth' country is obtaining fissile material for an explosive device. Even here, however, it may be possible to obtain components for sensitive enrichment or reprocessing plants from foreign sources. It is to an evaluation of the attempt by the international community over the years to halt or slow down the proliferation of nuclear weapons to 'nth' countries, by controlling the transfer of sensitive technology and fissile material and by other means, that we turn in the next chapter.

2 The International Non-proliferation Regime

Both superpowers believe that an increase in the number of nations (or sub-national groups) possessing nuclear weapons would threaten their control over 'world order'. The acquisition of nuclear weapons, in particular by countries over which they have little influence, in areas which are considered unstable, or whose leaders are perceived as irrational, is therefore seen by both superpowers to be against their global interests.[1] Consequently, the United States and the Soviet Union have taken the lead, sometimes in cooperation, in promoting measures to discourage or prevent further 'horizontal' proliferation of nuclear weapons.

This is not meant to suggest that non-proliferation is not in the interest of other countries. Indeed, over 120 nations have now signed and ratified the 1968 Non-Proliferation Treaty, thereby promising neither to acquire nuclear weapons nor to help other nations do so. Admittedly many of these promises were made under pressure or inducement from the superpowers and most of these countries could not attain a nuclear weapons capability anyway; but these signatures have also provided mutual reassurance between countries that neighbours that could develop that capability do not intend doing so.

Nevertheless, as the first nations to obtain nuclear weapons, it would seem self-evident that the two superpowers should be particularly concerned to prevent other nations from joining the nuclear club. Moreover, through their control over nuclear technology transfer and, more particularly, their supply of enriched uranium fuel, both countries had until recently the ability largely to determine nuclear developments in their respective spheres of influence.

By no stretch of the imagination can South Africa, the subject of this book, be considered in the Soviet sphere of influence. So this chapter focuses on the development of *Western* non-proliferation policies, where the lead has been taken by the United States. More recently however, United States influence over nuclear commerce, as in international affairs in general, has declined. Thus the policies of other Western nations and the need for a concerted Western approach to non-proliferation are discussed later in the chapter. Because of their historic importance for the global non-proliferation regime, and also because of their relevance to the South African situation, particular attention will be paid to the policies of both natural and enriched uranium-exporting countries.

FROM ATOMIC SECRECY TO ATOMS FOR PEACE

Following the end of the Second World War, the onus for proposing a regime for international control over the nuclear industry, to prevent other nations from obtaining nuclear weapons, rested with the United States, the only country possessing nuclear weapons and significant nuclear technology. The first such proposal was the Acheson–Lilienthal Report which formed the basis of the Baruch Plan presented to the United Nations in 1946. This proposed the progressive transfer of all nuclear installations, including uranium mines, to the control and, in the case of sensitive facilities, ownership by an international authority. The United States would not have surrendered her nuclear monopoly until the very last step had been taken. This proved unacceptable to the Soviet Union, who rejected the Baruch Plan, proposing instead an arrangement whereby the United States first gave up her nuclear weapons.

Although the USA did not abandon hope that a modified version of the Baruch Plan might be agreed, this initial Soviet rejection reinforced an American inclination to adopt a unilateral non-proliferation policy of atomic denial, her major concern being to prevent Soviet acquisition of nuclear 'secrets', possibly by espionage. Thus, under the 1946 US Atomic Energy Act, commonly known as the McMahon Act, which transferred control of American nuclear installations from the US Army to the US Atomic Energy Commission, most nuclear scientific and technological information remained classified and denied to all other countries, including even Britain and Canada (until the Act was amended in 1958) who had collaborated with the United States to develop the atomic bomb during the Second World War (despite the secret 1944 agreement between Churchill and Roosevelt that collaboration should continue after the war). No distinction was made in the 1946 Act between the military and civil uses of nuclear energy. Thus, in the initial post-war period, the United States, Britain, Canada and subsequently France continued their development of nuclear technology independently with little or no exchange of know-how with each other or any other nation.

The one exception to United States nuclear self-sufficiency, for which she remained dependent on her wartime allies, concerned the supply of natural uranium. Britain and the United States continued to collaborate through their jointly-owned Combined Development Agency in obtaining uranium for their weapons programmes. Most of the uranium procured went to the United States, initially from Canada and the Belgian Congo and later (in steeply decreasing order of quantity supplied) from South Africa, Australia and Portugal;[2] but Britain's role in the Combined Development Agency was highly valued by the Americans because of British influence with her former Dominions (Canada, South Africa and Australia) as well as with the Belgian mining company, Union Minière, in the Congo.[3] Besides the need to obtain a sufficient quantity of uranium for their rapidly increasing production of fissile material for weapons purposes, a major objective of this collaboration between Britain and America, to which both sides were committed under a wartime agreement, was to prevent other nations from obtaining uranium which was then considered a scarce resource.[4] The Combined Development Agency was thus authorised secretly to buy up all the uranium in the non-communist world and then to allocate it between Britain and America according to their requirements.

This policy of nuclear denial was initially very successful; but by the mid-1950s it had become necessary to obtain the cooperation of the uranium-producing nations in this covert non-proliferation policy, in a forum known as the Western Suppliers Group (the existence of which did not become known until 1975). Uranium deposits were found to be more widespread than had earlier been suspected; and the number of countries with uranium reserves or production capacity seemed likely to continue to increase. The USA's own uranium production capacity was rapidly increasing. Yet, with her development of the hydrogen (fusion) bomb, the USA's uranium requirements for fissile material for her weapons programme were to decline steeply at the end of the 1950s. For a decade beginning in the late 1950s, then, the task of the Western Suppliers Group nations was to keep each other informed of their uranium exports to non-member states and ensure that they were used for peaceful purposes only. The group initially comprised the United States, Britain, Canada, Australia and South Africa. They were later joined by Belgium, Portugal and France. As we shall see in the next section, these nations helped the United States draw up the first system of international safeguards for ensuring that nuclear installations were used for peaceful purposes only.[5]

So, by the mid-1950s the United States had found it necessary to seek the cooperation of uranium-producing countries to ensure the effectiveness of her non-proliferation policy. Moreover the policy of retaining a government monopoly over the ownership and production of nuclear materials, classifying nuclear technology and attempting to deny it to others seemed to conflict with the liberal ethos of scientists in general and the United States in particular. Indeed the policy was seen to have failed to achieve its purpose. The Soviet Union and Britain had already developed nuclear weapons and, following the Soviet Union's first nuclear explosion in 1949, non-proliferation had an altered and reduced priority for the Americans. The United States government also faced domestic pressure, from private industry and technologists in the Atomic Energy Commission, for the declassification of some fuel cycle technology in order that the USA could better compete with the Soviet Union and Britain in the development of civil nuclear power technology. In addition, other countries, in particular America's European allies, wanted to use nuclear power for peaceful purposes. The uranium mining industry also pressed for power reactor technology to be developed; and the other main uranium-producing countries, Canada, South Africa and Belgium, urged the United States to supply them with nuclear know-how in return for their cooperation concerning uranium supplies.[6]

These various pressures and developments formed both the background and the response to President Eisenhower's famous Atoms for Peace speech at the 1953 UN General Assembly. (There were other factors too: the Atoms for Peace speech was primarily a public relations initiative and a disarmament proposal. President Eisenhower proposed that the nuclear weapon states (the United States, Britain and the Soviet Union) should begin progressively to hand over their entire stock of uranium and fissionable material to a proposed International Atomic Energy Agency (IAEA) to be re-released for peaceful purposes only. Apart from the eventual establishment of the IAEA, however, little came of *this* proposal.) The assumptions behind Eisenhower's Atoms for Peace proposals were that peaceful nuclear technology could be distinguished from military technology and that the secrecy hitherto prevailing over the former could be lifted and international trade encouraged, provided that the United States and other technology suppliers (Britain and Canada) could ensure, by such means as periodic inspections, that recipients were using the technology solely for peaceful purposes.

An early result of Eisenhower's speech was the passage by Congress of the 1954 Atomic Energy Act which, unlike the 1946 Act, provided for nuclear exports to countries with which the United States had 'agreements for nuclear cooperation'. Because of their close cooperation over the supply of uranium, early agreements were made with Britain,

Canada and Belgium; but many similar agreements were soon made
with other countries. The major provisions of these agreements were for
the liberal exchange of scientific information, the training of foreign
scientists and the supply of research reactors and enriched uranium to
fuel them to foreign countries. All such supplies, which were made on
very generous financial terms, were safeguarded to ensure that they were
used for peaceful purposes only. It was hoped that, in the ensuing race
for the successful exploitation of the 'peaceful atom', United States
nuclear power technology would prevail and that the United States
would thus retain control over nuclear developments worldwide. The
US Atomic Energy Commission's monopoly of the production of
enriched uranium, which was supplied only to countries with whom the
USA had agreements for nuclear cooperation, was considered particularly important in enabling the United States to retain this control.[7]

This race between the great powers, notably the superpowers, for
income and influence over customers and the prestige of being seen
successfully to have developed civil nuclear power technology, occurred
at the same time as the superpowers were similarly devoting considerable scientific and technological resources to space and nuclear arms
races between each other. One arena where the race for the successful
exploitation of the 'peaceful atom' took place was in Geneva, where
successive UN conferences on the peaceful uses of atomic energy were
convened in 1955 and 1958, at which the major powers revealed their
development of nuclear technology in considerable detail for the first
time. So it was that, during the second half of the 1950s, most nuclear
fuel cycle technology (including reprocessing technology, but with the
notable exception of enrichment technology) was progressively declassified by the US Atomic Energy Commission, as well as by Britain and
Canada, who were closely consulted and collaborated in this policy.[8]

THE IAEA AND INTERNATIONAL SAFEGUARDS

In his 1953 Atoms for Peace speech, President Eisenhower had proposed
talks with the nations 'principally involved' in nuclear commerce on the
establishment of an International Atomic Energy Agency (IAEA) to
oversee the expansion of this commerce for peaceful purposes. The
United States wanted these talks to be between those nations 'principally
involved' in the uranium trade, namely the United States herself,
Britain, Australia, Canada, South Africa, France, Belgium and Portugal; and accordingly, in 1954 America began discussing a draft statute

for the proposed IAEA with these seven other nations.[9] The Soviet Union, objecting to the overwhelming influence of colonial powers in this negotiating group, did not at first participate in the talks. Similarly the non-aligned nations, led by India, objected that the proposed IAEA statute could be discriminatory, as it was being negotiated only by those nations which produced uranium or had advanced nuclear technology. However, possibly because she realised that the eight Western nations would unilaterally have adopted the statute in any case, the Soviet Union subsequently changed her stance and accepted the eight-nation draft as the basis for further negotiations. In 1955, Brazil, Czechoslovakia, India and the Soviet Union joined the eight Western nations; and these twelve nations effectively negotiated the IAEA statute in 1956, when the draft was approved by a conference of all member countries of the United Nations.[10] The IAEA formally came into existence in 1957, as a rather special member of the family of UN specialised agencies, with headquarters in Vienna. The twelve founding members of the IAEA retained a privileged status with seats on a Board of Governors which has greater powers *vis-à-vis* the Director General and the (annual) General Conference than is the case for other UN agencies.

The two main aims of the IAEA, which have often seemed conflicting, are (i) to encourage by international cooperation the use of nuclear technology for peaceful purposes, and (ii) to provide safeguards on nuclear installations and materials to ensure that they are used for peaceful purposes only. It has always been a difficult task for the IAEA to achieve a fine balance between its promotional role of technical assistance (largely to developing countries) and its regulatory role of safeguarding nuclear installations. The industrial nations have given greater support for safeguards whereas the less developed nations have sought to enhance the agency's promotional role.

The early work of the IAEA and the resources placed at its disposal were far more modest than President Eisenhower had envisaged in his Atoms for Peace address. He had suggested that the agency should act as a bank for all fissionable material and safeguard all nuclear facilities, first in the non-nuclear weapon states and eventually in all states, to ensure that they were used only for peaceful purposes.

The first major problem encountered by the IAEA concerned the negotiation of a safeguards system which, as the United States was obliged to accept, would be voluntarily applied. When the IAEA statute was being negotiated, there was disagreement between the Western powers, led by the Anglo-Saxon nations, and Soviet bloc and non-aligned nations, who had some support from France. For example, one area of disagreement was that the second group thought that fissionable materials (that is, plutonium and enriched uranium) should be safeguarded, whereas the Western powers wanted safeguards extended to cover 'source material' (in effect, natural uranium). The Soviet bloc and non-aligned nations objected that this would constitute an excessive infringement of nations' sovereignty. The non-aligned nations, led by India, which had not yet started producing 'source material' (uranium or thorium), pointed to the disproportionate influence that uranium-producing nations had in the IAEA and asserted that such a safeguards system, although supposedly voluntary, would discriminate against nations dependent on uranium imports which would necessarily be safeguarded. A compromise was reached when the Western powers acknowledged that, with uranium deposits and production becoming increasingly widespread, safeguarding the trade in source material would be impractical, over-restrictive and would bring the IAEA into disrepute. So when the IAEA statute was being agreed, it was decided that natural uranium would be brought into the material accounting system for safeguards purposes only when it was fabricated into fuel and cycled through reactors.[11] However, as we noted in the previous section, the Western uranium-supplying nations sought secretly to monitor the trade in uranium to non-nuclear weapon states to try to ensure that it was used for peaceful purposes only.[12]

The Soviet Union (and, for that matter, India and France) at first refused to cooperate with the IAEA safeguards system, which was instituted very slowly; but she reversed her stance in 1963 during the thaw in Cold War relations following the signing of the Partial Test Ban Treaty and as a result of her experience of cooperating with China in her nuclear programme which included the construction of the enrichment plant which was subsequently used to produce high-enriched uranium for China's first nuclear weapon test in 1964. Soviet non-proliferation policy concerning nuclear exports then became much more restrictive, as it has remained to this day.

The broad purpose of IAEA safeguards, as described by a former Assistant Director General of the IAEA, is 'to act as a *deterrent* or more accurately to give *information* (reassurance) that countries are behaving themselves'.[13] To achieve this purpose, the IAEA has a team of inspectors who carry out periodic inspections of nuclear facilities and their material accounts. These inspections are supplemented where necessary by photographic surveillance of nuclear installations and containment of nuclear materials by the application of special seals. The objective of IAEA safeguards was later elaborated in the standard safeguards agreement under the Non-Proliferation Treaty (known officially as INFCIRC/153 or, more colloquially, as 'The Blue Book') as being:

> the timely detection of diversion of significant quantities of nuclear material from peaceful nuclear activities to the manufacture of nuclear weapons or of other nuclear explosive devices or for purposes unknown, and deterrence of such diversion by the risk of early detection.[14]

However, in practice, the emphasis in the IAEA safeguards system rests on the 'timely' verification that such diversion has *not* occurred. If safeguards are violated by a country, in other words if it proves impossible to verify that diversion has not occurred, because of anomalies in the material accounts for example, the only sanctions available under the statute to the IAEA Board of Governors or General Conference are (i) withdrawal of technical assistance, (ii) partial or total suspension of the offending nation from the privileges and rights of membership of the IAEA and its committees and (iii), most important of all, *publicity*.[15] In particular, non-compliance or breach of safeguards may be reported by the IAEA Board of Governors to all member states and to the UN Security Council and General Assembly. So far as is known, there has never been any violation of IAEA safeguards, at least none serious enough for the Board of Governors to decide to invoke its sanctions powers.

Because of Soviet non-participation, the first voluntary IAEA safeguards system was in effect drawn up by the eight Western Suppliers Group nations in 1961, as these nations dominated the IAEA Board of Governors at that time. Installations were only safeguarded if nations voluntarily agreed to this; and at that time most nuclear installations outside the nuclear weapon states were subject to bilateral safeguards, notably those on research reactors provided under importing countries' bilateral agreements for nuclear cooperation with the United States. During the course of the 1960s, however, the IAEA gradually assumed responsibility for safeguarding most of those installations that had been previously safeguarded under bilateral agreements by the supplying nation (usually the United States). Two notable exceptions were natural uranium-fuelled reactors in India and Israel, supplied by Canada and France respectively before the IAEA safeguards system had been established. As we shall see in the next section, these two reactors were not voluntarily submitted to bilateral *or* IAEA safeguards.

By the mid-1960s it had become apparent that the development of nuclear power technology, notably American light water reactor technology, had at last reached the stage where it might be commercially viable for electricity generation. There was then the prospect that some countries might develop their own nuclear fuel cycle technologies or adapt imported technologies and become independent of the safeguarded supply of fuel and technology from the United States, Britain, Canada and the Soviet Union. The Western Suppliers Group was finding it increasingly difficult to monitor the uranium trade to ensure that uranium exported to non-nuclear weapon states was used only in safeguarded facilities. The superpowers thus perceived the need to establish a more comprehensive system of 'full-scope' safeguards, that is IAEA safeguards on *all* nuclear installations outside the nuclear weapon states, not just those which relied on imports of technology or fuel. Such a system of full-scope safeguards was provided for under the 1968 Non-Proliferation Treaty; and during the course of the 1970s this system came to cover nearly all nuclear plants outside the nuclear weapon states.

THE NON-PROLIFERATION TREATY

The superpowers took the lead in negotiating the Non-Proliferation Treaty (NPT) because of their common concern to maintain the post-war strategic world order. The Soviet Union was particularly concerned to prevent West Germany from gaining control of nuclear weapons. By means of their supply of nuclear technology and fuel, in particular their joint monopoly in the commercial supply of enriched uranium, the superpowers were able to ensure that most nations wishing to make use of nuclear technology signed the NPT; and by 1985 the treaty had been signed and ratified by over 120 nations. (It expires in 1995 unless, as seems likely, it is extended by the signatory states.)

There is a distinction under the Non-Proliferation Treaty between the obligations of the five nuclear weapon states (NWS) – the United States, the Soviet Union, Britain, France and China – and those of the remaining non-nuclear weapon states (NNWS). Of the nuclear weapon states, only the United States, Britain and the Soviet Union have signed the NPT. However, France has long stated that she would conduct her nuclear commerce as if she had signed the treaty; and until recently China had not exported significant nuclear technology or material, and has now also stated that she will require safeguards on all her nuclear exports.

By signing the NPT, non-nuclear weapon states agreed to forgo the possession of nuclear weapons, and each signatory promised not to assist any other country's acquisition of nuclear weapons (Articles I and II).[16] NNWS signatories were obliged under Article III to accept full-scope safeguards, that is safeguards on all their nuclear installations. As a gesture to indicate that they are also prepared to sacrifice some of their sovereignty, the nuclear weapon states have all now voluntarily agreed to submit some of their civil nuclear plants to IAEA safeguards, although they were not obliged to do so under the NPT.

Also to compensate for the overtly discriminatory nature of the NPT, as between the nuclear weapon states and the non-nuclear weapon states, the latter were guaranteed (under Article IV) that no restrictions would be placed in the way of their development of peaceful nuclear technology, and all parties agreed to facilitate such development.

Under Article VI, all parties to the NPT undertook to pursue arms control negotiations leading to a comprehensive test ban treaty, halting the nuclear arms race, nuclear disarmament and eventually to general and complete disarmament. In effect this meant that the nuclear weapon states, in particular the superpowers, have undertaken to make progress towards reversing the 'vertical' proliferation of nuclear weapons, in return for a general undertaking by all parties to halt 'horizontal' proliferation. Article VIII of the NPT provided for the convening of a Review Conference of all parties in 1975 and every five years thereafter, at which the NWS parties could be expected to give an account of their fulfilment of these obligations under the treaty. Although some non-aligned NNWS have threatened to withdraw from the treaty at these subsequent Review Conferences, which they may do under the treaty after giving three months' notice, no country has so far done so.

Despite their defects, the NPT and IAEA safeguards remain central to the non-proliferation regime. They give assurance to regional neighbours, nuclear suppliers and the superpowers alike that signatories are not developing nuclear weapons. There may not be a significant increase in the number of states signing the NPT; but the treaty remains of immense value as a moral deterrent to proliferation, setting a standard of behaviour against it.

Nevertheless, as can be seen from Table 2.1, besides those states refusing to sign the NPT because of its discriminatory nature, some non-nuclear weapon states have in addition refused to allow some of their indigenously-developed nuclear installations to be safeguarded. It will be noted that these are mostly developing countries of the southern hemisphere, whereas the major concern of the superpowers in the late

1960s and early 1970s was to obtain the NPT signature of key northern industrialised countries such as Italy, West Germany and Japan.

We may also note that, by the 1970s, nearly all of the countries shown in Table 2.1 had or were developing a uranium mining capacity or, ⁖ in the case of Israel, were able to import uranium (sometimes by devious means) free of the strict safeguards that had previously been insisted upon by the Western uranium-exporting countries. Indeed, there were suggestions that one of these uranium-exporting nations, South Africa, who, because of her racial policies, was becoming increasingly shunned by other Western countries, might have exported uranium without insisting that strict IAEA safeguards should be applied to its use in those key industrialised countries mentioned above, had these countries not decided to sign the NPT. Moreover, as we shall see in Chapter 4, by 1970 it is very likely that South Africa had already exported uranium to *Israel* without insisting that IAEA safeguards be applied to its use in the Dimona reactor.[17]

Table 2.1   Nuclear Facilities in Non-nuclear Weapon States not subject to IAEA or Bilateral Safeguards[a]

Fuel Cycle Stage	Number of Facilities				
	Argentina[b]	India	Israel	Pakistan	South Africa
Enrichment	1	—	—	1	1
Fuel fabrication	—	3	1	1	1
Heavy water production	1	7	1	2	—
Reactor	—	12	1	—	—
Reprocessing	(1)	3	1	2 or 3	—

[a] In addition to the fuel facilities shown, Argentina, India, Pakistan and South Africa all possess unsafeguarded plants for the conversion of uranium concentrate to oxide and/or hexafluoride (UF_6). Brazil also possesses an unsafeguarded UF_6 conversion plant.
[b] Argentina's pilot reprocessing plant is not specifically subject to safeguards; but, in the absence of an unsafeguarded reactor, the reprocessing plant is expected to come under safeguards when, as now, reprocessing safeguarded spent fuel.
Source: Information supplied to author by Stockholm International Peace Research Institute, February 1985.

France had supplied the unsafeguarded Dimona research reactor to Israel following the 1956 Suez War when both countries had felt vulnerable to oil supply interruptions and let down by lack of support from the United States in the face of rocket threats from the Soviet Union. Nuclear cooperations between France and Israel remained close until the 1967 Middle East war. With the help of a French company, Israel managed to construct an unsafeguarded reprocessing plant in the 1960s. She was therefore able to separate weapons-grade plutonium from spent fuel from the Dimona reactor; and there have been periodic rumours, including leaks from the United States Central Intelligence Agency, that Israel has possessed several nuclear weapons since the late 1960s or early 1970s, although Israel's officially-stated but ambiguously-phrased policy is that 'she will not be the the the first country to introduce nuclear weapons into the Middle East'.

A more dramatic challenge to the post-NPT non-proliferation regime came in 1974 when *India* exploded a nuclear device under the Rajasthan desert. The Indian government claimed that this underground test constituted a 'peaceful nuclear explosion' (PNE), the benefits of which are guaranteed to all NPT parties, under the Article V of the treaty, if supervised by 'an appropriate international body' (presumably the IAEA) in a way which has not yet been fully determined and that the Indian government would have considered discriminatory (its stated reason for not signing the NPT). The United States and the Soviet Union have in the past experimented with the use of PNEs for such purposes as major earth-moving projects and facilitating oil and gas production; but there is considerable scepticism amongst experts about whether there are any applications for which their use may be justified on economic grounds. For practical purposes, a peaceful nuclear device is indistinguishable from a weapon. So whatever her intentions, India had demonstrated by her 1974 explosion that she had a nuclear weapons capability. (Although she has not repeated the 1974 test, India has since continued to develop her rocketry and hence her nuclear delivery capability.)

India shares a disputed border with the People's Republic of China, a nuclear state since 1964, and there was a fierce border war between the two countries in 1962. However, it is also likely that the desire of the Indian government for greater international and domestic standing or respect provided a major motive for the 1974 test. Following the explosion, the reaction from the Indian media and the scientific and technocratic élite was generally favourable, at a time when the government was otherwise experiencing domestic political unrest. For a large section of the domestic and international audience, the explosion seemed to confirm India's role as a leading member of the non-aligned world and the Group of 77 developing countries. It was also widely seen as a symbol of resistance to world domination by the superpowers.

This was not however the reaction of the Canadian government, which had supplied the natural uranium-fuelled Cirus research reactor from which the plutonium for the explosive device had been obtained. (The USA had supplied the heavy water moderator, and plutonium had been separated from the spent fuel at the indigenously-developed unsafeguarded reprocessing plant at Trombay.) Like Israel's Dimona reactor, the Cirus reactor had been supplied before the advent of IAEA safeguards; but Canada had obtained peaceful-use assurances from India. The Indian government felt that these assurances had been honoured; but the Canadian government felt it had been deceived and withdrew nuclear and, for a time, all other aid. Within a couple of years there was also a delayed reaction to India's explosion elsewhere in the Western world. Fears were expressed, particularly in the United States, that another wave of nuclear proliferation had been initiated, this time in the Third World.

SENSITIVE NUCLEAR EXPORTS TO DEVELOPING COUNTRIES

Following the Indian explosion in 1974, concern naturally centred on nuclear developments in *Pakistan*, who also had a long-standing border dispute with India over the state of Kashmir. Like China, Pakistan had been to war with India, most recently in 1971 when India supported East Pakistan's breakaway as the independent state of Bangladesh. Pakistan's nuclear ambitions have since developed in parallel with those of India. Although all her nuclear facilities were safeguarded in 1974, Pakistan's attitude to the NPT, which she has not signed, is very similar to that of India. The Pakistanis have aspired to the same nuclear weapons capability as that of India as a matter of national honour; and her nuclear scientists and engineers have pursued this objective with seemingly religious fervour, despite the considerable strains the programme must have placed on the nation's resources. In fact it is probable that Pakistan has been able to get financial support for her nuclear programme from fellow Islamic nations. It is also thought that Pakistan has obtained possibly crucial technical support from China.

In 1974, Pakistan signed a contract to purchase a reprocessing plant from France. Concern was subsequently expressed, in North America in particular, that plutonium could be diverted from the plant and used to construct an explosive device. Because Pakistan was unwilling to sign the NPT or accept full-scope safeguards, and also to counterbalance her withdrawal of aid for India's nuclear programme, Canada terminated nuclear cooperation with Pakistan in 1976. The supply of uranium and heavy water for Pakistan's Kanupp CANDU reactor was thus withheld.

By the time of the 1976 US presidential election campaign, the initial low-key reaction in the United States to India's 1974 explosion had been replaced by widespread public concern about the prospects for nuclear proliferation in other Third Word nations. The American government exerted considerable pressure on both France and Pakistan to cancel the reprocessing plant sale. France eventually insisted on more stringent non-proliferation conditions which Pakistan could not accept, and the project was terminated in 1978.[18] However, the blueprints were left by the French company, and it is thought that Pakistan has subsequently been able to develop an unsafeguarded reprocessing capacity, just as she has developed an unsafeguarded capacity to fabricate natural uranium fuel and heavy water, thus frustrating the Canadian embargo.[19]

Moreover Pakistan had also meanwhile adopted a dual strategy of pursuing both the plutonium and the enriched uranium routes to a nuclear weapons capability. With the help of information stolen by a Pakistani metallurgist employed at the URENCO enrichment laboratory in the Netherlands, a pilot gas centrifuge enrichment plant of unknown capacity has been built at Kahuta, twenty miles from the capital Islamabad. This cannot easily be justified on economic grounds as Pakistan's sole power reactor, the Kanupp reactor near Karachi, is fuelled by natural uranium. Much of the equipment for the unsafeguarded enrichment plant came from Western countries through agents or front companies so that its eventual destination was not disclosed. Other items of equipment had other legitimate civilian uses and the purpose for which they were procured was disguised. Controls on this type of export were only tightened after these exports to Pakistan had taken place.[20]

However, it should be stressed that, notwithstanding these developments, there are significant constraints on Pakistan's leaders to stop short of announcing possession of or testing a nuclear explosive device. Besides possible withdrawal of substantial American military aid, a more immediate threat could come from the Israeli or Indian response to such a move. It is clear that Pakistan's nuclear programme is already facing severe resource constraints; and she would be hard pressed to compete with India in however pedestrian a nuclear arms race that might ensue. Thus, Pakistan's tactics are probably to adopt a more ambiguous posture (like Israel), dropping hints and leaks about her nuclear weapons option, possible 'bombs in the basement' and, perhaps, her wish (like India) to conduct 'peaceful nuclear explosions'.

Besides the French contract to supply a reprocessing plant to Pakistan, the other major deal in the mid-1970s, for the transfer of nuclear technology to a developing country which had not signed the Non-Proliferation Treaty, was an intergovernmental agreement for West German companies to supply *Brazil* with facilities for the complete fuel cycle. Despite considerable pressure from Washington on the West German government, *this* agreement was *not* cancelled, although it has been delayed and its scale much reduced.

When the agreement was signed in June 1975 it was valued at US$4.8 billion; but due to delays in implementation and escalating costs, it is now thought that the total cost of work carried out under the agreement could be around $30 billion. The work envisaged when the agreement was signed included (i) German aid for exploration for uranium, (ii) development of the West German jet nozzle enrichment technology and (iii) construction of a fuel fabrication plant, at least two power reactors (with the possibility of six more eventually) and a reprocessing plant. The power reactors, Angra 2 and Angra 3, were to be pressurised water reactors constructed on sites alongside the similar American-supplied Angra 1 reactor.[21]

For West Germany, the major attraction of this giant deal was that orders for Kraftwerk Union, her ailing power plant construction company, were guaranteed. There were suspicions (in the United States) that the provisions for the transfer of enrichment and reprocessing technology were added as 'sweeteners' in order to secure the contract for the reactors. However, the agreement also provided West Germany with the opportunity to diversify her sources of uranium at a time when prices were rising, competition for supplies was intense and Australia and Canada were attaching increasingly restrictive safeguard conditions to their uranium exports.[22]

For Brazil, the contract appeared to satisfy long-held nuclear ambitions which were driven by the need felt by the Brazilian élite to remain abreast of nuclear developments (peaceful or otherwise) in Argentina. The German contract offered Brazil the prospect of nuclear self-sufficiency and independence of American supplies, which were perceived to be becoming insecure and to which increasingly stringent non-proliferation conditions were being attached. Although plants constructed under the agreement are to be covered by IAEA safeguards and Brazil has given assurances that technology transferred will not be re-exported for twenty years or used to manufacture a nuclear explosive device, concern has been expressed that the technology may be modified in such a way that Brazil could claim it to have been developed indigenously.[23] A facility using this modified technology could then be constructed to produce unsafeguarded weapons-grade fissile material.

The nuclear contract was also considered to confer economic benefits for Brazil of energy independence at a time when oil prices were high and supplies appeared vulnerable to interruption. Brazil is largely dependent on imports for her oil and coal requirements, although electricity is mainly generated by hydroelectric means and is therefore cheap.

Given this cheap electricity, the jet nozzle enrichment technology was a logical one for Brazil to choose; and for STEAG, the West German company responsible for developing the technology, Brazil was an ideal country in which to develop the technology.[24] Under the joint development programme, agreed between the Brazilian company Nuclebras and STEAG, a 6000 SWU/a pilot enrichment facility has been built at Resende. This was to be followed by a 300 000 SWU/a demonstration plant, but a decision on this has now been postponed until 1988. Fuel fabrication and uranium hexafluoride conversion plants have also been constructed at Resende. However, problems have been encountered in developing the nozzle enrichment technology and it is unlikely to prove commercially competitive. Thus the original plan to establish a 1 million to 3 million SWU/a commercial plant by the early 1990s and for Brazil to become a major exporter of enriched uranium has been virtually abandoned.[25] There have also been delays in the construction of the Angra 2 and Angra 3 power reactors. No further reactors are likely to be ordered in the foreseeable future, and the reprocessing plant is not likely to be built for some years, until sufficient spent fuel has accumulated from the existing power plants. Indeed, faced as she is with an enormous foreign debt burden, the economic case for Brazil's nuclear programme seems increasingly questionable.

THE NUCLEAR SUPPLIERS GROUP GUIDELINES

In the early 1970s, the number of nuclear power reactors in the world was growing rapidly, and this growth was projected to accelerate as countries sought to reduce their dependence on imported oil, supplies of which were becoming both expensive and uncertain. As we have seen, some less-developed countries showed a desire to acquire enrichment or reprocessing plants, ostensibly as part of their civil nuclear power programme, but these plants would also enable these countries to produce weapons-grade fissile material if they so wished. By the mid-1970s, Americans had become concerned that IAEA safeguards on such plants might not be adequate to give assurance of non-diversion of such fissile material. The United States government pressed very strongly for the cancellation of French plans to transfer reprocessing technology to Pakistan and South Korea and the West German agreement to transfer both reprocessing and enrichment technology to Brazil. The French deals were eventually cancelled (as was a Taiwanese plan to develop a reprocessing capability) following strong American political pressure on the Asian countries concerned, but, as we have seen, West Germany resolutely refused to cancel her agreement with Brazil. North Americans were concerned that, unless restrained, European countries might conclude further agreements for the transfer of sensitive enrichment and reprocessing facilities as 'sweeteners' in order to secure contracts for the sale of power reactors in the highly competitive Third World market.[26]

We have seen that, by 1970, the American-led Western Suppliers Group of uranium-producing countries was no longer able to ensure that uranium was only used in safeguarded installations in non-nuclear weapon states. Uranium deposits had been found to be widespread. Uranium mining is not very different from any other mining technology; and the number of countries able to produce uranium, in relatively small quantities, but sufficient for their own consumption, had increased. So, for example, by the 1970s, Israel, India, Brazil and Argentina had all developed their own uranium mining capacity.

As a result of these developments, the US government, besides publicly urging the cancellation of the above-mentioned European export arrangements, secretly sought agreement with other industrial-ised nations on guidelines to be followed so that non-proliferation as well as commercial considerations would be taken into account in their nuclear exports. In the mid-1970s, frequent highly-secretive meetings of the main nuclear technology exporting countries (rather than, as before, the uranium-exporting countries) were held to this end. According to Pringle and Spigelman, this group of countries was a direct descendant of the Western Suppliers Group, but with the exclusion of certain uranium-producing countries, Australia, South Africa and Portugal, and the inclusion of potential technology-exporting countries, West Germany, Japan and the Soviet Union. (This was also the period of East–West *détente*.) Accordingly, this group of countries became known as the Nuclear Suppliers Group (NSG) or, more colloquially, the London Club (after its first and customary meeting place).[27]

Provisional agreement on a code of conduct governing member countries' nuclear exports was reached in 1975. By 1977, when the group last met, the membership of the London Club had expanded to fifteen, comprising Belgium, Canada, Czechoslovakia, France, East and West Germany, Italy, Japan, the Netherlands, Poland, Sweden, Switzerland, the United Kingdom, the United States and the Soviet Union. This enlarged group announced substantial agreement early in 1978 when member states sent identical letters to the IAEA setting forth the principles and detailed guidelines they would henceforward follow in their nuclear exports.[28]

A central feature of this joint policy statement was a 'trigger list' of items which were only to be exported if IAEA safeguards were applied to their end use. At the time, this list extended a similar list, drawn up by a committee of twenty-one nations known as the Zangger Committee, of exports by NPT signatories to non-nuclear weapon parties that would trigger full-scope safeguards under the Non-Proliferation Treaty.[29]

The NSG trigger list included natural and enriched uranium, plutonium, heavy water and graphite (the composition and minimum quantity to trigger safeguards being defined in the list) and the following fuel-cycle facilities and their component parts: reactors, fuel fabrication plants, heavy water production plants, reprocessing plants and enrichment plants. The list even defined the enrichment plant components, the export of which would trigger safeguards in the importing country. These included gaseous diffusion barriers, gas centrifuge assemblies, jet nozzle and vortex separation units, large axial or centrifugal compressors (corrosion resistant to uranium hexafluoride) and special seals for these compressors.[30] Here the NSG list went beyond the Zangger Committee list. However, whereas the Nuclear Suppliers Group no longer meets, the Zangger Committee continues to update its list, so that it now includes all items on the NSG list. (In 1984, the Zangger Committee went further by specifying materials and component parts for gas centrifuge assemblies (in an attempt to prevent exports of components similar to those made by Western firms to Pakistan). The Zangger Committee plans to undertake a similar task for component parts of reprocessing plants and other fuel-cycle facilities, the export of which by NPT parties to NNWS parties would trigger IAEA full-scope safeguards.[31])

Under the London Club guidelines, export of any item on the NSG trigger list to non-nuclear weapon states should trigger IAEA safeguards, assurance of non-explosive use and physical protection guarantees. These safeguards and assurances plus the original supplying country's consent would also apply to the construction or re-export of any reprocessing, enrichment or heavy water plant which utilised technology 'of the same type' or 'derived from' the originally transferred item. The practical problems in enforcing this last provision have already been noted in the context of the West German agreement to supply Brazil with fuel cycle facilities including nozzle enrichment and reprocessing technology.[32]

London Club members made other non-proliferation commitments besides the trigger list. France and West Germany accepted that there should be no more deals such as those made with Pakistan and Brazil for the export of reprocessing plants. (France subsequently cancelled her plan to build a reprocessing plant in Pakistan.) France and West Germany accepted the Nuclear Suppliers Group policy of 'exercising restraint' in their exports of sensitive nuclear technology and weapons-usable material.

The adoption of the NSG guidelines by France was considered by the Americans a major non-proliferation advance, as it was the first time that France had formally supported a superpower-sponsored non-proliferation initiative (her support for the earlier Western Suppliers Group policy on uranium exports having been half-hearted at best). Because of its discriminatory nature, France has refused to sign the NPT, although she has agreed to conduct her nuclear exports in line with the provisions of the treaty. French policy then was that countries may indigenously develop their own unsafeguarded nuclear plants, as she had done, but that French exports should not be seen to be increasing the prospects for further proliferation. So, although France does not insist on full-scope safeguards, she was able nevertheless to support the NSG guidelines.[33]

From a non-proliferation perspective, the French policy and the Nuclear Suppliers Group guidelines in general can be criticised for appearing to encourage nations to become self-sufficient in nuclear technology and fuel. Under the guidelines, London Club members are expected to ensure that their nuclear exports are used in safeguarded facilities; but full-scope safeguards are not required in the importing countries, as they are under the NPT. Importing countries may therefore have perceived advantages in not signing the Non-Proliferation Treaty. NPT parties, on the other hand, might justifiably have felt discriminated against. Some of them also felt that the agreement by London Club members to exercise restraint in their export of sensitive technology and material contravened Article IV of the Non-Proliferation Treaty.

Some importing nations could thus have received the signal from the London Club that nuclear technology and material are 'forbidden fruit'. It would have been considered particularly unfortunate if developing countries had received this message, as it can reasonably be argued on technical grounds that nuclear power is not suited to their economies.

Nevertheless, at a time when Third World countries were pressing for the establishment of a 'New International Economic Order' and when their economies had been particularly adversely affected by the sharp rise in oil prices, many of these countries may have concluded from the secretive deliberations of the Nuclear Suppliers Group (like those of the Western Suppliers Group before it) that the industrialised countries were trying to impose a nuclear cartel, albeit one controlling technology transfer rather than prices. It is largely to allay such suspicions that the London Club no longer meets, although the guidelines remain in force.

A final loophole in the London Club agreement, and one which has since widened, is that membership of the Club was restricted to industrialised nations of the northern hemisphere. Yet the major industrialising nations of the 'South', including Brazil, Argentina, India, China and South Africa, now have the capacity for significant nuclear exports; and some of these countries intend increasing their nuclear exports to each other and other developing countries (in exchange no doubt for political influence as well as economic returns). Analysts in the West have expressed concern that this trade may not be constrained by non-proliferation undertakings by these exporting countries.[34] However, although some of these countries will not subscribe to the London Club guidelines for political reasons (because they seem to discriminate against have-not nations), other industrialising nations may consider their status as technologically advanced nations enhanced by recent attempts by the United States to persuade them to follow the London Club guidelines in their nuclear exports.[35]

THE US NUCLEAR NON-PROLIFERATION ACT

The secretive deliberations of the London Club did not allay the mounting American concern over the advent of the 'plutonium economy'. Increasing amounts of spent fuel would be accumulating from power reactors. More countries seemed to want to reprocess this spent fuel to facilitate waste disposal, recycle the uranium and plutonium in thermal or fast breeder reactors or possibly, it was feared, 'misuse' the plutonium for weapons purposes. It was felt that plutonium could be quite easily and swiftly diverted from reprocessing plants by governments or terrorist groups, and that adequate international safeguards and national security procedures to give 'timely warning' of such diversion would be technically very difficult and perhaps even impossible to achieve. The 1974 Indian explosion had been of a plutonium device. United States pressure had forced the cancellation of reprocessing plants which were to have been constructed by French companies in Pakistan and South Korea; but there remained plans for the construction of commercial reprocessing plants in West Germany, France, the United Kingdom, Japan and Brazil, and other countries would be bound to want to emulate these. Public concern, about nuclear proliferation in general and the dangers of the plutonium economy in particular, became evident in the pronouncements of both candidates in the 1976 US presidential election campaign.[36] This concern eventually resulted in the passage into law of the 1978 US Nuclear Non-Proliferation Act (NNPA).[37]

Under the NNPA, which amended the 1954 Atomic Energy Act, all US exports of nuclear fuel and reactors to non-nuclear weapon states were to trigger full-scope safeguards in the importing country with effect from 1980. The semi-autonomous Nuclear Regulatory Commission (NRC) was to grant export licences only if the provisions of the Act were satisfied. These licences would be issued on a case-by-case basis for each export. For overseas countries' fuel which had been fabricated or enriched in the USA or cycled through American-supplied reactors, it would be necessary for these countries to seek prior consent from the US government before the material could be significantly transformed, in particular before it could be reprocessed. Agreements for nuclear cooperation with other countries were to be renegotiated to give the United States this right of prior consent over importing countries' fuel-cycle activities. An NRC refusal to grant an export licence could be overturned by the President only in exceptional circumstances if the refusal was judged harmful to American conduct of foreign policy or her security interests. (Even such a presidential order could be overruled by Congress if both the Senate and the House of Representatives concurred. However, this fresh assertion of congressional authority was subsequently nullified when the Supreme Court ruled in 1983 that the congressional overrule provision was unconstitutional.)

To demonstrate its concern over the advent of the plutonium economy and to set an example to other nations, the Carter administration unilaterally suspended America's own commercial fast breeder and reprocessing programmes and halted the construction of plants. It also initiated the International Nuclear Fuel Cycle Evaluation programme (INFCE): an intergovernmental enquiry into nuclear technology involving a broad cross-section of IAEA members. It was hoped that INFCE might conclude that fuel cycles which did not require the reprocessing of spent fuel should be adopted.

Although she had thus voluntarily retired from the 'back end' of the thermal reactor fuel cycle (for the time being), the USA could exert leverage over other countries' nuclear programmes through her exports for the 'front end' of the fuel cycle. Although she was losing much of her market share for the construction of power reactors, to France and West Germany in particular, the United States still dominated the world market for uranium enrichment. (It was not appreciated that even this market dominance was projected to be rapidly eroded soon.[38]) Most of the spent fuel which other countries wished to reprocess thus originated as uranium which had been enriched in the United States.

Besides provoking the resentment of developing countries which saw their access to peaceful nuclear technology impeded, intense criticism of the US Nuclear Non-Proliferation Act came from Western Europe and Japan, where there were already plans for building reprocessing plants to facilitate waste disposal and/or extract uranium and plutonium from spent fuel for their re-use as fuel. For these countries, the Act's requirement that the prior consent of the American government should be obtained before fuel originating or enriched in the USA could be reprocessed appeared to create intolerable uncertainty concerning nuclear fuel supplies, at a time when there was already uncertainty concerning oil supplies because of the actions of the petroleum-producing nations. Because of this West European and Japanese opposition to the NNPA, by 1986 the US government had still not been able successfully to renegotiate agreements for nuclear cooperation with Japan and Euratom, the nuclear supply agency for the European Community. Rather than risk a confrontation with her allies, the American government has therefore, since 1980, annually waived the prior consent rights provision of the NNPA for these countries.

The United States did obtain *some* support for her non-proliferation policy from other nations. In 1976 the United Kingdom and the Soviet Union had suggested that the London Suppliers Club should adopt a policy of requiring full-scope safeguards for all nuclear exports to non-nuclear weapon states. France (and other West European countries) had, however, objected on the ground that this would amount to an imposition of the Non-Proliferation Treaty on countries which had not signed it. The United Kingdom's nuclear exports were by now insufficient for her to be able to exert any significant non-proliferation leverage, and the Soviet Union was not prepared to require full-scope safeguards on her nuclear exports unless the other members of the Nuclear Suppliers Group agreed to do likewise. The USSR has thus continued to supply India with heavy water embargoed by Canada, offered to sell power reactors to India, supplied Argentina with heavy water and enriched uranium and is building a nuclear power station in Cuba.[39] All these countries refuse to accept NPT-type full-scope safeguards, and India and Argentina possess unsafeguarded facilities. Soviet policy is thus to require safeguards on her nuclear exports, but she does not insist on full-scope safeguards. However, she does require that all spent fuel from Soviet-constructed reactors (almost exclusively in the Soviet sphere of influence) should be returned to the USSR.[40]

The United States obtained more substantial support for her non-proliferation policy from Canada and Australia, both major uranium-exporting nations. Canada is the world's largest exporter of natural uranium. She is also a significant exporter of nuclear technology, notably the CANDU natural uranium-fuelled power reactor. Australia has the world's largest uranium reserves and was also projected to become a major uranium exporter.[41] Like the United States, Canada and Australia adopted a policy of requiring full-scope safeguards for their nuclear exports and were prepared to allow reprocessing (of spent fuel originating as uranium mined in their countries) only under strict conditions. Canada's concern that she may have contributed to proliferation in the Indian subcontinent has been mentioned already. Her strict non-proliferation policy pre-dated the US Nuclear Non-Proliferation Act. Adherence to the policy was enforced through her annual award of uranium export licences. Reluctance on the part of importing countries to agree to Canada's non-proliferation requirements (in particular her insistence on the right to give prior consent before countries could reprocess fuel of Canadian origin) led to a Canadian uranium embargo on the European Community and Japan throughout 1977.

Nevertheless, it was felt in Western Europe and Japan that, whereas the United States, Canada and Australia could impose these non-proliferation policies at little cost to themselves, since they were self-sufficient in uranium, they (Western Europe and Japan) were largely dependent on imported uranium. Because they were so dependent on imports for their energy supplies, these countries' aim was to achieve greater self-sufficiency by developing the breeder reactor which would make use of their stocks of depleted uranium. The long-term objective of West European and Japanese nuclear programmes was thus to reprocess spent fuel from thermal reactors and recycle the plutonium in these reactors or to surround it with a natural or depleted uranium blanket and use it in breeder reactors. These countries therefore viewed reprocessing as essential for achieving 'energy security', whereas the non-proliferation policies of the United States, Canada and Australia seemed to be adding to the insecurity of their energy supplies.[42]

However, due largely to decisions made or developments at hand before the United States, Canada and Australia instituted their non-proliferation policies, the leverage these Anglo-Saxon nuclear-exporting nations were able to exert was shrinking with their diminishing control over the markets for natural uranium and uranium enrichment.

THE ANGLO-SAXONS' LOSS OF NUCLEAR LEVERAGE

By the late 1970s, the French and West German market share of nuclear power reactor exports had been increasing at the expense of American companies for some years (though these exports were almost exclusively of light water reactors, a technology originally developed in the United States). US production of raw uranium concentrate, though large, had always only supplied her domestic market. Now the United States was importing an increasing amount of natural uranium, and this trend was projected to accelerate. Indeed, the United States had only been able to maintain a large uranium production capacity by using her enrichment monopoly to ensure that domestic electric utilities purchased only domestically-mined uranium. This embargo on foreign uranium imports was progressively lifted by the US government between 1977 and 1983.[43]

Canada and Australia were able to exert considerable influence in the uranium market; but this influence was reduced both by delays in the planned expansion of production capacity in Australia (due to domestic political reasons) and also by increased production by the African producers, Gabon, Niger, South Africa and Namibia.[44] There was therefore a tendency for countries which did not meet the strict Canadian and Australian non-proliferation requirements to import from these African countries. Uranium exports from South Africa and Namibia are further discussed in Chapter 4. The marketing of uranium production from Gabon and Niger is largely undertaken by French government-owned companies; but the government of Niger has also in the past supplied fellow Islamic nations, Iraq, Libya and Pakistan, with uranium generally far in excess of that needed for their known reactor programmes and with minimal or no non-proliferation conditions attached.[45]

Even consumers with exemplary non-proliferation credentials sought to diversify their sources of supply away from Canada and Australia because of the associated uncertainty and bureaucracy (the latter being largely due to the need to 'track' and 'label' the uranium through the fuel cycle in order for the supplying country to be sure that spent fuel was not reprocessed without its prior consent). This increased demand for African-mined uranium has in the past enabled African producers to obtain a premium on the price of their yellowcake (uranium concentrate). Indeed a 'grey market' in uranium, with no non-proliferation strings attached, has emerged. In addition, West European and Far Eastern electric utilities and government-owned mining companies sought to diversify their sources of supply further by funding exploration in other areas (as West Germany had done in Brazil).

For the reasons outlined above it has become impossible for a few mainly Anglo-Saxon Western nations secretly and successfully to monitor and control the international trade in uranium in the interests of non-proliferation as they did during the 1950s and early 1960s. Nevertheless, ever since she had launched the Atoms for Peace era, the United States had been able to exert substantial control over international nuclear developments by means of her monopoly in the supply of uranium enrichment. However, this monopoly position was also being eroded and was projected to be further eroded.[46]

The Soviet Union first broke the American monopoly in 1970 when she began to sell enrichment services in the West. In 1973, in an unsuccessful attempt to promote the privatisation of American enrichment plants, the Nixon administration altered the contracting arrangement for American enrichment supplies. This, together with the announcement of plans for expanded nuclear power programmes by Western governments following the rapid rise in oil prices after the 1973 Middle East war, led to a rush of orders by enrichment consumers (electric utilities). When the US government announced in 1974 that, due to insufficient capacity, it could not enter into any additional contracts to supply enrichment to overseas customers, uncertainty about energy security and the reliability of American supplies increased in Western Europe and Japan.[47] Existing plans for the construction of enrichment plants in Europe by the internationally-owned URENCO and Eurodif concerns were then pursued with greater urgency; and other Western nations announced enrichment programmes. As explained in the Appendix, the position today is that, largely as a result of these developments which took place during the first half of the 1970s, the world market for uranium enrichment is now vastly oversupplied (a situation which will continue well into the 1990s) and the United States has lost her monopoly position.

To make their non-proliferation policies effective, therefore, the Anglo-Saxon nuclear exporters (the USA, Canada and Australia) would have had to secure the cooperation of (i) the African producers of natural uranium – Niger, Gabon and South Africa (which also controls the territory of Namibia) and (ii) those European countries (and possibly, in future, Japan) which supply nuclear reactors and enrichment services.[48] As Lodgaard has stated, failure to obtain the support of these countries would mean that importing nations might

> turn to European suppliers for technology and equipment, to South Africa and France/Gabon/Niger for uranium, and to Eurodif/Coredif, Urenco, and possibly the USSR for enrichment services. Accordingly, European countries may prefer Canadian, Australian, and U.S. uranium for their domestic power programmes, so that enough South African uranium is available to support reactor orders from countries which do not fulfil the strictest requirements. This prospect is certainly noted by South Africa . . .[49]

South Africa's export policy is discussed in some detail in Chapters 4, 6 and 8, but we may note here that France in particular has also acquired considerable influence in international nuclear commerce through (i) her interests in uranium mining in Niger and Gabon (as well as in France itself), (ii) her dominant interest in the Eurodif enrichment venture and (iii) her position as a major exporter of nuclear power reactors.[50] Commenting on the changes in the pattern of supply of nuclear fuel and technology and their effect on the ability of the United States and, by implication, Canada and Australia, to achieve their stated non-proliferation objectives, Neff and Jacoby observed in 1979 that:

> These market changes are of profound importance to U.S. non-proliferation policy, because countries perceiving an advantage in independence of the United States will soon be able to achieve it . . . If the stakes are raised too high, or if large uncertainties about the security of supply from the United States continue, the balance of some nations' interests may be shifted away from the United States, to the detriment of both its nonproliferation influence and its commercial interests . . . U.S. market leverage is declining rapidly and so too is any influence based on this leverage. The continued U.S. use of fuel leverage only tightens near-term supply conditions and increases uncertainties, adding to the pressure to decide in favour of the very activities we are trying to restrain.[51]

This last comment suggests that American policy actually had the effect of *encouraging* the construction of enrichment plants, reprocessing plants and fast breeder reactors, rather than the reverse, which was the intention. Thus, for example, according to her own government officials, *Argentina's* decision to construct an enrichment plant (announced retrospectively in 1983) was precipitated by the American suspension of enriched uranium fuel supplies for her research reactors. These supplies were cut off because Argentina could not accept full-scope safeguards (although Argentina subsequently obtained enriched uranium from the Soviet Union). The 1983 Argentine announcement came as a great surprise, as the construction of the unsafeguarded 23 000 SWU/a plant at Pilcaniyeu (planned to come into operation in 1986) which, according to Argentine officials, employs the sophisticated diffusion technology, had been a well-kept secret. Moreover, for power generation, Argentina uses natural uranium-fuelled reactors and so would appear to have no need to develop expensive enrichment technology indigenously. However, Argentine officials sought to justify the development by stating that the use of slightly enriched uranium would improve the fuel efficiency of these reactors. In addition, besides the need for enriched uranium fuel for her research reactors, the construction of the Pilcaniyeu plant has been justified on the ground that it enables Argentina to supply enriched uranium fuel for research reactors built by Argentina in other Latin American countries. Argentina attaches great political value to such exports as they appear to demonstrate her nuclear dominance in a region where, in other respects, Brazil could justifiably claim to be the major power.[52]

Inevitably, by the 1980s the United States had to accept that leverage in the enrichment market had shifted to the Europeans, notably the French. Indeed, in 1981 and 1982, in order to prevent a deterioration in relations with India, Brazil and South Africa over the full-scope safeguards provision of the Nuclear Non-Proliferation Act, President Reagan allowed or acquiesced in these nations obtaining essential enriched uranium supplies from European producers, rather than, as contracted, the US Department of Energy.[53]

From the manner in which the Nuclear Non-Proliferation Act has been implemented, or rather circumvented, it would appear that the US government has now recognised that, due to the erosion of American dominance in nuclear commerce, it needs to seek the support of other Western nuclear-exporting countries for its non-proliferation policy. In the July 1981 statement of his administration's non-proliferation policy, President Reagan stated that the United States had to demonstrate that she was a 'predictable and reliable partner' in nuclear commerce to prevent trading partners 'going their own ways', with a consequent diminution of American influence in international nuclear affairs. In an effort to attain a convergence with West European and Japanese nuclear policies, the President also stated that the United States would no longer 'inhibit . . . reprocessing and breeder reactor development abroad in nations with advanced nuclear power programmes where it does not constitute a proliferation risk'. So, by the early 1980s, because of their reduced leverage over the markets for natural uranium and uranium enrichment and in an effort to attain a rapprochement over non-proliferation policy with their Western allies, the United States, Canada and Australia had all agreed to issue 'generic' or 'programmatic' consent for reprocessing of fuel originating or enriched in their countries, rather than exercise case-by-case review of such exports as they had previously intended.[54]

However, at the same time as these changes in the supply side of the nuclear market were taking place, there were also changes on a global scale in the fortunes and acceptability of nuclear power. *These* changes on the *demand* side were leading to surplus capacity in uranium production and enrichment and reduced commercial pressure for both (i) an increase in the number of enrichment and reprocessing plants and (ii) the advent of breeder reactors. Thus, as we shall see below, to this extent the aims of the US non-proliferation policy became more readily achievable.

URANIUM OVERSUPPLY: LESS CONCERN ABOUT THE PLUTONIUM ECONOMY

In the event, the INFCE consultations, at their conclusion in 1980, did not produce any 'technical fix'. What was supposedly a technical evaluation was inevitably dominated by political considerations and, in the end, the chief protagonists, the United States on one side and the West European nations and Japan on the other, found it politically expedient to agree on a compromise final report. Thus it was accepted that it was impossible to rank fuel cycles according to which were the most proliferation-prone; and the Europeans and Japanese interpreted this conclusion as giving a green light for their breeder programmes. The most that could be agreed was that the recycling of plutonium in thermal reactors might not be justified economically (the American view) but that some nations might wish to adopt plutonium recycling in order to facilitate waste disposal, help increase their energy security or conserve uranium resources (the European and Japanese view).[55] One commentator on the INFCE discussions contrasted the American concern with military security (non-proliferation) with the European concern with energy security. The American position emphasised the slow projected growth in nuclear power generation, whereas amongst the Europeans there was 'more optimism about the growth of nuclear power and more pessimism about uranium reserves (and particularly about the free availability of uranium, whatever the reserves might be)'.[56]

Six years later it is possible to say with hindsight that the American projection was by far the most accurate. Partly for social reasons to do with the public's acceptance, or rather non-acceptance, of nuclear power (due mainly to concern about its health and safety effects, a concern which intensified following the 1979 Three Mile Island power reactor accident in the United States) and partly because of the economic recession since 1980 and generally escalating capital and construction costs for nuclear power stations, the rate of growth in the number of nuclear power plants ordered worldwide since the mid-1970s, and hence the demand for uranium, has been very low, whilst the number of cancellations of orders for nuclear power stations has increased. In the early 1980s there was therefore a large surplus in uranium production and enrichment capacity and a steep fall from the high prices of uranium concentrate attained in the mid-1970s.[57] Stockpiles of both natural and enriched uranium built up, especially in the consuming countries. These stockpiles, which amounted to over three years' forward consumption in the early 1980s, together with greater diversification of sources of supply, gave uranium-importing nations more security of supply. A significant secondary trade even emerged, with some electric utilities selling surplus natural and enriched uranium. It was predicted that, even in the unlikely event of a sudden turnaround in the nuclear fuel market, due to a global economic revival and another change in the fortunes of the nuclear power industry (this time for the better), the uranium buyers' market would not change into a sellers' market until the 1990s.[58]

As uranium prices fell and supply sources became more diversified, the need perceived in Western Europe and Japan for further reprocessing capacity and for the 'plutonium economy' to be developed was reduced, both for economic reasons and for reasons of energy security. With worldwide overcapacity in enrichment supply projected to continue into the 1990s, there was also no immediate economic pressure for the construction of more enrichment plants.

Reduced economic pressure for both the construction of enrichment and reprocessing plants and the early adoption of fast breeder reactors helped to reduce the prospect of further proliferation of nuclear weapons capabilities, as did nations' diminished anxiety about the need to be self-sufficient over the entire fuel cycle. However, it should be noted that these changes occurred in spite of the Anglo-Saxon nations' non-proliferation policies rather than because of them. (To be more accurate, the general public rejection of nuclear power in the West was not the intention of these governments' policies, although it was in part the result.) Indeed the excess and more diversified capacity in uranium production and enrichment reduced the non-proliferation leverage at the disposal of the United States, Canada and Australia.[59] It should also be noted that, with the downturn in the nuclear industry, there was a temptation for nations to relax the non-proliferation conditions on their nuclear exports in order to secure jobs and maintain production capacity established in the boom years of the early 1970s. (It was suspected in some quarters that it was pressure from the domestic nuclear industry that led in part to President Reagan's announced relaxation in United States non-proliferation policy in 1981.) Indeed, whatever the official export policies pursued, excess capacity in all stages of the nuclear industry is likely to result in a 'grey market' in nuclear equipment, material and technologists available for buyers.[60]

NON-PROLIFERATION POLICY TODAY: THE EMPHASIS ON MOTIVATIONS

In the account above of the erosion of the American monopoly in the production of enriched uranium and her consequent inability unilaterally to persuade other countries to accept full-scope safeguards on their nuclear installations, we noted that Argentina, Brazil, India and South Africa, countries which did not accept full-scope safeguards and had earlier been supplied or had contracted to be supplied with enriched uranium from the United States, were able to obtain this enriched uranium from other sources in the early 1980s. Pakistan and Israel, the other states on the threshold of nuclear weapons possession which also had unsafeguarded facilities, did not depend on nuclear supplies from the United States. So the Nuclear Non-Proliferation Act posed even fewer problems for these countries. However, both nations depended on the United States for their considerable imports of armaments; and the Reagan administration substantially increased the USA's level of military and economic aid to both Israel and Pakistan (the strategic importance of the latter having increased following the 1979–80 Soviet military intervention in Afghanistan) despite the protests of the Arab nations and India respectively.[61] In the United States, this strengthening of military links with Israel and Pakistan was rationalised on non-proliferation grounds with the assertion that, by addressing these nations' security concerns, their *incentives* for acquiring nuclear weapons had been reduced.

Whilst a detailed discussion of 'nth' countries' possible incentives for acquiring nuclear weapons would not be appropriate here, a brief résumé of conventional wisdom on the subject is offered below.[62] Some suggestions have been made earlier in this chapter concerning the nuclear motivations of some of the countries mentioned above. South Africa's nuclear intentions are discussed in Chapter 8.

Broadly speaking, governments may be motivated to obtain nuclear weapons by either prestige or security considerations. Considering first the prestige motivation, a government may feel that, by demonstrating the capability to produce nuclear weapons, it acquires a high standing, both domestically and internationally, because the country is thereby seen to be scientifically, technologically and industrially 'advanced'. (Indeed, because they may feel that it raises *their* status, the bureaucratic and/or scientific and technological élite within a country may propel that country towards a nuclear weapons capability without there necessarily being much political control over that development.) A government may feel that, after the country has been shown to have a nuclear weapons capability, other nations, friend and foe alike, will take it more seriously in their bilateral military, scientific and trading relations. This respect could come as a result of a nation's indigenous development of nuclear technology, regardless of whether that nation has any military ambitions concerning the use of that technology.

In seeking to prevent a country from acquiring a weapons capability by denial of nuclear material or technology, the United States and other major powers shaping the non-proliferation regime may be merely increasing the country's determination to develop that capability. On the other hand, the recent apparent American downgrading in importance attached to non-proliferation (compared with other policy goals) may serve to diminish the value attached to nuclear weapons and technology for nations seeking an enhanced global status.

In practice, countries generally are and have been motivated to develop a nuclear weapons capability by both military *and* prestige considerations which may be difficult to distinguish. If, however, prestige motivations are dominant, a government may be content to let the nation's weapons capability become known by intelligence leaks, a 'peaceful nuclear explosion' or an atmospheric test which is anonymous yet whose authorship is readily attributable. India, Israel, South Africa and possibly Pakistan seem to have made it known in one or more of these ways that they have a weapons option. Even if the motivations are primarily military (as they are for Israel), there are constraints against an unambiguous declaration of nuclear weapons possession, whether by a weapons test or otherwise. There would be a strong possibility of the withdrawal of American economic aid (as mandated by congressional legislation) to such an 'nth' nuclear weapon state; and, despite the mixed results of non-proliferation policies to date, an international climate of opinion has been firmly established against further proliferation, as shown by over 120 signatures of the Non-Proliferation Treaty. Moreover, since India's 1974 explosion, the alibi that such explosions could be for peaceful purposes seems to have been generally discredited.

Continued 'vertical' proliferation – the escalating arms race between the superpowers – may weaken these constraints against further 'horizontal' proliferation. Notwithstanding the superpowers' agreements to limit the number of their strategic delivery systems and the warheads they contain, a tripling of their arsenals of nuclear warheads since 1968, and the lack of progess made by the nuclear weapon states in agreeing a comprehensive test ban treaty would seem to indicate both the apparent utility of nuclear weapons and the bad faith of the NPT sponsors, shown by their evident lack of commitment to Article VI of the treaty (which was their part of the bargain). Nevertheless, the United States and the Soviet Union still feel obliged to convey to the world the appearance of trying to make progress towards arms control and eventual nuclear disarmament (especially before the quinquennial NPT Review Conferences). Jozef Goldblat has described the relationship between vertical and horizontal proliferation and the consequent responsibilities of the nuclear weapon states as follows:

Doubts are sometimes expressed as to whether there exists a relationship between the two types of proliferation [vertical and horizontal]. Indeed, if at this stage any new country acquires nuclear weapons, it will do so presumably in order to intimidate or impress its immediate neighbours, or to enhance its international standing and gain more political prestige, influence and consideration in world councils, rather than to compete militarily with the present nuclear weapon powers, especially the USA and the USSR. Whether or not nuclear weapons will spread any further will also depend on the resolution of the most acute regional conflicts. Be that as it may, a treaty denying a powerful weapon to most nations in order to preserve a firebreak between the 'haves' and the 'have-nots' is not likely to withstand the pressures of a continued arms race. Since nuclear weapons appear to have political and military usefulness for the nuclear powers, the non-nuclear weapon countries may feel that they too must obtain these advantages. A dynamic process of nuclear disarmament is therefore necessary to de-emphasize the role and utility of nuclear weaponry in world diplomacy and military strategy and to generate political and moral inhibitions dampening the nuclear ambitions of certain non-nuclear weapon states.[63]

Although it may not be very impressed with the above argument, the American government, as mentioned at the beginning of this section, now favours a non-proliferation policy which pays closer attention to potential 'nth' nations' military incentives for acquiring nuclear weapons. In his 1981 non-proliferation policy statement, President Reagan said that the United States would henceforth 'strive to reduce the motivation for acquiring nuclear explosives by working to improve regional and global stability and to promote understanding of the legitimate security concerns of other states'.[64] Of course this statement begs certain questions concerning how this broad policy goal is to be interpreted. Its practical implementation would first depend on the American government's political and strategic judgement as to which states' security concerns are 'legitimate'. However, in general one can say that nations' security concerns may be addressed and their military incentives for possessing nuclear weapons reduced by the United States adopting one or more of the following approaches: (i) trying to solve regional disputes; (ii) providing security guarantees (possibly to the extent of providing a nuclear 'umbrella'); (iii) supplying conventional armaments; and (iv), if necessary, deploying US or allied troops.[65]

Conversely, refraining from taking any of these actions may increase nations' incentives for acquiring nuclear weapons. Thus a decline in the credibility of United States military support and security guarantees for certain nations may precipitate moves towards acquisition of nuclear weapons by countries not hitherto considered in this chapter. For example, when President Carter announced that US troops would be withdrawn from South Korea by 1982, that country was seen to be pursuing the nuclear weapons option with more determination, and this helped to persuade President Carter to change his mind. If America's strategic commitment to her allies in the northern hemisphere was to be called seriously into question, there might even be domestic pressure on more Western European governments and Japan to acquire nuclear weapons.

United States military strength and self-confidence is clearly essential if this form of non-proliferation policy is to be effective. In this context it should be recalled that the 1970s, the decade of major concern about proliferation, coincided with a period of relative American weakness when, largely as a result of her debilitating military involvement in Vietnam, the United States appeared less able to exert her military strength, particularly in the Third World.

An assessment of which countries' security concerns are 'legitimate' and which of the aforementioned policy measures should be adopted would also depend on a foreign policy judgement of American interests in the region concerned. Clearly, however, too explicit a linkage between military support and nuclear development in the country concerned could render the United States vulnerable to blackmail by that country. The United States may also seem to third parties to be rewarding the country for nuclear developments to date. A final danger, leading American non-proliferation policy-makers to approach the resolution of this 'dove's dilemma' with caution, is that conventional arms sales may enhance the nuclear weapon delivery capability of the recipient state.

CONCLUSION

The emphasis in non-proliferation policy has therefore now switched to attempting to address individual nation's possible motivations for acquiring nuclear weapons rather than the means by which that capability is acquired. Nuclear proliferation problems are now viewed in a regional context. It has become accepted that there is no universal panacea such that a unilateral Act of Congress or a multilateral treaty can prevent further proliferation. Technology denial may now be considered a wasting asset anyway, as technology will inevitably spread eventually. Moreover, although nuclear power technology and nuclear weapons technology are closely related, all those states known to possess nuclear weapons, or considered likely to possess them, have reached that position by means of a dedicated programme rather than by diverting fissile material from a nuclear power programme. In any case, developing and developed countries alike now seem to have a more realistic assessment of the commercial prospects for nuclear energy, which has failed to live up to earlier extravagant hopes. Any government embarking on an ambitious nuclear power programme is now more likely to appear profligate and spendthrift than 'modern'.

This changed approach to non-proliferation policy, with less emphasis on the denial of nuclear material and technology, is summed up in the expression that policy should be addressed to the problem of 'sensitive countries', such as Pakistan or Argentina, rather than 'sensitive technologies', such as enrichment or reprocessing. The American government now appears to regard the enrichment and reprocessing plants that have been established elsewhere, notably in Europe, as being justifiable and 'not constituting a proliferation risk'. Further capacity, such as enrichment in Australia, could be similarly justified. The hope may be that the resulting overcapacity and diversification of capacity may be used to argue persuasively, on economic grounds and grounds of increased security of supply, against the further spread of 'sensitive' technology to 'sensitive' countries.

Thus, discrimination between nations, whether it is between India and Pakistan or between 'sensitive' developing countries and Western industrialised nations, which are not 'proliferation risks' and have a well-developed nuclear technology base and where further development of 'sensitive' technologies can therefore be justified on economic grounds, is inevitable in the new approach, as it is in any non-proliferation policy. This time the countries discriminated against will not be able to point to the wording of a multilateral agreement or treaty or a unilateral act of legislation, as in the recent past, but will instead have to monitor case law as it develops with the implementation of the new non-proliferation approach.

In any case, notwithstanding the inevitable associated injustices, American policy-makers may have reached the sober assessment that essentially their proliferation problems have become limited to six nations: Argentina, Brazil, Israel, India, Pakistan and South Africa, whereas in 1963 President Kennedy had forecast that by 1975 there could be another fifteen to twenty nuclear weapon states. None of these six countries accept full-scope safeguards on their nuclear plants, and some of them probably already possess nuclear explosive devices. However, although most of their declared policies have left open areas of ambiguity concerning weapons possession, none of these six nations are likely openly to declare their possession of nuclear weapons in the foreseeable future, for a variety of reasons which are explored in the case of South Africa in Chapter 8 and which have been briefly suggested for some of the other five countries above. Moreover, for these six nations, acquisition of nuclear weapons capability (and, almost certainly for some of them, possession) has not been followed, as it was in the first wave of proliferation in the northern hemisphere, by the accumulation of huge stockpiles of weapons-grade fissile material, the development of the much more powerful thermonuclear or fusion bomb or the development of a vast armoury of increasingly sophisticated missiles for delivering these weapons. Nor do any of these six aforementioned states (with the possible exception of Israel) pose any serious threat to the territory of the United States or any other industrialised nation in the northern hemisphere.

As we have argued, it is likely that future American non-proliferation policy will focus on seeking non-proliferation assurances from these and other countries that they will require all their nuclear exports to be safeguarded. Unsafeguardedness would thus be confined to within the borders of these six countries and the five nuclear weapon states as defined under the NPT. The solid foundation of the non-proliferation regime, the Non-Proliferation Treaty and IAEA safeguards, remains indispensable, and every effort will be made to ensure that it is not eroded. Concerning nuclear export policy, the United States government now seems to recognise that its own leverage has been reduced. So a common approach by the industrialised nations is likely to continue to be pursued, although, to allay the suspicions of developing nations of discrimination and cartel-like activity, cooperation between industrialised nations is likely to be by means of quiet diplomacy, refining trigger lists, sharing intelligence about 'sensitive' nuclear installations in 'sensitive' countries and the like, rather than loud declaratory policy statements.

Nevertheless, notwithstanding a growing rapprochement over non-proliferation policy between the industrialised nations, there remains the prospect that leading countries of the southern hemisphere may develop their own unsafeguarded nuclear plants and allow less stringent safeguards on their growing nuclear exports than members of the London Club, despite attempts by the United States to obtain assurances from such second-tier nations that all their nuclear exports should be safeguarded. These remarks are particularly relevant in the case of South Africa; and it is to a consideration of that country's position and posture that the rest of this book is devoted.

3 South Africa's International Relations

THE OUTCAST STATE

There are a few countries in the international community with whom the overwhelming majority of the rest of the community of nations do not wish to been seen to have a close relationship. This select group of countries have been termed *pariahs*. Besides South Africa, they include Israel, Taiwan and perhaps South Korea. The governments of these countries are seen by their regional Third World neighbours as illegitimate, because territorial sovereignty appears to have been taken by a minority group from the people to whom it rightfully belongs.[1] These governments therefore come under united and overwhelming attack from non-aligned and socialist countries in international forums such as the United Nations, and they have been excluded from many of the UN agencies.

One common characteristic of the pariah powers is their paranoia about being deserted by the West. Yet, for a variety of reasons which are discussed later in the case of South Africa, Western nations have not found themselves able to break their ties with these countries completely. Indeed, because of these continuing ties with the West and the total lack of relations with the Soviet bloc, there is an asymmetry in the international relations of the pariah powers. Rather than term them pariahs, some students of international relations therefore consider it more appropriate to group them with developing countries with authoritarian right-wing governments which are dependent on support from the West. Such countries might include, for example, the former Iranian regime under the Shah, Zaire, Chile and some other Latin American countries.

In the case of South Africa, the reason for her isolation is, above all, the racial policy of the regime, based on the ideology of apartheid and enshrined in the laws and constitution of the country. Apartheid means the enforced separation and separate development of the races. It has been systematically instituted since the National Party came to power in 1948, although a racial constitution and some of the racial laws have been in force for very much longer. Apartheid reached its apotheosis in the 1950s and 1960s when the plan was formulated by Prime Minister

Verwoerd's government for the black majority population, which now numbers nearly 25 million, to become citizens of small impoverished rural homelands to which they have tribal links and which would be made independent states. Thousands of blacks have since been forcibly removed to these overcrowded homelands. However, it has been found impossible to implement this ideal fully. About half the black population live in separate townships surrounding the major cities in 'white South Africa', the economy of which is dependent on the labour of these people; and only South Africa has recognised those independent black homelands that have so far been established.

In South Africa, the franchise was formerly restricted to the white population, now numbering about 5 million; and, by means of discriminatory legislation, denial of political rights to the majority non-white population and repression of dissent, white dominance was preserved. Within the white population, since the 1948 election, power has been retained through the National Party by the Afrikaner (Afrikaans-speaking) majority of mainly Dutch but also French and German descent. Under a new constitution enacted in 1984, in part to allay international objections to the racial nature of the regime, the approximately one million Asians and nearly three million coloureds (people of mixed race) have been allowed to vote for their own legislatures; but the new constitution enables the National Party to retain control of the government, and a large majority of the Asians and coloureds have shown their opposition to it by boycotting the polls. Although no plans have been announced, there have been more recent indications that the government may co-opt homeland leaders and officials of the black townships who are prepared to cooperate in a federal or confederal system of government based on ethnicity. This would be welcomed by the powerful white business community, which is largely Anglo-Saxon or Jewish but which has a growing Afrikaner membership. In what are regarded by most blacks as cosmetic changes, some of the more clearly discriminatory laws have been repealed. However, whilst petty apartheid may have been reformed, there are few signs that the whites intend to surrender their power and privileges. Indeed, in a departure from the previous Westminster-style constitution, the new constitution provides for a state president, who is inevitably a white, with sweeping powers to appoint and dismiss government employees and veto legislation. Nevertheless, in contrast with the mood amongst the Afrikaner people during the 1950s and 1960s, there now seems to be no widely-shared vision of the future constitutional order in South Africa. Having hesitatingly and grudgingly embarked along the road of what it sees as reform, Afrikanerdom seems to have lost is cohesiveness and sense of direction.

Outside South Africa, opposition to apartheid has mounted as a result of a post-war global consensus which finds racism abhorrent and outdated and which seeks to promote increased civil rights and decolonisation worldwide. This consensus has been expressed notably from the 1960s onwards, for example, within the United States and in the United Nations. As African states further north progressively gained independence from European rule, South Africa became increasingly isolated. These newly-independent African nations were particularly opposed to the South African regime as they understandably found its policies insulting. In 1963, with pan-African nationalist idealism, they formed the Organisation of African Unity (OAU) to which virtually all African states (except for South Africa) belong. An OAU Liberation Committee is based in Dar es Salaam, and OAU opposition to South Africa is led by the initiatives of the southern African 'front-line states': Angola, Botswana, Mozambique, Tanzania, Zambia and Zimbabwe. Mention should also be made of Nigeria, the black African country with by far the largest population and economy (the latter based on oil production). Thus, although geographically distant from southern Africa, the Nigerian government sometimes attends meetings of the front-line states. The OAU is, however, divided between 'moderate' (pro-Western) and 'progressive' states, and the organisation has become weakened as the economies of African states have stagnated and their governments have tended to become unstable, inefficient and corrupt.[2]

Besides apartheid, the other major cause for international opposition to South Africa is her continuing occupation of South West Africa/ Namibia. South Africa was originally allowed to govern the former German colony under a mandate from the League of Nations; but the International Court of Justice ruled in 1971 that South Africa's failure to grant independence to Namibia meant that her continuing occupation of the country was illegal under international law. The South West African People's Organisation (SWAPO), claiming to represent the Namibian people (a claim recognised since 1973 by the UN General Assembly), is fighting South African forces in a low-level guerrilla campaign from bases in Angola in order to 'liberate' Namibia from South African rule. South African forces have responded by raiding deep into Angola and in the 1980s established a virtually continuous military occupation of southern Angola. Western nations, led by the United States, have attempted to mediate and negotiate conditions with SWAPO, the front-line states and South Africa under which the latter would grant a UN-supervised transition to independence under the 1978 UN Security Council resolution 435; but South Africa continues to prevaricate (establishing her own local 'transitional' administration in 1985) and international opposition to South African control over Namibia therefore continues.

South Africa perceived a marked deterioration in her strategic situation in 1975 when, following the 1974 coup in Lisbon, Angola and Mozambique gained independence from Portugal under Marxist governments friendly towards the Soviet Union. Independence for Zimbabwe (and probably eventually Namibia), quite likely under a similar government, then became inevitable sooner rather than later, and South Africa had lost the buffer of colonies separating her territory from most of the independent black African nations.

Of particular concern to South Africa was the psychological if not military setback she suffered in 1975–6 at the hands of Cuban troops which, with arms and advisers from Soviet bloc countries, had been airlifted into Angola with the help of the Soviet Union, in that country's first major involvement in sub-Saharan Africa. These Cuban troops then helped the newly-established but unelected Popular Movement for the Liberation of Angola (MPLA) government overcome other Angolan groups which had military backing from South African troops and US CIA-funded mercenaries. South Africa felt abandoned at that time because of what she perceived as inadequate support from the West, notably the United States. South Africa continues to provide military and logistic support to the National Union for the Total Independence of Angola (UNITA) which is still fighting the Marxist MPLA government from its base in south-eastern Angola; and the South African government, supported by the United States, has made the departure from Angola of the approximately 30 000 Cuban troops, still present helping to defend the MPLA government against UNITA forces, a condition for her agreeing to grant independence to Namibia.

THE CAMPAIGN AGAINST APARTHEID

Because of their common political and economic interests, OAU member states have obtained the support of other non-aligned nations, as well as the Soviet bloc, in their campaign to isolate South Africa. During the 1970s, the solidarity between African and Arab states was particularly noteworthy, as each group obtained the support of the other in their campaigns against South Africa and Israel respectively. Liberal and left-wing opinion and anti-apartheid and civil rights activists in Western countries have also supported the international campaign against South Africa, which aims at her isolation at every level of international contact with the West which, it is believed, helps sustain the present regime. Most success has been achieved in the isolation of South Africa at the sporting level; but we are here concerned more with military and economic areas of contact. At the military level, concerted international action to isolate South Africa has had some success, in particular with the imposition of a mandatory arms embargo by the UN Security Council in 1977. At the economic level, there has been a formal embargo on the shipment of oil by Arab producing countries since 1973 (in return for which most African nations then broke off relations with Israel). Most oil-exporting countries, including Britain, have followed by formally embargoing the export of oil to South Africa. The most significant step came in 1979 when, following the Islamic revolution, the embargo was joined by Iran. The Shah's regime had previously supplied South Africa with nearly 90 per cent of her oil imports; but South Africa has subsequently continued to obtain vital oil imports, albeit at some extra cost, by means of spot market purchases, swap arrangements and exploiting loopholes in the embargo with the help of international oil marketing companies.[3]

There is some opposition to apartheid from whites within South Africa, notably from church and student groups; but white people are generally united in support of the government's foreign and defence policies. Most whites perceive a common enemy in the Soviet-backed 'terrorism' of the African National Congress (ANC). Although its members are predominantly black, the ANC is a non-racial organisation. Its origins can be traced as far back as 1912. As spelt out in the Freedom Charter, adopted in 1955 by a mass meeting of South Africans of all races, the aim of the ANC is to achieve universal suffrage in a unitary, non-racial, democratic South African state, with a mixed economy and a non-aligned foreign policy. Along with the more exclusively black Pan Africanist Congress of South Africa (PAC), the ANC was banned following the unrest after the 1960 Sharpeville incident, when sixty-nine peaceful black protesters were shot dead by the police. The ANC has remained by far the more effective of the two organisations. The leaders of both groups remain in prison or have fled the country and are now in exile in the front-line states and Europe.

As political activity was made impossible, the ANC abandoned its long-standing reliance on peaceful protest. It first adopted a campaign of defiance, involving boycotts, strikes and civil disobedience, and then in 1961 formed a military wing, Umkhonto we Sizwe (Spear of the Nation). The main tactics of Umkhonto we Sizwe consist of attacks on police stations and the sabotage of strategic economic and military targets. It does not engage in terrorism in the sense of hijackings, taking hostages or large-scale indiscriminate attacks on civilians. ANC headquarters are now in Lusaka, Zambia. Most military training camps ('bases') are in Angola. There are also some camps in Tanzania. Most specialist training and arms are provided by Soviet bloc countries, some of the arms being provided through the OAU Liberation Committee. These are then smuggled into South Africa and hidden in secret caches. The ANC enjoys a close relationship (notably in the form of an overlapping membership) with the small pro-Soviet South African Communist Party which, needless to say, is also banned by the South African government.

The ANC continues to operate underground in South Africa, notably in the townships, raising people's political consciousness and helping groups sympathetic to its cause to organise strikes and consumer and school boycotts, one of the organisation's long-term objectives being to work for a prolonged general strike.

International opposition to the South African regime has been strongest following seemingly spontaneous and increasingly frequent outbreaks of township unrest and the ensuing government repression of dissent. Thus the 1963 UN Security Council resolution recommending an arms embargo was passed following the disturbances after the Sharpeville massacre and the banning of the ANC and PAC. The 1977 Security Council resolution mandating an arms embargo was passed following the detentions, bannings and death in police custody of Black Consciousness leader Steve Biko, which in turn followed the Soweto disturbances, when over 600 people were killed, most of them black schoolchildren shot by the police after protests in 1976 against their inferior education system. The ANC also received a boost at that time when hundreds of radical young blacks fled the townships for neighbouring countries and many were subsequently recruited by Umkhonto we Sizwe.

Then in 1984 and 1985, after demonstrations against rent increases in the townships and a campaign against the new constitution led by the newly-formed United Democratic Front, a multiracial umbrella organisation made up of more than 600 community, youth, student, women's and church groups (and therefore difficult for the government to ban), unrest again broke out and rapidly escalated in the black and coloured townships. Schools and shops owned by whites were boycotted. There were stone, petrol bomb and arson attacks on the police, police informers, township councillors and other blacks perceived to be collaborators with the government.

In July 1985 the government responded by declaring a state of emergency in the main trouble spots and the army presence in the townships was reinforced; but the usual repressive methods of live and rubber bullets, the sjambok, teargas, detention, torture, treason charges and bannings did not succeed in quelling the violence. By the end of 1985 over 1000 blacks had been killed since the unrest had started the previous year. Again most of these were young radicals seemingly unafraid of being shot by the police. The exiled ANC had called on people to make the townships ungovernable, but it was not altogether clear how much control the banned organisation exerted over the township youths.

Under international and domestic pressure, Western governments, led by the US Congress and (significantly, in view of that country's earlier close military and nuclear ties with South Africa) France, responded to this sequence of events by tightening the arms embargo, curtailing military and nuclear cooperation, and imposing their own extremely limited (and largely symbolic) forms of economic sanctions. Perhaps more significantly there was a flight of capital from South Africa and a collapse of the currency, the rand. South Africa found herself unable to repay her short-term debts to Western banks, and United States banks, under domestic pressure, refused to renew these short-term loans. South Africa was forced to suspend the repayment of capital on the loans and impose controls on the foreign exchange market. By early 1986 the unrest had become widespread, affecting the whole country; but the authorities continued to keep it contained within the townships. However, it looked as though the whites' worst fears of violence spreading to their own residential and business areas might be realised sooner rather than later.

South Africa thus faces a combination of internal and international opposition aimed at her total isolation and the eventual overthrow of the government. Bordered by three states, Angola, Mozambique and Zimbabwe, whose Marxist governments came to power between 1975 and 1980 through communist-supported revolutionary violence, the South African regime then came to the conclusion that it was being subjected to a Soviet-backed 'total onslaught', which it had to meet with a 'total national strategy', encompassing (besides the mix of reform and repression at home) military, economic, political and diplomatic dimensions overseas.[4] It is these dimensions of South Africa's 'total strategy' that we next discuss in turn.

THE MILITARY RESPONSE

It is appropriate to begin by discussing the South African government's military response to the crisis it perceived itself in from the mid-1970s onwards, for it was the South African Defence Force (SADF), led by General Magnus Malan, who is now the Defence Minister and a protégé of President P. W. Botha (who was then the Defence Minister), which was largely responsible for formulating the 'total strategy' at that time.[5] Indeed SADF personnel now permeate the civil service and have a key role in the State Security Council, the most important functional element of the new executive presidency. Although constitutionally only an advisory body, it is the State Security Council (comprising senior ministers, military, police and intelligence figures), and not the cabinet, which essentially takes major government decisions and manages the 'total strategy'.

According to the latest estimate of the International Institute for Strategic Studies, the South African Defence Force has 106 400 men (including 64 000 white conscripts) permanently under arms, plus 317 000 reserves capable of being mobilised quickly by a full call-up of the Citizen Force and a 130 000-man paramilitary Commando Force.[6] There are 12 000 white and 5400 black and coloured soldiers in the regular army plus, at any one time, 58 000 army conscripts. The navy comprises 9000 men (including 4000 conscripts) and the air force 13 000 men (2000 conscripts). For the defence of Namibia against SWAPO guerrillas there is a 21 000-man South West Africa Territory Force formed from Namibian conscripts of all races. However, for general internal security, the government relies first on the South African and Namibian police who have wide discretionary powers, mastermind intelligence and operate against guerrillas within each country's borders. The South African Police is composed of 19 500 whites and 16 000 non-whites, and there are 20 000 reserves.

Table 3.1 shows South African defence expenditure for selected years for the period since the Second World War. It can be seen from the table that the two periods of rapid build-up of defence spending and capability have been the early 1960s and the mid-1970s, corresponding with the periods of most intense international opposition to the regime. By 1976, South African defence spending amounted to one-third of the defence expenditure of the whole of Africa, excluding Egypt.[7] Since then military spending has continued to rise, though at a less rapid rate, until the 1984–6 disturbances, following which it seems set to accelerate again and remain at a level of over 5 per cent of GDP and 20 per cent of total government spending. Comparison with figures for other industrialised nations suggests that scope remains for still further expansion in the defence budget.

Table 3.1   South Africa's Defence Expenditure, 1955–80 (selected years)

Year	1955	1960	1965	1970	1975	1980
US $ million (1980 prices and exchange rates)	200	200	800	900	2100	3100
Rand million (current)	40	40	180	260	930	2420
Per cent of GDP	1.0	0.8	2.3	2.1	3.4	3.9

All figures rounded.

Sources: Stockholm International Peace Research Institute, *World Armaments and Disarmament, SIPRI Yearbook 1974*; Stockholm International Peace Research Institute, *World Armaments and Disarmament, SIPRI Yearbook 1985*.

The strength of South Africa's armed forces is far greater than that of any black African state to the north and is particularly awesome in terms of armoured combat vehicles and air power.[8] The army has 250 tanks, mostly Centurions, and 1600 Eland armoured cars, plus numerous scout cars and armoured personnel carriers with artillery, up to 155mm calibre, and surface-to-air missiles.[9] The air force has 6 Buccaneer and 5 Canberra bombers and at least 70 Mirage fighters, mostly supplied before the 1977 UN arms embargo, but since augmented by local manufacture. The navy has commissioned locally-produced Minister fast-attack craft of Israeli (Reshef) design, having previously relied on British-built frigates and French-built Daphne-class submarines, of which it had three of each at the time of the 1977 embargo.

South Africa mainly relied on British armaments until Britain voluntarily embargoed supplies in 1964, in response to the 1963 UN resolution. South Africa then turned to other West European suppliers, notably France and Italy and, latterly, Israel. Some of the weaponry South Africa now possesses may be considered as a stockpile, amassed to meet future contingencies when the 1977 mandatory UN arms embargo begins to have some effect on the military balance in southern Africa. However, South Africa has also now reached a high degree of self-sufficiency in arms manufacture, with some arms actually being produced for export. Indigenous weapons production is coordinated by the state-owned Armaments Development and Manufacturing Corporation (Armscor), but most arms production is subcontracted by Armscor to private companies. Besides Mirage aircraft and Reshef warships (mentioned above), South Africa is now producing her own Cactus missiles (based on the French Crotale missile), Impala jet trainers (based on Italian aircraft technology) and Eland armoured cars (based on the French Panhard armoured car).[10]

Nevertheless, South Africa remains at least partially dependent on foreign licences and spare parts for her weapons production and maintenance, and, as these become more difficult to obtain, with her growing isolation, she will gradually fall behind industrialised countries in the sophistication of her armaments. Although South Africa is expected to be able to import *some* modern weaponry (through commercial arms dealers overseas) in defiance of the UN embargo, growing media exposure will make such transactions more difficult and more costly than in the past. Such comments also apply to 'grey area' or dual-use items, which can have both civilian and military uses, such as computers, components, radar systems, spotter planes, transport planes, coastguard equipment and Land Rovers.[11]

Some of South Africa's defence spending has gone into capability for curbing civil unrest and performing counter-insurgency tasks; but much of it has gone into a build-up of conventional weaponry which has been used to conduct hot-pursuit, pre-emptive or punitive raids against ANC or SWAPO guerrilla presences in neighbouring countries. South Africa is hereby employing the same tactics against guerrilla insurgents as those used by Israel and the former white government of Rhodesia. South African military strategists have studied these examples carefully and acknowledge their applicability to their own situation.[12]

South Africa has also provided logistical support in the form of supplies, training and sanctuary to armed dissident groups within the neighbouring countries of Angola, Mozambique, Lesotho and, probably, Zimbabwe. This military support is increased or reduced according to the freedom these countries allow the ANC or SWAPO to operate within their borders. As such operations, in particular the transit of arms, may be difficult for the host country to control, South Africa reserves the right of the SADF to enter these countries, ostensibly to deal with 'terrorists'.

However, there is always the danger, from the point of view of the South African regime, that such actions, which have often included attacks on unarmed civilians and refugees, may seem a provocative

violation of the territory of sovereign states and may produce a response
from external powers, notably the Soviet Union. For example, when a
South African armoured column drove fifty miles into Mozambique in
January 1981 and attacked buildings occupied by ANC personnel in
Matola, a suburb of the capital Maputo, killing twelve people and
capturing three, Mozambique invoked her 1977 Treaty of Friendship
with the Soviet Union. Ten days later, two Soviet warships were in
Maputo harbour to 'show the flag'.[13]

Nevertheless, despite continuing South African raids into and
destabilisation of neighbouring countries, the Soviet presence in the area
since 1981 has been practically non-existent; and Western countries
remain the major (but not only) suppliers of arms and military training
to nearly all the front-line states, except Angola. This Soviet restraint
may be a reflection of a more general global policy since her counter-
productive military intervention in Afghanistan at the end of 1979, but it
also reflects the fact that, unlike the West, Soviet bloc countries have few
economic interests in southern Africa and are unable or unwilling to
offer front-line states significant economic support. (The Soviet Union
also suffered strategic setbacks further north in Africa in the 1970s, in
Egypt, Somalia and Guinea, which may have made her wary of further
substantial involvement in the continent.) African countries in turn
recognise that their economic and trading relations are predominantly
with the West, that they rely on the West for aid for their fragile and
precarious economies, and that these relations with the West would be
gravely compromised if they invited Soviet bloc troops in or offered the
Soviet Union base facilities. With the notable exception of the Cuban
troops in Angola, significant Soviet bloc involvement in the area is
therefore essentially limited to the provision of arms and training in their
use to the ANC, SWAPO and some of the front-line states. South
African propaganda has none the less tended to exaggerate the flow of
Soviet bloc arms to and the presence of Soviet bloc advisers in these
countries; and increased Soviet involvement in the area may not be
unwelcome to South Africa, under certain circumstances, as it highlights, to the domestic white electorate and some sections of Western
public opinion, the Soviet threat to Western interests in the area. On
balance, although the Soviet Union is likely to remain cautious and not
get physically engaged in the region, the likelihood is that her supply of
arms and technical assistance (for manning anti-aircraft defences, for
example) will continue as long as South Africa continues her tactics of
military incursions into neighbouring countries.[14]

In fact such actions by the South African government may be

prompted less by military necessity and more by a desire to demonstrate overwhelming military might and convey both a sense of hopelessness to supporters of the struggle against apartheid and a sense of security to her own white population. For this reason, South African military intervention into neighbouring states is likely to increase as her internal security deteriorates. It is no coincidence that the Matola raid followed soon after ANC bomb attacks in South Africa and the election of President Reagan in the United States and within three days of the announcement of a general election in South Africa.[15] Thus, the element of overkill in South Africa's military capability can be explained both by the need perceived by South Africa's rulers (like those of Israel) to leave no room for doubt concerning her invulnerability in the minds of her own population and the people of neighbouring African states and the West and by the inability or unwillingness of outside powers to do anything about it.

RELATIONS WITH AFRICAN STATES

Whilst she has maintained a continuing and overwhelming military superiority over neighbouring African states and has continued her armed incursions into their territories, ostensibly in order to attack ANC or SWAPO guerrillas, South Africa has been at pains to emphasise to her neighbours that the purpose of her military capability is defensive and that she has no hostile intentions towards their governments or people. Although the official policy of neighbouring states is not to allow ANC bases on their soil, South Africa has wanted these countries to go further – to cooperate in preventing ANC guerrillas from operating within their countries and to sign formal non-aggression treaties with her. Though this last demand has generally been resisted by neighbouring states, South Africa achieved a most notable success in having it satisfied in March 1984 when she signed the Nkomati non-aggression pact with Mozambique.

Under the Nkomati Accord, each country undertook that neither would threaten or use force against the other and that neither territory would be used as a base for military or subversive activities against the other. It was subsequently revealed that Swaziland had secretly signed a similar agreement with South Africa in 1982. Following these agreements, the Mozambique and Swazi governments drastically curtailed the official activities of the ANC in their countries and rounded up South African refugees, most of whom were ANC supporters. The governments of Botswana and Lesotho have done likewise. (There are very few ANC refugees in Zimbabwe.) Most of these refugees have been sent further north to countries such as Angola, Zambia, Tanzania and Ethiopia. For South Africa, the pre-1975 cordon sanitaire separating her territory from her opponents seemed to have been at least partially restored.

However, despite the Nkomati Accord, the rebel Mozambique National Resistance (MNR) subsequently continued its acts of sabotage against the Mozambique economy and its attacks on the inhabitants of the country. It was the increasing scale of such attacks that had forced Maputo to sign the Nkomati agreement in the first place. Moreover there were indications that supplies and logistic support for the MNR were continuing to come from South Africa, probably with the support of elements within the South African Defence Force (although it was uncertain whether this support had been officially sanctioned by the Botha government, which was obviously embarrassed by these revelations of South Africa's apparent violation of the Nkomati agreement).

Nevertheless, despite continuing to employ her destabilising tactics, South Africa continues to state that she has no aggressive intentions towards any other African country. Indeed, South Africa has tried to attract nearby countries into a closer economic relationship, which her leaders have in the past termed a 'Constellation of States', with herself in the centre. The purpose has been to entice these neighbouring states into a dependent relationship, which would make it impossible to isolate South Africa economically without at the same time harming the economies of neighbouring countries even more. If South Africa could split the OAU and demonstrate her cooperation in some fields with some African countries, it would be harder for other countries to persuade the international community to increase her isolation.

South Africa has had mixed results in achieving her aim of seeking closer relations with African states, but it has remained a recurrent theme of her foreign policy, known at different times as the policy of *détente* or 'outward movement'. Some success was achieved in the early 1970s, when South Africa had particularly close economic and political relations with Malawi and some of the Francophone states further north, such as Gabon and the Ivory Coast, and was also engaged in talks with Zambia and Tanzania concerning a settlement of the Rhodesian issue. As the South African Foreign Minister put it at the time:

> The West is becoming aware of our fruitful cooperation with other countries in Africa, its attitude and disposition towards us are

improving, and I believe this will happen to an increasing degree. We must simply accept that our relations with the rest of the world are determined by our relations with the African states.[16]

Following the collapse of the Portuguese empire and independence for Angola and Mozambique, this 'outward policy' also collapsed in 1975; but in 1979 the policy re-emerged in the concept of a 'Constellation of States', whereby the economic dependence on South Africa of nearby countries and her own tribal homelands was to be cemented by means of regional development funding and a customs and monetary union. This plan was in turn made inoperable by the election in 1980 of an independent Marxist government under Robert Mugabe in the key state, Zimbabwe. Then again, for a short time following the 1984 Nkomati Accord, South Africa appeared as both the regional peace-maker and economic powerhouse. The West strongly supported the accord as it seemed both to exclude the Soviet Union and restore some stability to a region where it had considerable economic interests. (Indeed the key relevant Western powers with interests in the area, Britain, the United States and Portugal, had acted as brokers to the accord.) For the first time for many years, a South African prime minister was received by Western governments, when P. W. Botha made a tour of West European capitals in June 1984. The image of the South African regime as the regional peace-maker was then in turn shattered both by its attempts to suppress the 1984–6 revolt in the black townships and by the continuing activities of the MNR in Mozambique.

Yet South Africa continues to dominate the southern African region economically just as she does militarily. This economic domination was established in the colonial period; but South Africa has maintained strong trading links with all the southern African states, Botswana, Lesotho, Malawi, Mozambique, Swaziland, Zaire, Zambia and Zimbabwe, even after these nations gained their independence. These countries remain dependent on South Africa to varying degrees for trading outlets to the sea, essential supplies (including food, consumer goods and mining equipment) and remittances from migrant workers, most of them employed in the South African gold mines.

Zimbabwe is in a strategic position to influence relations between South Africa and other countries in the region, and, following her independence in 1980, southern African states (excluding South Africa) joined to form the Southern African Development Coordination Conference (SADCC) with the aim of cooperating, with the help of Western aid agencies, to reduce their economic dependence on South

Africa. In response, South Africa has pursued a policy of literally sabotaging alternative economic links (using her own agents or with the help of dissident groups such as UNITA and MNR) and, more generally, keeping the front-line states off balance, exploiting their economic dependence on her by manipulating aid and credit flows, electricity and telecommunications links and transport access (of goods and manpower), by alternate use of carrots and sticks (opening and closing borders, and the like) to suit her political objectives. These have been to demonstrate (i) the economic dependence of southern African states on South Africa, and (ii) that black African states are incapable of taking any independent initiative. More generally the South African regime has hoped to show domestic and international audiences alike that black rule, especially black Marxist rule, does not work and that blacks cannot effectively govern themselves. South Africa has also used these tactics of economic destabilisation, as well as military destabilisation, to try to force neighbouring countries to curtail the activities of the ANC and to sign non-aggression treaties. A signal achievement of this objective came when the Mozambique government was forced to choose between martyrdom and survival, and signed the Nkomati Accord. It is largely because of these South African policies and a general reluctance on the part of Western companies and governments to see a realignment of economic links in the area that the results of the SADCC initiative have so far been extremely limited.

RELATIONS WITH THE WEST

It has always been necessary for South Africa to pay constant heed to the reaction in the West concerning her domestic racial policies, her military posture and her relations with other African states, for it is only the Western industrialised nations that can provide some relief to her growing isolation. South Africa is protected in the United Nations Security Council from any significant economic sanctions and from stronger condemnation of her suppression of domestic unrest, her failure to grant independence to Namibia and her military raids into neighbouring countries, only by the veto power of the permanent Western members, notably the United States and Britain. However, since the end of the Second World War, when South Africa was closely allied with Britain, her relations with the West in general (and Britain in particular) have gradually become more distant and strained.

Like her economic ties with nearby African states, white South

Africa's economic, cultural and ethnic ties with the West in general (and Britain in particular) are a legacy of the colonial era. Western nations in general (and Britain in particular) have considerable economic interests in South Africa dating from these earlier times. Then, as now, South Africa's main role in the Western economy was as a supplier of a wide range of raw materials, most notably gold. (South Africa is still the world's largest gold producer.)

In return, South Africa still provides a sizeable market for the export of manufactured goods and machinery from the West. Western companies in general (and British companies in particular) have made substantial investments in South Africa, and, unlike in the rest of Africa, such investments remain generally highly profitable. There is thus an interdependence in South Africa's economic relations with the West, with the West depending on the supply of cheap minerals, some of them of key strategic importance, and the return on investments from South Africa, and South Africa in turn depending on the supply of capital and technology from the West.

Besides those arguing in the West for South Africa's increased isolation, there are therefore more influential people who argue that, in order to protect Western interests there, close relations must be maintained with the South African regime. It is argued that, by maintaining a 'dialogue' with South Africa, the dangerous 'laager mentality' of intransigent Afrikanerdom is avoided or at least lessened, and there is more opportunity for the West to influence the Nationalist government's racial policies. Western political and business leaders generally feel that, by maintaining relations and keeping open channels of communication with the South African government, a negotiated settlement to the Namibian independence issue remains possible and it is more likely that there will be an evolutionary and relatively peaceful transition to racial justice in South Africa, rather than the violent and revolutionary transition to majority rule which would be so damaging to Western interests there.

However, the West faces grave risks in maintaining close relations with South Africa. Apart from provoking domestic opposition in the West, such a policy provides a welcome boost for Soviet propaganda and also alienates important Third World nations, including the front-line African states, in which the West in general (and Britain in particular) also has interests.

Western industrial nations have generally allowed Britain and increasingly (as British influence and interests in South Africa have declined in relative terms) the United States to shape overall Western policy towards South Africa. With President Carter's concern to promote human rights worldwide, it seemed for a time, during the second half of the 1970s, that American policy towards South Africa might become rather more adversarial. However, aside from supporting the 1977 mandatory UN arms embargo and some tightening of the regulations concerning US exports of 'dual purpose' items having both military and civilian uses, little of substance changed in American policy, the only change being in the tone of the American government's ritual denunciations of apartheid. (The US government had voluntarily imposed an arms embargo even before the 1963 UN Security Council resolution was passed.) The European Community Code of Conduct concerning investments in South Africa was adopted and, in America, the essentially similar Sullivan Principles were widely accepted; but both initiatives were concerned more with allaying domestic and international opposition to such investments than with exerting pressure on the South African government.

The advent of the Reagan administration in 1981, with a policy of 'constructive engagement' in southern Africa, with more emphasis on private 'dialogue' than public posturing, marked a return to the approach favoured by the Nixon administration, as formulated in Option 2 of the notorious 1969 National Security Study Memorandum number 39,[17] with more use of 'carrots' than 'sticks' to try to influence South Africa to modify apartheid and grant independence to Namibia. As the Carter and Reagan approaches are much nearer to each other than the associated rhetoric would suggest, the short-term prospect is for little substantive change in the overall Western policy of 'dialogue' with South Africa; but over the longer term South Africa is likely to become steadily more isolated from the West.

SOUTH AFRICA'S STRATEGIC SITUATION

Some Western analysts believe that, as well as its economic interests in South Africa, the West has important strategic interests there, due to the strategic position of the Cape of Good Hope, around which much of the West's oil supplies pass. Following the closure of the Suez Canal, the level of oil traffic rounding the Cape grew to 18 million barrels per day in 1976 from 0.8 million barrels per day in 1965. According to one source, writing in 1982, some 2300 ships, including 600 oil tankers, pass the Cape every month. Half of these ships enter South African ports, for repair and supplies, etc.[18]

It has long been South Africa's hope that, because of the West's strategic dependence on her mineral exports and the Cape route, she might be allowed under the American nuclear umbrella.[19] In the past, the South African regime has tried to become an ex-officio member of the North Atlantic Treaty Organisation and has supported moves to extend the boundary of NATO responsibilities south of the Tropic of Cancer. However, such proposals have always been blocked by NATO members such as Norway, Denmark, Canada and the Netherlands; and South Africa has had no more success in persuading South American countries or the major Western naval powers to join with her in a South Atlantic Treaty Organisation.[20]

In fact the strategic significance of the Cape route has been recognised by the major world powers, in particular the British, for well over 100 years. Until the 1960s, the small South African Navy was fully integrated with the British Royal Navy; but, following the Sharpeville massacre and South Africa's enforced departure from the Commonwealth in 1961, the defence relationship between Britain and South Africa became progressively more distant.[21] The 1955 Simonstown Agreement, under which the base near Cape Town was used by the Royal Navy, was terminated by Britain in 1975. Subsequently the South African government announced that the South African Navy would be designed for the coastal defence of her home waters and that the West would have to police the shipping lanes around the Cape by itself.[22]

However, South Africa's accompanying hint that she might take a neutral stance in the East–West strategic balance of power was widely considered to be bluff and not taken seriously. The regime was judged to be making a virtue of the military self-reliance forced on it by its pariah status. In fact South Africa has frequently and consistently offered the use of her port facilities to Western navies, and she has expanded the Simonstown base for them should they wish to make use of it. Sections of the Western naval establishment might wish the West to respond positively to such offers, particularly in view of the Soviet naval build-up in the Indian Ocean during the 1970s; but the domestic and international political constraints (discussed above) to the West having closer relations with South Africa preclude such a response. Indeed, it has been argued that a Western naval presence in South Africa would be more likely to *provoke* a Soviet response, such as the acquisition of base or port facilities in Angola or the southern Indian Ocean, than be a *result* of the sizeable but sometimes exaggerated Soviet naval presence in the Indian Ocean and South Atlantic. Indeed, because of the East–West nuclear balance of terror, the strategic value of the Cape route in a global conflict is generally considered to have lessened since the end of the Second World War. Suggestions that the Soviet Union might be prepared to initiate a global war by impeding the flow of oil and raw materials around the Cape during peacetime are hardly taken seriously by Western analysts. It is generally recognised that, in a wartime emergency, South African bases and port facilities would still be available to the West; but in the meantime, any suggestion that South Africa's offer of such facilities might be accepted would incur greater political costs than strategic benefits.[23] As Bissell concluded in 1982,

> the plain message even from the new Reagan administration was that Simonstown would not be used by the US Navy. As long as the State Department controls policy on such issues and South Africa continues to pursue its basic policies of racial separation with only marginal changes, military cooperation is not possible on such overt questions. At the same time the multiplicity of contracts between the two countries ensures that military issues will arise.[24]

Such conclusions clearly do not preclude less overt cooperation. Thus, results of intelligence-gathering by South Africa and the United States continue to be shared;[25] and South Africa continues to pass naval intelligence to the major Western naval powers from the Silvermine communications installation (near Simonstown) which monitors shipping in the southern oceans – from New Zealand to Brazil.[26]

FREE MARKET OR SIEGE ECONOMY?

The same contradictions are displayed in South Africa's economic relations with the West as in her defence policy. The South African government wishes the country to be considered one of the Western industrialised nations. Indeed, since the discovery of gold on the Witwatersrand 100 years ago, extensive white immigration, massive injections of foreign capital, huge profits, industrialisation and rapid economic growth have followed. The standard of living enjoyed by white South Africans is now one of the highest in the world. South Africa continues to welcome foreign investment, which she sees as giving Western nations an interest in the preservation of the existing order. Consistent with her emphasis on the importance of her mineral resources to the West, South Africa draws attention to her liberal mining laws and her scrupulous fairness in fulfilling contracts and not introducing restrictive tax or ownership policies. South Africa's anti-communist rhetoric dictates that she preaches the virtues of capitalism.

Yet her economy possesses some features of a developing country, or even a socialist state.

The South African economy, though strong, is still heavily dependent on the export of minerals, particularly gold, for foreign exchange earnings which account for a major share of her gross domestic product. The rise in the price of gold and the high though volatile level of that price during the 1970s 'saved' South Africa at a time when she was facing growing isolation and would otherwise have experienced severe economic difficulties. The mining labour force is predominantly black; and most of the legislation that culminated in the apartheid system was designed to make black migrant labour available for mining at the lowest possible cost. Labour remains cheap and readily available from the black homelands and neighbouring states. Unemployment is high; the economy of the black rural homelands is largely based on remittances from those menfolk working in the mines, farms and factories in 'white South Africa'.

Whilst preaching the merits of capitalist free enterprise and seeking to preserve her trading relations with the West, South Africa has also prepared for the possible imposition of economic sanctions. Her economy would be particularly vulnerable to an effective embargo on her importation of oil, one of the few commodities in which she is not broadly self-sufficient. However, oil accounts for only 20 per cent of South Africa's total energy requirements; and two-thirds of this is used for transportation (South Africa being particularly dependent on continuity in the supply of diesel fuel). The government is thought to have stored the equivalent of 2 years' oil consumption in abandoned mine shafts, for use in an emergency. Using coal liquefaction technology originally developed by Germany during the Second World War, the state-controlled SASOL corporation has now built three oil-from-coal plants which provide at least a third of the nation's oil consumption, production from these plants having increased by about twenty times the amount it was in 1980 when only one SASOL plant was in operation.[27]

To prepare for the adoption of a 'laager' or siege economy, should effective economic sanctions ever be imposed by the international community, other state-controlled corporations have been utilised. Besides SASOL and the Armaments Development and Manufacturing Corporation (Armscor), which have been mentioned already, these include: the Iron and Steel Corporation (Iscor), the Industrial Development Corporation (IDC) and the Southern Oil Exploration Corporation (Soekor). In its preparation for siege, the South African government commands the widespread support of the Afrikaner electorate which believes that technological achievements like the SASOL oil-from-coal process and the 'unique' uranium enrichment process (discussed in Chapter 5 below) enhance the nation's prestige and appearance of invulnerability in the eyes of the outside world. (There is no significant environmental movement in South Africa to oppose such examples of 'big technology'.)

Nevertheless, notwithstanding the regime's attempts to make the country self-reliant, the South African economy remains highly dependent on the flow from the West of capital and advanced technology in the form of private investment, bank loans, imports of capital and high technology goods, and skilled immigration from Europe (particularly Britain). Her economy remains bound to the West and therefore vulnerable to external influence. Global recessions have caused black unemployment to rise and have thus, in part, led to unrest in the townships. Such unrest has in turn been followed by flights of capital from South Africa (as Western investors and creditors have lost confidence in the country's stability and have disinvested and withheld credit) and by a net emigration of whites, as happened following the Sharpeville, Soweto and 1984–6 disturbances. During the 1980s global recession, South Africa has found it increasingly difficult to support the economies of Namibia and the black homelands; and the domestic political and economic costs of waging the war along the Namibian–Angolan border have mounted.

The scarcity of capital and skilled manpower, referred to above, has forced the South African government to take some hard decisions concerning the allocation of resources for projects deemed essential for strategic purposes in both the civilian and military sectors of the economy.[28] South Africa has therefore welcomed foreign partnership in scientific research, technological development and capital investment. When this is obtained, she is reassured of her value to the West.

THE LEAGUE OF THE DESPERATE

However, such cooperation has been increasingly withheld, particularly in the military and nuclear spheres. South Africa has therefore had to turn to the other pariah nations mentioned at the beginning of this chapter, which, like herself, are dependent on the West but which, again like South Africa, do not enjoy unimpeded access to Western supplies and technology in these strategic areas. These pariah powers then find themselves in similar circumstances with similar interests.[29] They also find that they have complementary resources which attract each other: South Africa's raw materials (particularly uranium and steel), Taiwan's technology, Iran's oil (available before the overthrow of the Shah) and Israel's military know-how. They are therefore seen to be loosely bound together in an informal arrangement variously dubbed the 'Club of Pariahs', the 'alliance of the disenchanted' and the 'league of the desperate'. John de St Jorre has characterised the attitude of this group of nations as follows:

> The grouping may be loose and ephemeral – its basic objectives are tactical rather than strategic – but it merits attention because most of the countries involved possess a respectable military capability, some mastery of modern technology . . . and potential leverage in terms of vital resources or strategic locations. They view themselves as 'middle-level' powers, strongly anti-communist, nonaggressive, internally stable, and devotedly loyal to the Western alliance. Their individual motives for closer links with each other vary, but most of them feel that their unswerving friendship with the United States and Western Europe has not been properly rewarded and that the isolation they suffer from has been unfairly thrust upon them. In such circumstances they see no harm in turning their backs on the world community and showing the West that they have minds of their own. South Africa is the most active member of the pariah's club, perhaps because it is also the most isolated. And it is the nexus with Israel that has aroused the greatest controversy . . .[30]

Both Afrikaners and Israelis have deep religious roots; both view themselves as a 'chosen people'; both may be portrayed as minorities struggling for survival in their homelands; both feel beleaguered; both see themselves in a lone struggle against terrorism. The Afrikaners' 'laager mentality', a collective determination to resist against seemingly overwhelming odds, may be likened to the Israelis' 'Massada complex'. There are also personal links between the two countries: the South African Jewish community is both affluent and influential, and contributes more per capita to the Zionist cause than any other Jewish community in the world.[31]

Despite earlier traits of anti-Semitism within South Africa's ruling National Party, there have always been close intergovernmental relations between Israel and South Africa. These blossomed during the 1970s following the 1973 Middle East war, when Israel felt deserted by her European and African friends. During the war, Israel received spare

parts from South Africa for weapons systems originally supplied by
France. In 1976, South African Prime Minister Vorster visited Israel,
where he inspected naval installations and signed a pact to promote
economic and scientific cooperation between the two countries. Cabinet
ministers were to meet each year to review progress.[32] Trade between the
two countries was worth US $100 million by that time and had
quadrupled in value since 1972. South Africa is the main supplier of raw
diamonds for the Israeli diamond-cutting and polishing industry which
traditionally provides most of Israel's export earnings (but now comes
second to her earnings from arms exports). There is a joint steel project
by the two state-controlled industries, through which South Africa
supplies Israel with 25 per cent of her steel consumption. Israel
participates in an electronics factory near Pretoria. A huge ten-year coal
export deal has been signed that will help reduce Israel's dependence on
imported oil.[33]

South Africa's main motive in fostering these close relations with
Israel (and, to a lesser extent, the other pariahs) is to obtain scientific and
technical know-how – in particular military technology. Israel and the
other pariahs are interested in South Africa's natural resources.
Together, the South African and Israeli intelligence agencies provide a
most effective coverage of the whole of Africa, South African
intelligence covering southern Africa and the Israeli intelligence agency,
Mossad, covering the northern half of the continent. According to
Bissell,

> The South Africans and Israelis consult on counterinsurgency tactics;
> indeed a few Israeli observers were in Angola in 1975–76 with South
> African forces. When the South Africans bought Israeli patrol boats,
> the crews were trained at Israeli bases. The Israelis are also reliably
> said to have sold radar equipment to them, refurbished tanks, and
> supplied machine guns. In turn, South Africa provided special alloy
> steel for Israeli tank manufacture.[34]

According to another informed observer, Robert Harkavy,

> Israel has sold missile patrol boats to South Africa, is reported to have
> assisted it with electronic surveillance gear for counterinsurgency
> warfare, and may also have aided in refurbishing and upgrading
> Pretoria's large Centurion tank force (Israel has had much experience
> extending the lives of its own old Centurions). South Africa also uses
> Israeli small arms, probably Belgian-produced on license and
> obtained through private dealers.[35]

There are, however, limits to the cooperation possible between South Africa and Israel (and the other pariah powers). It is probable that, for Israel, the relationship with Pretoria is a tactical convenience, whereas, for South Africa, the relationship is of far greater strategic importance. For Israel there are strong domestic and international political reasons to limit cooperation. She has stated that she will abide by the 1977 United Nations arms embargo on South Africa; and, should her relations with her Arab neighbours and the West improve so that she gradually feels less isolated, Israel may wish to reduce her links with South Africa, for fear of jeopardising her resumption of good relations with black African countries, which may then be more important to her than her links with South Africa.[36] (South Africa would then suffer a similar setback to that which she has recently experienced in her relations with France: whereby, following the 1977 UN arms embargo and France's completion of the construction of the Koeberg nuclear power station in South Africa (see Chapter 5), bilateral links between France and South Africa have been sharply reduced.)

Ultimately, if for no other reason than that of geographic separation from each other, all the pariah powers depend far more on their links with the West than on each other to ease their isolation and their security problems. To conclude (in the words of John de St Jorre again):

Israel can help considerably in the field of technology, and the South African government will endeavour to initiate more bilateral industrial enterprises to cement what are fundamentally relationships of tactical convenience. But it is difficult to imagine this phenomenon materially altering South Africa's fundamental dependence on the West. The Western orientation has been too broad and too all-pervasive for it to be disrupted easily. It has also been part of the white South African's innermost beliefs, the concept of his being a Western man . . . and that may be the hardest bond of all to break.[37]

4 Uranium Mining in Southern Africa

THE DEVELOPMENT OF SOUTH AFRICA'S URANIUM RESOURCES

In the late 1940s and 1950s South Africa obtained the cooperation of Britain and America in the development of her nuclear science and technology and the exploitation of her uranium resources.[1] This was in exchange for a South African agreement to supply Britain and America with uranium for their nuclear weapons programmes. In an arrangement agreed with South African Prime Minister Smuts at the end of the Second World War and implemented by the Nationalist government which came to power after the 1948 general election, the wartime allies, through their jointly-owned Combined Development Agency (CDA), supplied money and expertise for the exploitation of South Africa's uranium resources. As explained in Chapter 2, after the passage of the 1946 US Atomic Energy Act (the McMahon Act), the CDA represented the only major continuation of the wartime collaboration in nuclear development between Britain and America, who otherwise pursued their separate nuclear courses. Following the war, both countries were keen to obtain as much uranium as possible. Although uranium is now recognised to be widespread in its abundance in the earth's crust, it was considered at the time a scarce resource. (Recent official estimates of Western world uranium resources, including those of South Africa, are shown in Table 4.1. Historic South African and world uranium production and projected future capacity are shown in Table 4.2. Non-communist resources and production only are shown: the Eastern Bloc and China are self-sufficient in uranium, neither importing nor exporting significant amounts.)

We have seen in Chapter 2 that the aim of the Combined Development Agency was to buy up all Western world production. As shown in Table 4.2, uranium resources were exploited and procured by the CDA mainly from the Belgian Congo, Canada, Australia and South Africa itself. Initially all South African production was sent to the United States, which was concerned to avoid overdependence on the Belgian Congo (now Zaire), the resources of which were becoming rapidly depleted. Nevertheless Britain's role was valued by all parties. It was felt in

Table 4.1　Western World Uranium Resources (1000 tonnes U)[a]

	Reserves[b]	Total Resources[c]
Algeria	26 (2)	26 (1)
Argentina	19 (1)	44 (1)
Australia	314 (21)	730 (17)
Brazil	163 (11)	256 (6)
Canada	176 (12)	695 (16)
Central African Republic	18 (1)	18 (0)
Denmark (Greenland)	0 (0)	43 (1)
France	56 (4)	113 (3)
Gabon	19 (1)	34 (1)
India	32 (2)	62 (1)
Namibia	119 (8)	188 (4)
Niger	160 (11)	213 (5)
South Africa	191 (13)	460 (10)
Spain	16 (1)	25 (1)
Sweden	2 (0)	82 (2)
USA	131 (9)	1299 (30)
Other	26 (2)	39 (1)
Total (rounded)	1470	4400

[a]　Figures in brackets are per cent of total (may not add to 100 due to rounding).
[b]　Reasonably assured resources mineable at costs of less than $80/kg U.
[c]　Reasonably assured resources and estimated additional resources recoverable at costs of less than $130/kg U.

Source: OECD Nuclear Energy Agency and IAEA, *Uranium Resources, Production and Demand* (Paris: OECD, 1983).

America that Britain's influence in Africa and with her former Dominions helped to 'deliver' these countries' uranium.[2] Later in the 1950s it was perceived that South Africa's uranium resources would be of great value to Britain herself as she envisaged the development of a nuclear power programme along with her weapons programme, although, in the event, Britain's power programme did not take off until the 1960s.[3]

According to the definitive paper on the early development of South Africa's uranium mining industry, the South African mining companies were

　　. . . amazed . . . at the expeditious way in which delivery of material to the project was made, due largely to the extremely high priority

given by all of the three Governments directly concerned with the
South African production of uranium . . . . It can safely be said that no
major industry in the history of South Africa has been developed as
rapidly as the uranium industry.[4]

Production continued on a large scale from 1953 to the mid-1960s,
reaching a peak of 5000 tonnes of uranium in 1959, but falling off later
when the British and American military stockpiling programmes
declined and it was found that America could meet her uranium
requirements from her own production. The Combined Development
Agency was wound up in 1960, but contracts were stretched out and
shipments continued to the US Atomic Energy Commission until 1966
and to the UK Atomic Energy Authority until 1973.[5]
    The pattern of growth of South Africa's uranium production during
the 1950s followed by a decline in the early 1960s (with production not
recovering until the 1970s, by which time nuclear power programmes in
the industrial countries had finally materialised) was similar to that of
the United States and Canada. During the initial period of high
production in the 1950s and early 1960s, the US Atomic Energy
Commission acquired roughly 85 per cent of Western world uranium
production, much of the balance going to the United Kingdom. France
developed her nuclear weapons somewhat later, independently of the
USA and Britain and largely based on her own uranium resources and
those of her African colonies, Madagascar and Gabon.[6] South Africa's
subsequent commercial exports of uranium for power reactors are
discussed in the next section; but a useful rule-of-thumb when considering the evolution of the uranium trade is provided by one expert's
assessment in 1981 that, of the 600 000 plus tonnes of uranium produced
in the last forty years, one-third has been used or set aside for military
purposes; another third has been or is being used in nuclear power
reactors; and the remaining third is being stockpiled, mainly by electric
utilities, but also by governments (and much lesser amounts by mining
companies and traders).[7] Broadly speaking, nearly all the uranium
produced before the 1960s was used for nuclear weapons or was
stockpiled by nuclear weapon states; nearly all the uranium produced
since the 1960s has been used for nuclear power generation or has been
stockpiled in countries with large nuclear power programmes. What did
or did not take place in the 1960s hiatus in demand for uranium is one of
the topics discussed in the following sections.
    In South Africa, uranium is produced as a by-product of gold from
the mines in the Witwatersrand and the Orange Free State, or it is

Table 4.2 Western World Uranium Production (tonnes U)[a]

Country[b]	Production[c]							Projected Capacity[d]	
	1950	1955	1960	1965	1970	1975	1980	1985	1990
Australia (1954)	—	180 (2)	930 (3)	260 (2)	250 (1)	—	1 560 (4)	3 800 (8)	3 300 (7)
Canada[b]	200 (7)	970 (13)	9 780 (31)	3 380 (22)	3 530 (19)	3 510 (18)	7 150 (16)	11 500 (25)	12 100 (25)
France (1949)	100[e] (4)	180[e] (2)	1 040[e] (3)	1 610[f] (10)	1 250 (7)	1 730 (9)	2 630 (6)	3 900 (8)	3 900 (8)
Gabon (1961)	—	—	—	n.a.	400 (2)	800 (4)	1 030 (2)	1 500 (3)	1 500 (3)
Niger (1971)	—	—	—	—	—	1 310 (7)	4 100 (9)	4 000 (9)	4 000 (8)
Namibia (1976)	—	—	—	—	—	—	4 040 (9)	3 900 (8)	3 900 (8)
South Africa (1952)	—	2 150 (28)	4 920 (15)	2 260 (14)	3 170 (17)	2 490 (13)	6 150 (14)	6 330 (14)	6 460 (13)
USA (1942)	420 (15)	3 100 (41)	14 460 (45)	8 150 (52)	9 900 (53)	8 900 (47)	16 800 (38)	10 300 (22)	12 200 (25)
Belgian Congo[b]	2 040 (74)	970 (13)	920 (3)	—	—	—	—	—	—
Total	2 760	7 550	32 050	15 670	18 610	19 070	43 970	46 660	49 360

n.a. Not available (see note f)

[a] Figures in brackets are per cent of total Western production/capacity.

[b] Date in brackets is year of first production. Before 1939 uranium ore was produced in small quantities, primarily for the contained radium, in the Belgian Congo, Canada, Czechoslovakia, Portugal and the USA.

[c] Countries shown have been responsible for at least 98 per cent of Western world annual production. Other nations which have produced comparatively small amounts include Argentina, Brazil, Japan, West Germany, Portugal, Spain, Sweden and Mexico.

[d] As projected in December 1983 (In the USA in particular not all capacity is likely to be utilised). Countries shown are projected to provide at least 95 per cent of Western world production capacity to 1990. Other countries whose capacity is forecast in the range 100–800 tU by 1990 are Argentina, Brazil, India, Mexico, Portugal and Spain.

[e] Includes production in Madagascar.

[f] Includes production in Gabon (approx 400 tU).

Sources: European Nuclear Energy Agency and IAEA, *Uranium Production and Short Term Demand* (Paris: OECD, 1969); OECD Nuclear Energy Agency and IAEA, *Uranium Resources, Production and Demand* (Paris: OECD, 1973, 1979, 1982, 1983); Thomas L. Neff, *The International Uranium Market* (Cambridge, Mass.: Ballinger, 1984) Appendix B.

extracted from the tailings dumps and slimes dams left over many years, after gold has been extracted from the ore produced by these mines. (The exception is the production of uranium, as a by-product of copper, from the Rio Tinto-Zinc-controlled Palabora mine, which is marketed differently, but which accounts for less than 5 per cent of South Africa's uranium production.) Mines were more recently opened of whose output uranium was considered a co-product or even the primary product; but the profitability of these mines was still dependent on their gold production and, with depressed prices of both gold and uranium most recently, these mines have been closed again.[8]

At present South Africa is unique in largely producing uranium as a by-product. This makes it easier for the mining companies to maintain a steady production as the price fluctuates. When the price is low, uranium can be stockpiled, in concentrate or in the tailings, rather than sold. It is believed that South Africa holds a considerable quantity of such stocks. Indeed South African uranium production is more dependent on the market for gold than that for uranium.[9] The relationship is not a simple one, however. When the price of gold is high, the gold mining companies' policy is to work lower-grade seams, and this normally results in lower uranium production. However, under these circumstances, if the high gold price is maintained, uranium production could again rise in the medium term as new mines and seams are opened up. Nevertheless, cost considerations suggest that for the remainder of this century South African uranium production will remain relatively static as high-grade producers, notably in Canada and Australia, expand their production (see Table 4.2).

URANIUM EXPORTS

Responsibility for sale of South African uranium to the Combined Development Agency rested with the government's Atomic Energy Board established under the Atomic Energy Act of 1948. When sales for the British and American arms programmes declined, new markets had to be found. The CDA's monopsony was ended when the first private sale of uranium took place in 1958.[10] In 1967 the Atomic Energy Act was repealed and a new act, the Atomic Energy Act number 90, left responsibility for the processing and marketing of uranium with the Nuclear Fuels Corporation of South Africa (NUFCOR), a private service company owned by those gold mines which produce uranium and the half dozen or so principal mining finance houses. It is thought that, through its numerous interlocking shareholdings, the giant Anglo American Corporation may have a controlling 50 per cent share in NUFCOR, which is also closely associated with the Chamber of Mines.[11] NUFCOR is responsible for collecting ammonium diuranate slurry from the mines and milling it to produce uranium oxide concentrate at its central calcining plant. The uranium exported by South Africa is thus of a very uniform quality.

In the late 1960s, as sales to the CDA were coming to an end, the international uranium market was very depressed. Government-held stocks were high and uranium demand for power reactors had not yet developed to any significant extent. The US market was closed by protectionist measures, notably the stipulation under 1964 legislation that all uranium enriched for US consumers (power utilities) from 1966 should be of US origin.[12] The United States, it should be recalled, had a global monopoly of the enrichment market at the time.[13] The main uranium producers in Australia, Canada, France and South Africa responded to this situation in the early 1970s by secretly cooperating in a market-sharing arrangement to induce a price rise. Between March 1974 and March 1976, the spot market price for uranium rose from \$8/1b U_3O_8 to over \$39/1b U_3O_8.[14] There were other reasons for this dramatic price rise, including (i) the effect of the 1974 oil price hike, (ii) announcements of large nuclear power powers by Western governments, (iii) uncertainty concerning enrichment contracts with the US government, (iv) the delay in expansion of Australian uranium production due to domestic political opposition and (v) the announcement to its customers by the Westinghouse power plant construction company that it could not meet their uranium orders as contracted; but the non-American producers' action was undoubtedly a major factor. In fact United States companies were also involved in the cartel; but the leading members were NUFCOR, three or four Canadian mining companies (some of them government-owned), the French government-owned Commissariat à l'Energie Atomique (CEA), which controlled the marketing of uranium produced in France, Niger and Gabon, and the UK-based Rio Tinto-Zinc corporation, which controlled current or planned production capacity in Canada, Australia and Namibia (as well as production from the Palabora mine in South Africa).[15] The cartel was also supported by the Australian and Canadian governments. The cartel members met secretly, usually in Paris or Johannesburg, on several occasions between 1972 and 1974. In response to the worldwide rise in the price of uranium and the revelation of the cartel's existence, cartel members were sued in the US courts by Westinghouse, which was in turn sued by American and Swedish consumers. However the price has since declined, the supply side of the uranium market is much more competitive, and the cartel is assumed to have been disbanded. Indeed, in the subsequent buyers' market, South African producers perceived some advantage in the out-of-court settlement under which they were to supply Westinghouse with a large tonnage of uranium.[16]

Information about the sale of South African uranium since the 1960s is difficult to obtain. Under the Atomic Energy Act number 90 of 1967, which was extended to cover Namibia, and the Nuclear Energy Act number 92 of 1982 which replaced it, it is a serious offence for anyone other than the South African government to publish material relating to the prospecting, production and pricing of uranium.[17]

Nevertheless it is clear that South Africa's main customers are no longer the United States and Britain, but other West European nations and Japan. It seems that, whereas Japan was South Africa's largest customer in the mid-1970s, she has now diversified her supplies, possibly to avoid politically undesirable dependence on South African supplies. Since the late 1970s, West Germany has thus been South Africa's main customer, and indeed South Africa has been West Germany's main supplier (closely followed by Australia and Canada).[18]

Historically France has obtained most of her uranium from her own production and that of her ex-colonies, Niger and Gabon. In 1977 the French government claimed that South Africa supplied only 6 per cent of her needs.[19] However, the French nuclear power programme is one of the largest in the Western world, and France is a major uranium consumer. In 1977, the French CEA's nuclear fuel subsidiary COGEMA thus negotiated with NUFCOR a contract for approximately 900 tonnes of uranium a year to be delivered between 1980 and 1990 in exchange for a loan granted to the Randfontein gold and uranium mine managed by the Johannesburg Consolidated Investment Company.[20] Under a similar arrangement between Belgium's Synatom fuel company and the Harmony gold mine (managed by the Barlow Rand Company) South Africa was due to supply 50 per cent of Belgium's uranium demand by 1985.[21]

Before the 1979 Islamic revolution, Iran had signed a large contract with South Africa for the purchase of uranium for her ambitious nuclear power programme. This was cancelled when the power programme was suspended following the Iranian revolution; but, luckily for South Africa, the contract was replaced by another with Taiwan to supply 4000 tonnes of uranium oxide between 1984 and 1990.[22] Indeed South Africa has managed successfully to diversify her markets for uranium. Spain is

another large customer; and, before the outbreak of renewed disturbances in South Africa's black townships in 1984–6 and the consequent
domestic political pressure on the US government to ban imports of
South African uranium, there was the prospect that uranium exports to
the United States might once more have increased following the lifting of
the aforementioned embargo (although, with depressed prices and huge
stockpiles overhanging the market, the US government faces similar
domestic pressures as in the 1960s to reimpose an embargo).[23]

Nevertheless the United States and United Kingdom are unlikely to
become significantly dependent on uranium supplies from South Africa
again, due to the domestic opposition from anti-apartheid groups such
dependence would bring. The dependence of the European Community
as a whole on uranium supplies from South Africa (the second largest
uranium supplier to the Community after Canada) has already been
criticised in the European Parliament.[24] For the European and Japanese
authorities, such domestic opposition to imports of South African
uranium must be weighed against the desire to avoid overdependence on
supplies from Australia and Canada, with continuity of supplies from
these sources perceived to be at risk because of the non-proliferation
conditions attached by the governments of these countries (see Chapter 2).

URANIUM EXPORTS AND NON-PROLIFERATION

At the dawn of the nuclear age it was considered essential for the success
of any non-proliferation policy that the international trade in uranium
should be monitored. Thus the first official non-proliferation proposal,
the 1946 Acheson–Lilienthal Report, proposed international UN
controls over the whole fuel cycle – including uranium mining. We have
seen in Chapter 2 how, following the rejection of the Baruch plan by the
Soviet Union, the jointly British and American-owned Combined
Development Agency sought to purchase all uranium produced in the
non-communist world; and how, when the CDA's monopsony ended,
Britain and America sought the cooperation of other uranium-producing countries in the Western Suppliers Group in their covert monitoring
of the uranium trade. In the late 1950s and early 1960s a major concern
of the American government was that the Western Suppliers Group
should ascertain Israeli purchases and use of uranium. In 1963 South
Africa had given the other members of the Group details of her recent
uranium deliveries to Israel; but by 1968 the system had broken down.[25]
Israel's nuclear programme could no longer be effectively monitored.

With the global increase in the number of nuclear installations and uranium-producing countries, it seemed to the American government that a more comprehensive system of international safeguards was needed.[26]

Besides the attention given to her supplies to Israel, the political significance of South Africa's uranium exports may be adduced from the reported strong American opposition to South Africa's agreement in 1963 to supply France with a large quantity of unsafeguarded uranium.[27] At the time, Franco-American relations were difficult and Canada had refused to supply France with unsafeguarded uranium. The South African deal was much appreciated by the French government as France was beginning a power programme and her rate of acquisition of a stock of fissionable material for atomic warheads was at its height. At this time France also hoped to be able to export natural uranium-fuelled power reactors free of American-imposed safeguards (as required under the Western Suppliers Group policy), although in the event this ambition was never realised. It is noteworthy that these South Arican sales of uranium to France and Israel occurred when the uranium market was depressed and producers were desperately looking for new customers to replace the British and American weapons programmes.

So, during the 1950s and most of the 1960s, a 'responsible' South African uranium exporting policy was seen, particularly by the Anglo-Saxon nations, to be an important pillar of the non-proliferation regime. However, as South Africa became increasingly isolated in international relations and it became clear that she was unlikely to sign the Non-Proliferation Treaty, South Africa was gradually excluded from negotiating forums such as the 'London Club' which were continuing to build the non-proliferation regime.[28]

Nevertheless South Africa's status as a major uranium producer meant that her uranium exporting policy could not be ignored by those nations, in particular the United States, which were taking the lead in constructing this regime.

When nations were formulating their attitude to the Non-Proliferation Treaty in the late 1960s and early 1970s, South Africa's officially-stated policy was that she 'would not allow her uranium sales to be used to increase the number of nuclear weapon states', and this somewhat ambiguously-worded formulation has remained her position on non-proliferation.[29] Although NUFCOR is responsible for the commercial aspects of uranium sales, export permission is required from the Atomic Energy Corporation, which has replaced the Atomic Energy Board, and which is in turn answerable to the Minister of Mineral and Energy

Affairs. The Atomic Energy Corporation has stated that it requires non-nuclear weapon state customers to give peaceful and non-explosive use guarantees and accept IAEA safeguards for the imported uranium; but this non-proliferation policy is a unilateral undertaking which South Africa could presumably withdraw in the future if she perceives it to be in her interests to do so. She has not signed any written agreement with other Western countries to maintain this policy in the future. Moreover, unlike Australia and Canada, South Africa does not require from her customers full-scope safeguards or the right to give prior approval for spent fuel reprocessing.[30] South Africa's non-proliferation export policy is further discussed in Chapter 6. The international political and economic leverage accruing to South Africa by virtue of this relatively relaxed policy is also discussed in Chapters 2, 8 and 9.

THE RÖSSING MINE IN NAMIBIA

South Africa's role in the mining of uranium in Namibia should finally be briefly mentioned. All uranium production in Namibia comes from the Rössing mine which is managed by the South African subsidiary of the British-based Rio Tinto-Zinc corporation (RTZ), the leading shareholder in the mine. Other shareholders are French, West German and South African companies, with government-owned interests dominant and the South African government-owned shareholder (the Industrial Development Corporation) having a predominant say over policy matters. The development of the open pit mine, which was the largest uranium mine in the world when it opened, was a direct consequence of a contract signed in 1968 between RTZ and the United Kingdom government-owned British Nuclear Fuels Limited (BNFL) for the supply of 7500 tonnes of uranium between 1977 and 1982.[31] The financial viability of the mine was assured when Japanese utilities signed contracts for 30 000 tonnes of uranium to be delivered between 1977 and 1990.[32]

As we saw in the previous chapter, South Africa's control of Namibia has been declared illegal by the United Nations. The UN General Assembly has appointed a UN Council for Namibia which in 1974 issued 'Decree Number 1 on the Protection of Namibia's Natural Resources' which states that the export of Namibian mineral resources is illegal.[33] The British government's attitude to Decree Number 1 is that the UN General Assembly-appointed Council for Namibia has no legal authority there.

In 1980, because of production delays, the delivery period for the supply of Namibian uranium to the UK was extended from 1982 to 1984. However responsibility for UK procurement of uranium has been transferred from BNFL to the British Civil Uranium Procurement Organisation on behalf of the Central Electricity Generating Board, and this organisation favours a policy of diversifying supply sources away from Namibia and RTZ.[34] (Britain's other major source of uranium is an RTZ-controlled mine in Canada.) Moreover Britain possesses vast stocks of uranium and so has no great need of supplies from Namibia at present. Accordingly it was announced in 1983 that the Namibian contract would not be renewed after it expired in 1984.[35]

South Africa's atomic energy legislation preventing disclosure of details of uranium production and exports has been extended to cover Namibia. This fact, and RTZ's reticence, have made it difficult to ascertain the destination of Namibian uranium.[36] However it is believed that for the duration of the BNFL contract Britain absorbed 25 per cent of Rössing's production which in turn accounted for 65 per cent of Britain's uranium imports. Because of political pressure, the German partner Urangesellschaft has reduced its interests in the Rössing operation, but West Germany still receives uranium from Namibia.[37] Under similar pressure from Third World countries, the Japanese Prime Minister announced the cancellation of Japan's contracts in 1974. However, contracts for the same amount were then signed with the RTZ parent company, the uranium being sent from Namibia through a Swiss subsidiary. Some Namibian uranium goes to South Africa through the South African General Mining Union Corporation, which has an interest in Rössing. This uranium is probably re-exported from South Africa. Thus France's socialist government, which came to power pledged to halt the importation of uranium from Namibia, is able to claim that 'France imports uranium only from South Africa', although the French interests in the Rössing mine are due to receive 11 080 tonnes of uranium from the mine between 1981 and 1990.[38] Iran cancelled a 10 670 tonne contract for Namibian uranium (to have been supplied between 1978 and 1990) when the Shah was overthrown, but lesser amounts may have been sold to Spain, Italy and the Netherlands; and Taiwan may receive uranium from Namibia commencing in 1989 under a contract signed between RTZ and the island's power utility, Taipower.[39]

Uranium is the only product of the Rössing mine, unlike in South Africa where uranium is produced as a by-product of gold mining. The Rössing deposits are of very low grade, but the mine has been very profitable. The extent of the reserves indicated in 1982 that the mine had a twenty-three-year life at the current level of production.[40] However the prospects for continuing orders from Western consumers are not good due to the current political situation in Namibia and the state of the uranium market. Recent indications therefore are that Rössing might have to cut production or stockpile uranium.[41] Indeed it may already be doing so behind its veil of secrecy. There are other uranium deposits in Namibia, and rights are held to them mainly by South Africa-based mining companies; but their exploitation is considered most unlikely at least until Namibia's political future is resolved.[42]

There is no information available on any safeguards required on the sale of uranium from Rössing,[43] but it is unlikely that the non-proliferation conditions are any stricter than those on South Africa's uranium exports. Indeed it is likely that Britain and France feel free to use uranium obtained from Namibia for their nuclear weapons arsenals.[44]

5 The Development of South Africa's Nuclear Capability

EARLY NUCLEAR RESEARCH AND DEVELOPMENT

As with the exploitation of her uranium resources, South Africa's capability in fundamental nuclear research was gained in the 1950s and 1960s mainly with British and American help. The South African Atomic Energy Board (AEB) was established in 1949 as a result of the passage of the South African Atomic Energy Act of 1948; and during this time there was a very close relationship between the AEB, the US Atomic Energy Commission (USAEC) and the UK Atomic Energy Authority (UKAEA, formerly the Ministry of Supply). The USAEC and UKAEA relied on the AEB for a large share of the supply of uranium needed for the American and British weapons programmes. Thus the USAEC and the UKAEA felt obliged to cooperate in the development of South Africa's capability in nuclear science and technology. As we saw in Chapter 2, Eisenhower's 1953 Atoms for Peace initiative could in part be viewed as a formal recognition of the importance of the uranium-supplying countries. An agreement for nuclear cooperation between the United States and South Africa (in effect between the USAEC and the AEB) came into effect in 1957. The agreement is similar to those negotiated between the United States and forty other countries during the 1950s under the 1954 US Atomic Energy Act, passed after Eisenhower's 1953 speech. It has subsequently been amended three times, the last amendment being in 1974, when the agreement was extended to the year 2007. The agreement provides for the training of South African scientists in the USA, and the American supply of nuclear fuel and technology subject to peaceful use guarantees and safeguards. A. J. A. Roux, President of the Atomic Energy Board throughout this period and a central figure in South Africa's nuclear development, has said that:

> We can ascribe our degree of advancement today in large measure to the training and assistance so willingly provided by the United States of America during the early years of our nuclear programme when several of the Western world's nuclear nations cooperated in initiating our scientists and engineers into nuclear science.[1]

The British role in South Africa's nuclear development was inevitably more modest than that of the Americans; and a cooperation agreement between the UKAEA and the AEB was later allowed to expire, although high-level exchanges continued until the early 1970s. Britain now claims that nuclear cooperation is limited to safety and medical aspects of nuclear technology. In Commonwealth forums, for example, Britain now makes a virtue of her non-cooperation with South Africa's nuclear development.[2] Nevertheless, South Africa, which has always suffered from a lack of trained manpower, has managed to acquire technological expertise (in the nuclear field in particular) only by the steady recruitment, throughout the post-war period, of scientists and technologists, particularly from Britain. Moreover, as will be seen later in this chapter, South Africa now has little need for formal nuclear cooperation with Britain.

Under the United States–South African agreement for nuclear cooperation, America supplied a 20 megawatt (MW) research reactor known as Safari-1 and 93 per cent enriched uranium to fuel it, most of the fuel being fabricated in the United Kingdom. 'Safari' is an acronym for 'South African Fundamental Atomic Research'. The reactor, which went critical in 1965, is sited at the Atomic Energy Board's research centre at Pelindaba near Pretoria. Although of weapons-grade, the fuel and the reactor have been safeguarded by the IAEA, and diversion of fissile material for weapons manufacture is thought to have been highly unlikely.[3] It is generally agreed that the construction and operation of the reactor provided South Africa with invaluable experience for the subsequent development of her nuclear industry.[4] This is probably of more significance than the research uses to which Safari-1 has been put, namely materials-testing and the production of isotopes for minerals prospecting and medical and agricultural use. Other fundamental research carried out at Pelindaba has included work on nuclear fusion and reactor fuel development. Nuclear research is also carried out by universities and the government's Council for Scientific and Industrial Research (CSIR).[5]

As a result of the experience gained in operating Safari-1, and the expertise acquired by scientists trained in the West, South Africa was able to design and build her own reactor, Safari-2, also known as Pelindaba-Zero, which went critical in 1967. To add to the confusion of names, Safari-2 was originally known as Pelinduna, an acronym for Pelindaba Deuterium Uranium Sodium (Na). Deuterium refers to the heavy water moderator, supplied by and later returned to the United States. Sodium (Na) refers to the coolant. At the time, South Africa had no firm plans for uranium enrichment and she wished to develop a reactor fuelled by natural uranium, in order not to depend on an overseas supply of fuel. However, difficulties were experienced in obtaining an assembly which could be made critical; and it was found that, by using 2 per cent enriched uranium instead of natural uranium, the number of fuel elements could be reduced from nineteen to four. Safari-2 was not submitted to IAEA safeguarding, but it had a negligible power output and produced very little plutonium, and was therefore not thought to be a risk from a weapons-proliferation viewpoint. The fuel was again supplied by the United States. The main purpose of Safari-2 was as an exercise in the independent design and construction of a reactor. There were, however, certain inherent problems in the design. To have developed it for power production would have been extremely costly, and even after a large power reactor had been constructed on the same design, it was very doubtful whether it would have been able to compete with the relatively cheap power provided by power stations fuelled by South African coal. Safari-2 was therefore soon allowed to run down. It was eventually dismantled in 1970. The official history of the South African Atomic Energy Board states that, at the time (the late 1960s), it faced the choice between allocating large sums of capital expenditure for the construction of a pilot power reactor, on the Safari-2 design, or the construction of a pilot enrichment plant. To have constructed both would have been prohibitively expensive.[6]

MR VORSTER'S 1970 ANNOUNCEMENT

This was the known state of South Africa's nuclear development in July 1970 when the Prime Minister, Mr Vorster, announced to the South African Parliament that South African scientists had developed their own process for uranium enrichment, and that a pilot enrichment plant was being built on a site adjoining Pelindaba. The site was to be known as Valindaba, a name deriving from the local African language, meaning 'We do not talk about this at all' (whereas Pelindaba means 'We do not talk about this any more').[7]

The development of an enrichment capability had indeed been (and continues to be) kept secret. According to Newby-Fraser, the project was classified and known as the 'Gas Cooling Project', later to be divided into three components and hence known as the 'XYZ project'. Newby-Fraser states that the project continued to get the personal backing of the then Prime Minister Verwoerd in spite of numerous technical difficulties, and that, when Dr Verwoerd visited the project site in 1965, 'it was possible to separate uranium-235 from uranium-238 in a helium-uranium hexafluoride mixture'. Mr Vorster's 1970 announcement, according to this source, was made because it was no longer possible to keep the project secret.[8]

Mr Vorster justified South Africa's development of enrichment technology on economic grounds. At the time (the early 1970s), South Africa, along with many other countries, planned a large nuclear power programme, using reactors fuelled by low-enriched uranium (and not natural uranium as had originally been intended). This, said Mr Vorster, 'can only be followed if the supply of enriched uranium can be guaranteed, which, in the difficult world in which we live, implies own production'. Mr Vorster emphasised South Africa's peaceful purposes and extended an invitation to other non-communist nations to help exploit South Africa's new enrichment process.[9]

Following Mr Vorster's statement to Parliament, it was announced that a government-owned company, the Uranium Enrichment Corporation of South Africa (UCOR), was to be set up with a capital of 50 million rand (US$67 million at the 1970 exchange rate) to build the pilot enrichment plant.[10]

There were no indications that the pilot enrichment plant would be subject to international safeguards. At the time of Mr Vorster's announcement to Parliament in 1970, South Africa's official position regarding the Nuclear Non-Proliferation Treaty (NPT) was that she was waiting for new arrangements for IAEA safeguarding to be announced before she made a decision on whether or not to sign the treaty. Mr Vorster professed his concern that IAEA inspections might infringe the commercial secrecy of her enrichment process (and her uranium ore milling process).[11] The Pretoria government has maintained this stance with regard to the NPT to the present time.

THE NATURE OF THE SOUTH AFRICAN ENRICHMENT PROCESS

Following Mr Vorster's 1970 announcement to Parliament, there was intense speculation and considerable scepticism overseas about the nature of what Mr Vorster claimed was South Africa's 'unique' enrichment process. It was wondered whether other countries – and, if so, which – had helped South Africa develop the process.[12] If the process was indeed 'unique in conception', some observers thought that the South Africans might be using an ion-exchange process, as they were advanced in this technology, having developed it (with British and American help) for the extraction of uranium from ore. However an authoritative report in the *Financial Times* stated that informed sources in Britain were:

> convinced that the South African scientists do now have a process different from the three currently under discussion in Europe as potentially economic routes to enrichment (the gaseous diffusion process, the electromagnetic separation process, and the gas centrifuge). Moreover, they are sure it is one which uses 'hex'.[13]

These various enrichment technologies mentioned above are outlined in the Appendix; but it should be noted here that an ion-exchange process would not use uranium hexafluoride ('hex') as the feed, whereas it was already known that South Africa was developing a hexafluoride conversion capacity.[14] One could speculate then that nozzle enrichment technology which *was* known about in Europe (it was developed in West Germany, and extensive details have been published in the open literature), and which uses 'hex' as the feed, was not then considered an economic process under *European* conditions (of high energy costs), but that South Africa, whose electricity costs are lower, *may* have been developing a version of this process.

South Africa did in fact show interest, both before and after Mr Vorster's 1970 announcement, in enrichment technologies developed elsewhere. When, in 1970–1, the USA had offered her classified diffusion technology to ten selected nations, there was clearly some disappointment in South Africa that she was not one of those selected.[15] South Africa had already shown an interest in participating in the URENCO centrifuge project with West Germany, the Netherlands and Britain; but by 1971 it was apparent that it was extremely unlikely that South Africa would be allowed to join this project, although another approach was made in 1972. South Africa has also shown interest in American work on laser enrichment, and Israeli technologists are said to be working at Pelindaba on enrichment technology.[16]

The early 1970s was a period when rapid growth in nuclear power plant construction was foreseen. There was therefore rising demand for enrichment services and intense international competition concerning where and with which technology additional enrichment plants would be built. Mr Vorster's 1970 announcement must clearly be seen in this context. In fact, it now appears that Mr Vorster's offer to other nations to join in exploiting South Africa's 'new and unique' enrichment process was really a request for much-needed capital and assistance with developing the basic technology.[17] Spence has suggested that Prime Minister Vorster's offer was really 'an attempt to make a virtue out of a necessity'.[18] Not surprisingly, South Africa found it difficult to attract the interest of foreign collaborators with an undisclosed technology; and her refusal to disclose the technology or allow IAEA safeguards on the pilot plant increased suspicions that South Africa's intentions were not as peaceful as they were stated to be.[19]

In late 1973 and early 1974, speculation began to focus on the probability that South Africa's enrichment process was a version of the Becker nozzle process developed in West Germany. News reached the trade press that components being manufactured for the pilot enrichment plant bore a marked similarity to those used for the Becker nozzle process.[20] In 1975 the West German press reported the agreement between UCOR and the Essen-based Steinkohlen Elektrizitäts AG (STEAG) (the West German government-controlled company responsible for the commercial exploitation of the Becker process) 'to compare the two variations of the jet-nozzle process'.[21]

Details of the South African enrichment process were first revealed officially in a paper given by A. J. A. Roux, the chairman, and W. L. Grant, the general manager of UCOR at a European Nuclear Conference in Paris in April 1975. It became clear then to Professor Becker (and to many other observers) that the process, which the South Africans called the 'Advanced Vortex Tube Process' or 'High-Performance Stationary-Walled Centrifuge', bore marked similarities to his own separation nozzle or jet nozzle process.[22] The main innovation claimed by the South African scientists was the 'helikon' cascade arrangement;[23] but, as explained in the Appendix, the need to use the helikon technique arose from the low cut used by the South Africans and the consequent need to use an axial flow compressor to handle several streams of gas of different composition without mixing and hence reduce energy consumption. Further information on the helikon technique was provided by Roux, Grant and their colleagues at an IAEA conference on nuclear energy in Salzburg in May 1977, when it was claimed that Dr Grant had discovered the process himself.[24] However, observers had noted that several South African scientists had been trained in Professor Becker's laboratory in Karlsruhe. Roux and Grant had also both visited the Karlsruhe laboratory, these exchanges being provided for under an intergovernmental West German–South African cultural agreement.[25]

THE STEAG–UCOR RELATIONSHIP

It became more clear that the South African process was a version of the Becker nozzle technique when details of cooperation between STEAG and UCOR were revealed following the publication by the African National Congress of documents stolen from the South African embassy in Bonn in 1975.[26] There is no doubting the authenticity of the documents. They are cited extensively (in its defence) in the 1978 publication of the West German government, *Fact v. Fiction*, which officially denied the allegations that accompanied the documents' release.[27] These allegations were that the West German government had assisted in the transfer of enrichment technology to South Africa and that key components for the South African pilot plant, such as compressors, isotope measuring instruments and the separation elements themselves (the jet nozzles), had been exported from West Germany, in some cases via third countries. The evidence may be inconclusive, but perhaps the best documented case concerns the alleged export of compressors by the Gutehoffnungshütte–Sterkrade subsidiary (GHH) of Maschinenfabrik Augsburg–Nürnberg AG (MAN).[28] It is interesting to note that, in its refutation of this allegation, the West German government claimed that GHH made small radial-flow compressors for the German nozzle enrichment process. The fact that large axial-flow compressors were being exported proved that their purpose could not be for an enrichment plant.[29] Yet the innovation claimed for the South African process, the helikon cascade technique, required just such an axial-flow compressor (or rather two of them for each module) to be used.[30]

So far as the relationship between STEAG and UCOR is concerned, briefly it seems to have evolved as follows:

After initial contacts in the 1960s between West German scientists and the South African Atomic Energy Board, STEAG applied to the West German government in October 1973 for permission to sub-license the jet nozzle process to UCOR. The West German cabinet postponed a decision and, sensing some opposition to the application, it was withdrawn by STEAG the following day.[31] However, technological cooperation between UCOR and STEAG continued when, within a year, STEAG stated in a press release that the two companies had signed a contract:

> to carry out a joint comparative economic feasibility study of both uranium enrichment processes. Should the study lead to favourable results, it is intended to consider building a commercial enrichment plant in South Africa by using the jointly available technology . . .[32]

The phrase 'jointly available technology' indicates that there were at least similarities between the two enrichment processes, as does the aborted plan to sub-license the jet nozzle technology to UCOR. South Africa however wished to keep her plans secret and, also for reasons of prestige, thus continued to claim that the process had been developed 'entirely by South Africans': a claim that may also have been partly designed to protect her West German partners from political embarrassment.[33]

Besides wishing to sell her enrichment technology and obtain orders for component manufacturers, the motivation of the West German government (which had a controlling interest in STEAG) may have been the desire to obtain a secure supply of enriched uranium, free from the irritating non-proliferation conditions and the threat of interruption in supply being attached by the United States. It should be noted that STEAG, an electric utility, had a particular interest in obtaining a secure supply of uranium and had directed its attempt to sell nozzle technology towards uranium-producing countries.[34] It may be significant, as Kapur asserts, that in 1975 South Africa won a contract against competition from Australia for the supply of natural uranium to West Germany.[35] It should also be noted that at about the same time, and motivated by similar considerations, West Germany signed a contract for the supply of nuclear technology to Brazil which enabled STEAG to sub-license the nozzle technology to Brazil. Because of the energy-intensive nature of the nozzle process, both Brazil and South Africa, because of their low-cost energy resources, the former based on hydroelectric power, the latter on cheap coal production, were logical choices of actual or potential uranium-producing countries towards which STEAG's sales drive was directed.[36] It is in this context that one can understand the remarks of Graf Lambsdorff, the West German government's spokesman on economic affairs, who visited Pelindaba at the beginning of 1975. He told Parliament in Bonn in April 1975 that:

In Canada and Australia – everyone knows this – the readiness to deliver [uranium] is restricted. Whereas in Brazil and South Africa it is better. We should adjust ourselves to this. I am convinced we cannot, in a decisive way, take exception to the fact that the political situation and the social order in those countries are not to our taste, to put it mildly. We must, in my opinion, carry on the uranium enrichment in these countries – not just contracts for delivery – with German participation in order to obtain a really secure supply basis.[37]

In the event, when the conditions for the supply of capital and natural uranium feed for a large commercial enrichment plant could not be agreed, STEAG withdrew from the agreement with UCOR in March 1976. It seems that each partner wanted the other to supply the uranium feed for the plant. Of course, South Africa had a large uranium production capacity, but most of it was contracted to overseas customers, who in turn already had contracts for its enrichment with American and European suppliers. South Africa was not able to guarantee sufficient natural uranium feed for a commercial enrichment plant, and, without the feed, STEAG was not willing to help find the capital required for its construction. In any case, it is likely that, by 1976, UCOR had learned all it needed to known about the nozzle technique. Enrichment plant components could now be produced in South Africa, and there was no further need for STEAG's help. Moreover, with the publicity that followed the publication of the documents stolen from the Bonn embassy, there could have been embarrassing political problems for both partners if the cooperation had continued.

CHANGING PLANS FOR ENRICHMENT CAPACITY

Meanwhile, UCOR was continuing with the construction of the pilot plant. In April 1975, Prime Minister Vorster announced in Parliament that part of the pilot plant was operating, though construction of the plant, which is also known as Mini-Z, was not completed until the following year.[38] The official history of the Atomic Energy Board states that the pilot plant became fully operational on 4 March 1977.[39] The actual production of enriched uranium by the plant has never been officially revealed, but the figure of 6000SWU/a (6 tonnes of separative work per annum) for its full capacity is quoted by diverse authoritative sources.[40] The 1981 report of the UN Secretary-General on South Africa's nuclear capability stated that material published in South Africa suggested that the pilot plant could be as large as 10 000SWU/a (10t SWU/a).[41] In the past, South Africa has had plans for following the construction of Mini-Z with a somewhat larger prototype plant, known as Proto-Z, with a capacity of 50 000SWU/a (50t SWU/a).[42] There have also been reports that enrichment capacity in South Africa now varies from 20 000SWU/a to 40 000SWU/a (20–40t SWU/a) with actual production usually at the lower end of this range.[43] Such reports may refer to such an enlarged prototype plant, but it is difficult to assess their reliability.[44]

South Africa had planned to construct a 5 million SWU/a (5000t SWU/a) commercial enrichment plant, which would have started production in 1984 and reached full capacity in 1986. At the IAEA conference in Salzburg in 1977, Roux and his colleagues disclosed that negotiations with 'interested foreign parties' over the contracts for the construction of this plant were under way and, in some cases, were 'at an advanced stage'.[45]

With hindsight, South Africa's plan, announced in 1975, for the construction of a 5 million SWU/a (5000t SWU/a) plant can be seen to have been excessively ambitious. It was already then becoming obvious that, with the worldwide slump in orders for nuclear power plants, there would be considerable excess capacity well into the 1980s for enrichment plants then in existence or under construction.[46] Furthermore, there had been a major escalation in the estimated cost of a 5 million SWU/a (5000t SWU/a) plant, such that a massive amount of foreign capital would have been required.[47] One of the reasons for this cost escalation was that the US government prevailed upon European countries to agree to withhold components, such as computers.[48]

There was also the problem of obtaining the uranium supply contracts that would guarantee that such a plant would be utilised at anything near its planned capacity. In October 1975, the *International Herald Tribune* reported that South Africa had negotiated an agreement with Iran, whereby Iran would invest in a commercial enrichment plant in return for the supply of enriched uranium for the Shah's own ambitious nuclear power programme;[49] but it was doubtful whether this contract alone would have been sufficient to enable the project to go ahead. (The contract was later terminated when Iran's nuclear power programme was suspended following the 1978–9 Islamic revolution.) In the sellers' market for uranium of the mid-1970s, South Africa may have felt that she had sufficient influence as a producer to force consumers to sign contracts for enriched uranium. This South African leverage would have been reinforced by the control exerted by South Africa's parastatal Industrial Development Corporation over the export policy for the Rössing mine in Namibia. However, as it became clear by the end of the 1970s that the market prospects were for a glut rather than a shortage of uranium for some time to come, European and Japanese consumers, who by then had plans for their own enrichment industries, would have been more able to resist South African pressure to sign enrichment contracts.[50]

Besides the escalating capital costs and the difficulties in securing enrichment contracts, South African nuclear officials admitted that a major problem was the high energy consumption of their enrichment process.[51] In congressional testimony in the US, Ronald Siegel of the

Massachusetts Institute of Technology suggested that in spite of her low-cost coal production, electricity supplies to a South African commercial enrichment plant would have to be subsidised to make the product competitive.[52]

To help the attempt, made again at the 1977 IAEA meeting in Salzburg, to gain foreign backing, South Africa dropped hints about numerous interested visitors to Pelindaba and even said she would allow IAEA safeguards on the commercial plant. This was seen as an effort to attract foreign backers who otherwise would have been wary of being seen to be cooperating with South Africa in the construction and operation of an unsafeguarded enrichment plant. However this gesture was clearly inconsistent with South Africa's refusal to allow safeguards on the pilot plant, which was based on the same technology, because, according to South Africa, they might infringe the commercial secrecy of her 'unique' technology.[53] The change of policy concerning safeguards was also not as significant as it appeared, as South Africa still maintained that she would accept safeguards on the plant only if she were not 'limited in the promotion of the peaceful uses' of nuclear technology and that details of the enrichment process were not disclosed. These conditions left a large loophole through which South Africa could withdraw from her commitment to allow safeguards on the larger plant if she perceived it to be in her interests. She has been able to exploit this uncertainty to extract concessions from the United States, in the form of continuing nuclear supplies for example, with the implied threat that the commitment to allow the larger plant to be safeguarded might be withdrawn (with consequent damage to US non-proliferation objectives) if such concessions were not forthcoming.

In the event, in a reversal of policy, the South African Minister of Mines announced in 1978 that the pilot enrichment plant would be converted into a relatively small production plant of 200 000 to 300 000 SWU/a (200–300t SWU/a) by 1981–2.[54] The government would decide later whether to expand this into a commercial plant, 'depending on economic circumstances, development plans for South Africa's nuclear energy programme and the demand for enriched uranium on the world market'. Observers suggested that, besides the escalation of costs, the reason for shelving plans for a commercial plant and instead building a small production facility was that this might enable fuel to be produced in time for South Africa's planned nuclear power reactors at Koeberg, the American supply of enriched fuel for which was then becoming highly doubtful.[55] The capacity announced for the plant, 200 000 – 300 000 SWU/a (200 – 300t SWU/a), would be sufficient to produce the 50t or so of low-enriched uranium needed for the annual fuel reloads for the Koeberg reactors.[56]

Because of budgetary constraints, initial production for this plant is now not thought likely before 1987, and it has been confirmed that it will only provide South Africa's own enrichment requirements. There are now no plans for large-scale exports of enriched uranium, although small amounts may well be exported after South Africa's own needs have been met.

To adapt Cassuto,[57] uranium enrichment has *not* enriched South Africa in the economic sense, and it is not likely to do so in the foreseeable future: enrichment services supplied for South Africa's own consumption from the small production plant are likely to be very uncompetitive, despite official talk at one time during the mid-1970s of supplying 14 per cent of the Western world's demand for enrichment. However it is doubtful whether South Africa's motives for establishing an enrichment capability were ever purely economic and, as we shall see, her capacity is of incalculable political and strategic value.

URANIUM HEXAFLUORIDE CONVERSION

Reference to Figure 1.1 indicates that South Africa must have developed the capacity to convert uranium oxide concentrate into gaseous uranium hexafluoride (UF_6) which is used as the feed for her enrichment plants. There is some evidence that this capability may have been acquired from Britain.[58]

Research and development work on hexafluoride conversion technology was carried out by the Atomic Energy Board in collaboration with the mining industry, in the shape of NUFCOR. By 1969, South Africa was already producing uranium tetrafluoride (UF_4), an intermediate product in hexafluoride conversion. A UF_4 plant was later purchased and erected by NUFCOR. Besides uranium concentrate, the other main feed material for hexafluoride conversion is hydrogen fluoride. Revealing the importance attached to hexafluoride conversion, Newby-Fraser has recounted the steps taken to ensure that South Africa was self-reliant and not dependent on foreign sources for hydrogen fluoride production, and how Prime Minister Verwoerd personally authorised funds for development work on hexafluoride conversion.[59]

In the early 1970s, uranium hexafluoride (hex) was being produced on a laboratory scale. In 1975 a small (200t/a UF_6) production plant was commissioned at Pelindaba which began producing hex on an industrial scale the following year, becoming fully operational in 1978. The process was acknowledged to be inefficient, but it provided sufficient feed for the pilot enrichment plant. In the meantime, the Atomic Energy Board was working in intimate collaboration with UCOR with a view to establishing a full-scale UF_6 plant at Valindaba.[60]

However, the United Kingdom Atomic Energy Authority (UKAEA) had a contract with NUFCOR for first refusal for the conversion of South Africa's uranium concentrate exports.[61] In particular, all uranium exports to West Germany were converted in the British hex plant (now owned by British Nuclear Fuels Limited). It is possible, but by no means certain, that faced with the erosion of their commercial position, the UKAEA and associated industrial interests decided either to license British technology to South Africa or to cooperate with South Africa in the development of her own conversion technology. In any case there was no announcement; but in 1970 the head of the South African Atomic Energy Board (and UCOR), Dr A. J. A. Roux, announced that research on hex had been carried out by South Africans in collaboration with 'overseas interests' and that South Africa was in a position to build her own conversion plant.[62]

Currently there are five large commercial conversion facilities in the Western world: two in the USA and one each in the UK, France and Canada. They range in size from 5000 to 15 000 t/a UF_6 production. Below this size, plants become uneconomical. A South African plant would be competitive only if Namibian as well as South African uranium were used as feed.[63] The latest information is that South Africa's larger conversion plant should be in operation in 1986: in time to provide feed for the 200 000 – 300 000 SWU/a enrichment plant when that is completed around 1987. The capacity of South Africa's larger conversion plant is being kept secret, but UCOR states that it will be large enough to permit exports of hex,[64] presumably after providing feed for the enrichment plant.

One suspects that countries having a large market share of conversion capacity (such as the USA, UK and France) will resist this, and South Africa may face similar problems (albeit on a lesser scale) establishing a commercial conversion plant for UF_6 export to those she faced with her commercial enrichment plans. Nevertheless, South Africa has signed uranium export contracts with countries in Western Europe and the Far East which stipulate that such uranium may first be upgraded (converted to uranium hexafluoride and then possibly enriched) when South Africa possesses the capacity for this.

THE KOEBERG POWER REACTORS

Ever since South Africa's initiation into the nuclear era by Britain and America in the 1950s, the intention had been that South Africa would use nuclear technology for electricity generation. When Prime Minister Vorster announced in 1970 that South Africa had developed her own enrichment technology, one of the reasons given for this was to provide sufficient fuel for South Africa's own nuclear power stations, which were planned to generate 20 000 MW(e) by the end of the century.[65] Within a few years, the price of oil was escalating rapidly and South Africa faced the prospect of having her oil supplies cut off, as Arab producers imposed an embargo on supplies to South Africa. The need to rely more on nuclear power for her energy needs appeared to be of greater urgency.

South Africa is fortunate is producing a large amount of low-cost coal, from reserves located in the Transvaal and Natal. Well over three-quarters of her electricity is generated from coal-fired power stations. However, South Africa wished to reserve as much coal production as possible for the SASOL oil-from-coal plants and for export. Since 1970, South Africa has rapidly become one of the world's largest coal exporters, and this trade is seen as providing political as well as economic returns.

South Africa does not have readily available hydroelectric power sources. Most of South Africa's hydroelectric power consumption comes from the Cabora Bassa dam on the Zambezi River in Mozambique. Following Mozambique's independence in 1974 under the Frelimo government, which was clearly not friendly towards South Africa, and with the future prospect of increased political instability, overdependence on this power source was clearly seen as being unwise.

However, as costs for nuclear power rose, and forecasts for future electricity consumption were lowered during the 1970s, South Africa's ambitions were modified. A chain of nuclear power stations to provide desalination of seawater as well as electricity had been the original idea. (Water is one of the few resources in which South Africa is deficient.) This became seen as being grossly uneconomic; and the only location where nuclear power might be economically viable was found to be in the Cape Province, where electricity demand was high and where the long distance from the Transvaal coalfields made coal-generated electricity expensive. Nuclear power stations could be situated on the coast and seawater used for their cooling systems.[66]

The culmination of government deliberations, as the economic prospects for nuclear power in South Africa changed, was the award by the state-owned Electricity Supply Commission (Escom) of a contract for the construction of two 920 MW(e) pressurised water reactors (PWRs) at Koeberg, a coastal site about 30km north of Cape Town. The contract was awarded to a French consortium of three companies, Framatome, Alsthom and Spie Batignolles, in 1976. The power stations would come under IAEA safeguards, and French interests were to provide much of the finance and training for the project. The reactors were to be fuelled with 3 per cent enriched uranium, the enrichment to be provided by the US Department of Energy under a contract lasting until 1992. The fuel would be fabricated by a Franco-Belgian company, Franco-Belge de Fabrication de Combustibles, in which Framatome had an interest.[67]

The French consortium won the contract against competition from a West German consortium and another one of American, Dutch and Swiss companies. In fact, the contract was about to be awarded to this latter group, but, at the last moment, it was given to the French consortium because, it was felt, anti-apartheid opposition in the United States and the Netherlands might impede its implementation. It has also been suggested that the contract was given to the French consortium in return for France's continuing arms supplies to South Africa.[68]

French leaders have denied charges that, in helping to construct the Koeberg power stations, France was contributing to South Africa's nuclear weapons capability. The official response to such accusations was that South Africa's weapons capability derives from her unsafeguarded enrichment plant. The Koeberg reactors were to be safeguarded and the spent fuel would be sent to France for reprocessing. (Radioactive waste will then be returned to South Africa, where a site in the northern Cape Province has been selected for disposing of low- and medium-level waste.) However, as we shall see in Chapter 6, the French government came under considerable pressure following the revelation in 1977 that South Africa might be about to conduct a nuclear explosion in the Kalahari Desert. France stated that she did not intend to supply any more reactors to South Africa; but in view of reports in late 1982 that she might in fact consider doing so, the cynicism which greeted France's earlier announcement may have been justified.[69]

The original completion schedule for the power plants was for Koeberg-1 to be finished at the end of 1982, and Koeberg-2 a year or so later. Few construction problems were encountered and it seemed that the deadline would be met. To have completed the plants so quickly, when nuclear power station construction times were lengthening in most other countries, would have brought great credit to both South Africa and France, the latter anxious to win further orders elsewhere. It would have been seen as an indication of both countries' organisational ability in managing a modern and highly prestigious technology. However, a fire at the site in July 1982, responsibility for which was claimed by the African National Congress, put back the start-up date. Security against attempted sabotage had already been reported to be very tight at the Valindaba enrichment plants as well as the Koeberg construction site, where precautions apparently included plans for defence against a possible sea-based attack.[70]

The ANC gained an even more impressive propaganda coup in December 1982 when four bomb explosions at the site, for which the organisation's armed wing Umkhonto we Sizwe again claimed responsibility, further delayed the date when the reactors could go critical. The explosions took place before fuel had been loaded into the reactors, so there was no danger of release of radioactivity; but considerable damage was done to the electric cabling and control rod mechanism.[71]

Koeberg-1 finally went critical and was connected to the power grid in 1984. With Koeberg-2 connected in 1985, the two stations will supply most of the electricity needs of the Western Cape and about 10 per cent of the nation's electricity consumption. For the medium term, South Africa has vague plans for a further coastal station, located either at Koeberg or in the Eastern Cape, to be completed around the turn of the century;[72] but she will face great difficulties since, following the 1985 township disturbances, the United States and the European Community stated that there will be no more significant nuclear exports to South Africa. So she will now probably find it impossible to import further power reactors or otherwise acquire the technology.

PROBLEMS WITH ENRICHED URANIUM FUEL SUPPLIES

By the mid-1970s, it was clear that South Africa's nuclear programme was encountering increasing international opposition both from groups opposed to apartheid and from those concerned about possible further nuclear proliferation. Hence South Africa experienced difficulty attracting Western financial and technological support for her enrichment plans, and STEAG gradually withdrew from its relationship with

UCOR. The Koeberg contract was awarded to France partly because it was felt that opponents within other Western countries might obstruct their fulfilment of the contract. Nevertheless France subsequently announced that no further reactors would be supplied. The United States was also preventing the supply of equipment for enrichment plants. However it was over the supply of enriched uranium fuel from the USA, both for the Safari-1 research reactor and the Koeberg power reactors, that South Africa encountered the most problems.

When the United States had tried to impose stricter conditions for the supply of fuel for the Safari-1 reactor in 1967, France had offered to replace the American supply of high-enriched uranium fuel. This offer was in return for South Africa's supply of natural uranium a few years earlier, for France's predominantly military programme, at a time when France was experiencing difficulties (caused by the United States) in obtaining sufficient supplies.[73] The tactic worked, because America subsequently renewed her contract for the supply of the Safari-1 fuel, although only after South Africa had given certain assurances about her non-proliferation policy with regard to her uranium exports.

However in 1975 legal action by the congressional Black caucus in the United States blocked shipment of fuel elements for Safari-1. In 1977, anticipating the passage of the Nuclear Non-Proliferation Act (NNPA), which made full-scope safeguards a condition of nuclear export, and continuing South African refusal to allow her enrichment plant to be subjected to safeguards, the US government finally cancelled the frozen contract under which enriched uranium fuel had been supplied for Safari-1.

It had been hoped that South Africa's enrichment plant would be completed in time to supply enrichment for the Koeberg reactors, but construction delays meant that South Africa would have to rely on overseas enrichment production for Koeberg at least until the mid 1980s. For the remainder of the 1970s and the early 1980s there were almost continuous negotiations between the USA and South Africa about the enrichment contract for Koeberg, with the USA stating that the contract would be honoured only if South Africa agreed to full-scope safeguards *and*, in a new condition not required by the NNPA, signed the Non-Proliferation Treaty (NPT).[74]

Because of the halt in fuel supplies, Safari-1 was only run at 5 megawatts from 1977 onwards, and the reactor was shut down on alternate weeks. Some of the research programmes were curtailed.[75] Then, in an announcement timed for the day before the white electorate went to the polls in a general election in April 1981, the Minister of

Mines and Energy announced that the South African Atomic Energy Board had successfully produced 45 per cent enriched uranium fuel elements which thus enabled Safari-1 to continue operating at 5 megawatts. The chairman of the AEB stated that Safari-1 would continue to be subject to IAEA safeguards and that the reason that 93 per cent enriched fuel, for which the reactor had been designed, was not used, was to allay international concern about the possibility of the fuel being used for nuclear weapons. Although 45 per cent enriched uranium could be used to produce a weapon, 'it would be a very clumsy bomb'. It is possible, of course, that the pilot enrichment plant did not have sufficient separative work capacity to be able to enrich the fuel further, but as the fuel core of Safari-1 consisted only of 5kg of 93 per cent enriched uranium, which would require about 1000SWU (1 tonne of separative work: see Table A.1) this seems unlikely. The modification of Safari-1's operating conditions so that it only used two or three kilograms of 45 per cent enriched uranium was more probably due to the need to use the remaining separative work capacity of the pilot enrichment plant for 'other purposes'.[76]

The April 1981 announcement was significant for two reasons: first, it was the first time that South Africa's enrichment plant had been shown to be capable of producing 'weapons-grade' high-enriched uranium; and second, it had been acknowledged that South Africa now had a fuel fabrication capability. The latter development was not altogether surprising as South Africa was known to have been developing this capability, which is far less arduous technologically than enrichment.[77] However, in view of the facts that fuel for the American-designed Safari-1 reactor had hitherto been fabricated in Britain and America, that scientists from these countries were known to be working at the Nuclear Research Centre at Pelindaba, and that South Africans had worked and been trained at Oak Ridge in the USA and Harwell in the UK, where Safari-1 fuel had been fabricated during the 1960s and early 1970s, one is bound to speculate whether South Africa's fuel fabrication capability was acquired with the help, directly or indirectly, of the nuclear establishments in those countries.

Be that as it may, the fuel fabrication and enrichment required for the Koeberg reactors was on a far larger scale than that required for Safari-1. The initial fuel load for Koeberg-1 was 75t of low-enriched uranium which would require nearly 250 000SWU (250t SWU), compared with a maximum of 5kg of high-enriched uranium requiring little more than 1000SWU (1t SWU) which was needed annually for the Safari-1 reloads.[78] By 1981, it was clear that, to the South Africans' disappointment, the new Reagan administration in the United States was maintaining President Carter's policy of requiring South Africa's signature of the NPT before the enrichment contract for the Koeberg fuel would be honoured. The initial fuel load for Koeberg-1 was due to be delivered to South Africa by mid-1982, ready for the reactor to go critical at the end of that year. If the fuel was not delivered and the power plant kept idle, Escom would face not only a large financial loss, but also the possibility of having to make power cuts. (South Africa was then facing an energy shortage: several coal-fired power stations had been ordered, but had not yet come on stream.)

South Africa had already made the necessary payments and delivered the natural uranium feed to the US Department of Energy (DOE) by August 1981. In return the DOE 'constructively delivered' 80t of low-enriched uranium to South Africa.[79] This meant that, legally, sufficient enriched uranium for Koeberg-1's first load had been obtained by South Africa; but it remained stored in the USA. The contract had been fulfilled; but South Africa still had to get an export licence from the US Nuclear Regulatory Commission; and this was out of the question unless she accepted the full-scope safeguards provision of the US Nuclear Non-Proliferation Act (NNPA).

THE PROBLEM SOLVED

The problem was eventually solved when, at the end of 1981, South Africa obtained low-enriched uranium from European electric utilities which had enriched uranium surplus to their requirements because of delays in reactor construction there.[80] A utility constructing a power station in Switzerland (with minor French and West German ownership) sold South Africa 130t of LEU, and more was obtained from the Belgian utility, Synatom. The fuel had been enriched by the Eurodif plant in France. The transactions were arranged through an American broker, Edlow International. This made it possible for all parties to deny having supplied enrichment services to South Africa. (Original reports in the *Washington Post*, quoting US government sources, that the enriched uranium had come from China, and that it was not safeguarded, were apparently deliberate disinformation.)[81] At the same time, South Africa was able to sell about a third of the enriched uranium she still had in the USA to a Japanese utility. It was assumed she would be able to sell the remaining two-thirds sooner or later.

Before this elaborate deal had been revealed it had been thought most likely that South Africa would get the enrichment from France. During the Carter administration, three-way diplomatic negotiations had taken place, involving the USA, France and South Africa. The Americans recognised that France had a strong interest in ensuring that South Africa obtained the first fuel load for the French-supplied Koeberg reactors. If the plant started running on time, this would demonstrate that France was a reliable and efficient supplier of nuclear technology. However, France agreed that she would only supply the enrichment under the same conditions as the United States, though this meant that she had a rather contradictory policy of insisting on full-scope safeguards for the supply of enrichment but not for fuel fabrication. It would in fact have been embarrassing for the newly-elected socialist President Mitterand to have been seen to be cooperating with South Africa in evading American non-proliferation efforts. Thus, when South Africa announced that she had obtained enriched uranium, she was able to state categorically that it did not come from her own enrichment plant, the United States or France. However it was believed that France, through her control of Eurodif which had performed the enrichment service, *had* helped to arrange the transaction;[82] and the reaction of the United States government to the news seemed to be one of unconcern. If it had not actually encouraged the deal, it seemed to have acquiesced in it.

The details of this transaction have been recounted because the acquisition by South Africa of at least 130 tonnes of enriched uranium fuel, almost enough for the first fuel loads of both Koeberg-1 *and* Koeberg-2, effectively removed remaining American leverage over South Africa's nuclear programme. As Table A.1 shows, annual reloads will require much less enriched uranium: about 50 tonnes for the two reactors together. (This could be produced by less than 200 000SWU if, as has been reported, South Africa's semi-commercial production plant, due to come on stream in 1987, operates at 0.3 per cent tails assay.)[83] South Africa could thus presumably either obtain her annual fuel reloads for the Koeberg stations from European utilities in a way similar to the way she obtained the first fuel loads, or she could run the Koeberg plants at reduced power until she is able to produce sufficient enriched uranium from her own larger production plant.

In the meantime, South Africa's only enrichment contract for the Koeberg fuel has been with the US Department of Energy. South Africa continued to honour the contract by delivering natural uranium feed and then selling the enriched uranium product (which she was not allowed to take out of the United States under the NNPA) to other utilities, as she had done with the first fuel load. However this annual charade was making a mockery of the NNPA every time it was performed, and South Africa was losing money over the transactions. In the end, after the US DOE postponed South Africa's requirement to deliver feed and take the product several times, the contract was indefinitely suspended at the request of the State Department in early 1984. The request was made after South Africa had made concessions concerning her non-proliferation stance regarding safeguards on her semi-commercial enrichment plant and on her nuclear exports (see Chapter 6). The Reagan administration was reported as wanting 'to remove the enrichment contract issue in an effort to forge better relations with South Africa generally'.[84]

CONCLUSION

This account of South Africa's nuclear development has shown that, over the last fifteen years or so, South Africa has become increasingly self-reliant and, to the extent that she has had to rely on foreign help, she has chosen to be dependent on European rather than American sources.[85] South Africa is now almost totally independent of outside assistance for the 'front end' of the fuel cycle – from uranium mine to reactor (see Table 5.1). The one exception is that she has not yet acquired the capability for fabricating pressurised water reactor fuel for the Koeberg stations. She remains dependent on fuel fabrication by France. However, the Nuclear Development Corporation (which succeeded the Atomic Energy Board in a 1982 reorganisation) has stated that this capability is being developed,[86] and when one considers that South Africa has already demonstrated the capability to fabricate fuel for the Safari-1 research reactor, and when one further considers the fuel-cycle stages already mastered, this would seem a relatively easy task for South Africa.

There have been reports of fuel-cycle facilities not mentioned in this chapter. In particular there have been occasional reports of a South African reprocessing plant; but such reports have never been properly substantiated. South Africa has no need for 'back end' facilities, and, by not developing them, she has avoided suspicion that she may be extracting plutonium for weapons purposes from spent fuel from the (safeguarded) Safari-1 and Koeberg reactors.[87] Nevertheless a hot cell complex for handling spent fuel is being constructed at Pelindaba;[88] and more recently there have been reports that the United States government

103

Fuel cycle stage	Location[b]	Description	Size (maximum production)	First year of operation or planned operation[c]	IAEA safeguards[d]	Source of technology[e]
Uranium mining and concentration	Transvaal and OFS	Mostly by-product of gold mining	6146t U (in concentrate) [1980 production]	1952	n.a.	US and UK assistance
Hexafluoride conversion	Pelindaba	Pilot production plant	200t/a UF_6	1975 (1978)	No	Possible UK assistance
	Valindaba	Commercial production plant	Not revealed	1986	?	
Fuel fabrication	Pelindaba	Fabrication plant for Safari-1 research reactor reloads	less than 10kg/a	1981	No	Possible UK and/or US assistance
Enrichment	Valindaba	Pilot plant	6000SWU/a	1975 (1977)	No	Probable West German assistance
	Valindaba	Production plant	300 000SWU/a	1987	?	
Reactors	Pelindaba	Safari-1 research reactor	20 MW (th) (5MW (th) from 1977)	1965	Yes	USA
	Pelindaba	Safari-2 research reactor (also known as Pelindaba-Zero or Pelinduna Critical Assembly)	negligible power	1967 (closed from 1970)	n.a.	Indigenous
	Koeberg	Koeberg-1 power reactor	920MW (e)	1984	Yes	France
	Koeberg	Koeberg-2 power reactor	920MW (e)	1985	Yes	France

[a] Known installations (in December 1985) only. Possible additional installations such as prototype enrichment plant or reprocessing facilities are not included.
[b] OFS – Orange Free State; Pelindaba is the National Nuclear Research Centre near Pretoria; Valindaba adjoins Pelindaba; Koeberg is 30km north of Cape Town.
[c] Date in brackets is year when fully operational.
[d] n.a. Fuel cycle installations of this type or size are not normally subject to safeguards; ? = safeguards situation uncertain.
[e] This is not necessarily meant to imply that technology transfer was officially sanctioned by government of source country.

has obtained intelligence information that a heavy water production capability is being developed, with possible unspecified assistance from a Swiss corporation.[89] If found to be correct, such reports might seem surprising in view of South Africa's decision in the 1960s to pursue the enriched uranium fuel cycle in her development of nuclear technology. Heavy water is generally used as a moderator for reactors fuelled by natural uranium only. However, as we shall see in Chapter 8, South Africa has learned at first hand the strategic significance, for the global non-proliferation regime, of the geopolitical distribution of such sensitive capabilities as uranium enrichment; and heavy water production capacity would also come into this category. It would normally be subject to IAEA safeguards. In the 1960s, when South Africa was operating the Safari-2 reactor, for which heavy water was used as the moderator, officials considered the development of a heavy water plant.[90] The feedstock for heavy water production is hydrogen; and South Africa has a significant hydrogen production capacity in connection with her SASOL oil-from-coal plants. However, by early 1986, these reports of South African heavy water production had not been substantiated.

As mentioned already, following the passage of the Nuclear Energy Act in 1982, the Atomic Energy Board was replaced by the Nuclear Development Corporation (NUCOR). NUCOR and the Uranium Enrichment Corporation (UCOR) have become subsidiaries of the Atomic Energy Corporation of South Africa, which has overall responsibility for nuclear policy and licensing matters. The 1982 Act imposes continuing secrecy over nuclear affairs. It provides for up to twenty years' imprisonment for publication of nuclear secrets. It is however known that the Atomic Energy Corporation is building another nuclear research centre besides the one at Pelindaba. This is being built near Mossel Bay on the southern Cape coast.[91]

6 South Africa and Nuclear Proliferation

International concern that South Africa may possess nuclear weapons derives from her possession of an unsafeguarded enrichment plant which can produce weapons-grade fissile material, her failure to sign the Non-Proliferation Treaty (NPT) and evidence since 1977 that she may have been preparing for testing or may actually have tested a nuclear explosive device. This evidence and South Africa's policy position concerning proliferation are discussed later in this chapter. South Africa's enrichment plant and the reasons given for not allowing it to be safeguarded were discussed in the previous chapter. South African signature of the NPT would imply a commitment to have *all* her nuclear facilities subjected to the safeguards of the International Atomic Energy Agency (IAEA). So it would be useful to begin by outlining South Africa's attitude to the agency.

SOUTH AFRICA AND THE IAEA

We saw in Chapter 2 how, as a prominent member of the Western Suppliers Group of uranium-producing nations that were monitoring and controlling the uranium trade (most of which was being used for British and American nuclear weapons), South Africa played a major role in the formation of the IAEA in 1957 and in developing its first safeguards system. In the 1950s and early 1960s, South Africa was considered a leading and (in terms of her nuclear export policies) responsible IAEA member. South Africa in turn found IAEA membership of great value as it gave her access to the latest information on nuclear science and technology, for example through its library and technical assistance programme.[1] In 1974 Spence summarised South Africa's attitude to the IAEA and the benefits derived from membership as follows:

> South African contribution to the work of the [IAEA] . . . has emphasised the importance of concentrating attention on the technical aspects of the agency's work, rather than allowing it to become an organ of the political and ideological debate. There can be no

doubt that South Africa attaches great importance to its standing within the agency and welcomes the opportunity to participate on terms which have not been available in other international organizations, where its delegates were compelled to resign or run the risk of ostracism.[2]

Quester's assessment in 1973 was very similar:

South African participation in the IAEA has all along been serious, responsible and expert; the nation is quite important not only because of its uranium deposits but also because of the advanced status of its nuclear industry. Agency deliberations indeed have been remarkably free of the anti-South African polemics which tend to characterize other specialized agencies of the United Nations.[3]

However, as the above quotations imply, South Africa was becoming increasingly isolated internationally in the 1960s and 1970s. With opposition to apartheid intensifying, spurred by events in South Africa in the early 1960s (in particular the Sharpeville massacre) and the mid to late 1970s (in particular the Soweto disturbances), and by the increasing membership of newly-independent African and other Third World countries of the United Nations and its agencies, it was inevitable that South Africa would encounter political opposition in the IAEA, despite her wish that it should remain a technical agency.[4]

Thus is did not come as a surprise when, in June 1977, as opposition to South Africa's policies was reaching a climax, she was removed from the IAEA Board of Governors, a position she had held since its inception by virtue of being a producer of 'source material' (uranium) and the African nation with the most advanced nuclear technology. South Africa's place was taken by Egypt who, it was felt by Board members voting for the change, would better represent African interests. South Africa's 'illegal' exploitation of Namibia's uranium resources was pointed to; but, in general, it was heightened opposition to South Africa's apartheid policies and her continuing occupation of Namibia, rather than her nuclear policies, which were the cause of the political opposition to South Africa in the IAEA.[5]

At the 1979 General Conference of the agency in New Delhi, a resolution was passed rejecting the credentials of the South African delegate. South Africa was thus barred from the Conference in the same way that she is invariably excluded from sessions of the United Nations General Assembly. She has not attended subsequent General Conferences of the IAEA. In 1981, South Africa was removed from the agency's

Committee on Assurances of Supply; and subsequently, in response to a 1982 UN General Assembly resolution, the IAEA General Conference has barred South Africa from receiving technical assistance from the agency and threatened further sanctions if South Africa does not submit all her nuclear facilities to IAEA safeguards. These moves against South African participation in the IAEA have been decided by the overwhelming vote of Soviet bloc and non-aligned countries, despite the opposition of Western nations.

The decision to exclude South Africa from the Committee on the Assurances of Supply (CAS) highlights a dilemma for the international community in general and the West in particular. The committee was set up in response to nations' complaints that the non-proliferation policies of some of the nuclear suppliers, notably the United States, were creating uncertainty in importing countries, thereby encouraging them to move towards nuclear self-sufficiency with the danger of creating the very problems the nuclear suppliers' policies aimed at preventing.[6] It was hoped that the deliberations of the CAS would restore trust between nuclear importing and exporting nations. As a leading exporter of uranium (and possibly, in the future, enriched uranium), South Africa seemed to Western nations to have an important role in the CAS. Her exclusion from the committee meant that suspicion might increase that she was pursuing irresponsible nuclear export policies. Moreover, it seemed possible that, if South Africa's international isolation increased, she might eventually be expelled (or resign in anticipation of expulsion) from the IAEA altogether. This would raise awkward questions about international safeguards on the Safari-1 and Koeberg reactors (although presumably Western nations could institute their own safeguarding system) and the international safeguards system in general.[7] For this reason, the USA and Western countries may be able to persuade Soviet-bloc and non-aligned countries to refrain from taking this final step of ostracising South Africa from the IAEA.

These various moves against South Africa in the IAEA should be seen in the context of what is regarded in the West as the increased 'politicisation' of the United Nations and its agencies by non-aligned, Third World and Soviet-bloc countries. Like South Africa, Western nations, in particular the USA, would like the IAEA (and other UN agencies) to concentrate on their technical functions, such as developing safeguards techniques, and not let international politics 'intrude'. Because of the increasing 'intrusion' of political questions, such as North–South issues, into IAEA deliberations, the USA no longer refuses to contemplate the eventual disbandment of the agency. Thus, when the 1982 General Conference rejected the credentials of the Israeli delegate (a move similar to the rejection of the South African delegate's credentials in 1979), because of Israel's bombing of the Osirak reactor in Iraq and her lack of support for the IAEA safeguards system,[8] the US delegate walked out of the meeting and announced that the United States would have to re-assess her policy towards the agency. Subsequently the USA postponed her payment of dues to the agency and refused to participate in IAEA meetings, although payments and full participation were resumed early in 1983.

SOUTH AFRICA'S NON-PROLIFERATION POLICY AND THE NPT

Thus, although South Africa was closely involved in the founding of the IAEA and fully participated in its activities in the 1960s, she found herself increasingly excluded from its deliberations in the 1970s. In the 1950s and 1960s South Africa also played a leading part in Western non-proliferation policies, through her membership of the Western Suppliers Group; but as the Group increasingly failed to be able to monitor or control nuclear trade, in particular the trade in uranium, Western nations adopted other multilateral and unilateral non-proliferation approaches in which South Africa was not closely involved. South Africa has therefore formulated a non-proliferation policy of her own. She has stated that she 'will not allow South African uranium to be used to expand the number of nuclear weapon states'. This statement allows for continued uranium sales to nuclear weapon states such as Britain and France, but it leaves open areas of ambiguity. For example, what of states such as Israel which may have developed nuclear weapons covertly? Even if such weapons possession become known, it would be impossible to ascertain the source of the nuclear material. South Africa could always claim that her uranium was supplied after the recipient nation had already acquired nuclear weapons.[9] This is not meant to suggest that South Africa has participated in nuclear proliferation in this way or would necessarily consider doing so; but she may perceive some political advantage in leaving open such areas of ambiguity about her policy, even if they were not intended when the policy was originally formulated.

South Africa outlined her official attitude to the Non-Proliferation Treaty (NPT) when the draft treaty was debated at the 1968 UN General

Assembly.[10] This remains the most detailed record of her attitude to the NPT and her stance has not fundamentally altered since that time. The country's UN ambassador, Mr. R. Botha, stated that South Africa's main concern was that IAEA safeguards might infringe her commercial secrets. Later, following the announcement of her enrichment programme in 1970, South Africa's main concern was that IAEA safeguards might compromise the commercial secrets of her enrichment technology.[11] But at the time (1968), South Africa was, or said she was, most concerned that details of her gold production and uranium extraction technology might leak out through safeguarding arrangements. There was, according to the South African ambassador, no guarantee in the NPT that uranium extraction and concentration plants might not at some future date come under IAEA safeguards provided for in signatory countries. In fact the NPT safeguards arrangements under INFCIRC/153 did not subsequently provide for such safeguards, although any natural uranium imported or exported by signatory states should be reported to the IAEA.[12] Reference was made in Chapter 4 above to the secrecy imposed by the South African government concerning her uranium exports. This secrecy has also been justified on commercial grounds.[13]

South Africa was also concerned that the 'potential benefits from any peaceful applications of nuclear explosions' might be withheld – contrary to Article V of the NPT. With regard to superpower armaments, she doubted whether the draft treaty contained 'sufficiently positive and effective provisions concerning the reduction and eventual elimination by the nuclear weapon states of their existing stockpiles of nuclear weapons'. Moreover South Africa expressed doubts about the credibility of the guarantee provided by the nuclear weapon states, in the UN Security Council resolution of June 1968, of Security Council action in support of a non-nuclear weapon signatory which was the victim of aggression by a nuclear weapon state.

Few other countries took these stated South African objections to the NPT at face value, although her evident distrust of United Nations arrangements was consistent with South Africa's general attitude to that organisation, and her objections to the discriminatory aspects of the treaty mirrored those of many other countries. Although South Africa has never ruled out eventual signature of the NPT, most observers have felt that her stated objections to the treaty hide a desire to retain the nuclear weapons option, whilst appearing to keep open negotiations (primarily with the USA) concerning her eventual signature.[14]

There was further clarification of South Africa's non-proliferation policy in January 1984 when the chairman of the Atomic Energy Corporation, the body responsible for licensing uranium exports, stated that South Africa's nuclear export policy would be 'in line with the spirit, principles and goals' of the Non-Proliferation Treaty and the Nuclear Suppliers Group guidelines. This statement removed some of the ambiguity surrounding South Africa's policy, as it meant that exports to non-nuclear weapon states of natural uranium and other items on the London Suppliers Club list, such as enriched uranium and enrichment technology, would trigger IAEA safeguards and peaceful and non-explosive-use guarantees. This was always thought to have been her policy, but it had not previously been so explicitly stated.

The American government warmly welcomed this statement of South Africa's intention to behave responsibly in her nuclear exports, and reciprocated by suspending its enrichment contract for the Koeberg reactors, although no formal connection was made between the two announced moves.[15]

However South Africa may also be seen to have gained respectability from the implicit recognition, by the publicity given to the announcement by the American government, that South Africa's enrichment capability made it desirable, from the Americans' viewpoint, that she be granted ex-officio membership of the developed nations' nuclear cartel, the Nuclear Suppliers Group. It is conceivable that South Africa may in the future attend unpublicised informal meetings with Western NSG members to discuss the trigger list and nuclear export policy.[16] It is at such meetings, and not the public formal meetings of the IAEA, that the international non-proliferation regime is being continuously adapted to changing circumstances. South Africa may thus be seen to have returned to the 'top table', joining the leading industrial nations determining the non-proliferation regime, a position she last held in the 1950s and early 1960s when she was a member of the Western Suppliers Group which operated in a similar fashion.

South Africa's non-proliferation posture would now seem to bear a marked similarity to that of France. Both nations have vowed not to contribute to further proliferation in their external nuclear affairs. Both have stated that they will observe NPT and NSG rules in their exports; but both refuse to sign the NPT. Both nations have made their non-proliferation undertakings unilaterally, independently and of their own volition.

South Africa would probably feel free to reconsider her undertakings (more likely by bending than by repudiating the rules of the London Club) if Western nations stopped treating her as one of the family in their economic and strategic relations. What leverage there is in nuclear relations with the West would seem now to rest with South Africa. Quester has summarised South Africa's non-proliferation policy in general and her attitude to the Non-Proliferation Treaty in particular as follows:

> South Africa can certainly observe the treaty without signing it. As an important supplier of critical materials rather than a receiver, it can afford to mold a policy of its own, demanding safeguards over most or all of its sales. For the interim, there are some clear bargaining arguments for such a non-committal position, whereby South Africa would cooperate with the NPT system but would not be bound to do so forever. On a yearly basis the threat of unsafeguarded uranium sales could thus be held in reserve to deter overly stringent boycotts and embargoes in order to force the United States and Britain to accommodate South African interests where such accommodation is crucial. In this light, it would be optimal for South Africa neither to surrender nor to exercise the option of spreading nuclear weapons.[17]

This assessment of South Africa's non-proliferation posture was given in 1973; but the posture does not seem to have changed much since, except that for 'uranium', one may now add 'enriched uranium and enrichment technology'. We will return to a consideration of the motives underlying South Africa's non-proliferation policy in Chapter 8; but we should now consider the evidence that nuclear weapons have spread to South Africa itself.

THE 1977 KALAHARI INCIDENT

Suspicions about South Africa's own nuclear capability and intentions were dramatically heightened when, in August 1977, it was revealed that a Soviet satellite had photographed installations in the Kalahari Desert which appeared to form a nuclear explosion test site. The installations in the northern Cape, near to the borders with Namibia and Botswana, included a large hole in the ground and a tower. In separate personal messages, Soviet President Brezhnev asked the United States, British, French and West German governments to join in preventing an imminent nuclear explosion.

There followed a unique exercise in East–West cooperation. US President Carter immediately ordered photographs from American reconnaissance satellites, which appeared to confirm the Soviet allegations. Following intense diplomatic activity President Carter announced, two weeks later, that:

> South Africa has informed us that they do not have and do not intend to develop nuclear explosive devices for any purpose, either peaceful or as a weapon; that the Kalahari test site, which has been in question, is not designed for use to test nuclear explosives; and that no nuclear explosive test will be taken in South Africa now or in the future.[18]

It has been pointed out that this statement does not preclude cooperation by South Africa with other nations in a nuclear explosion outside South Africa's territory.[19] Nor does it preclude South Africa obtaining a nuclear device from another country.[20] Later in the year, following denials by South African leaders that any assurances had been given, President Carter revealed the text of a letter sent to him earlier by Prime Minister Vorster which showed that President Carter's earlier statement had followed the wording of Prime Minister Vorster's letter very closely.

In fact, shortly after President Carter's statement, South Africa's Finance Minister Senator Horwood said that South Africa reserved the right to depart from its assurances that its nuclear programme was for peaceful purposes only. Should South Africa decide to use its nuclear potential in any other way, it would do so according to its own needs, and it alone would make the decision: 'I, for one, reject absolutely and entirely that anyone should tell us what we should do.'[21] As mentioned, Prime Minister Vorster denied that any promises had been given. Since South Africa had already independently decided on a peaceful nuclear programme 'the question of "*promises*" never arose – least of all in the context that "promises" had been exacted.'[22]

South African official sources suggested the satellite photographs had been misinterpreted (South Africa was not allowed to see them), and that the site photographed was a military airport construction site.

It was clear that South Africa had been subjected to intense diplomatic pressure by the West. This showed when the pressure was finally released, and Prime Minister Vorster let off steam before the National Party Congress in August: 'If these things continue and do not stop, the time will arrive when South Africa will have no option – small as it is – but to say to the world: "So far and no further. Do your damnedest if you wish."'[23] These remarks should be seen in the light of South Africa's possible political or prestige motives for her nuclear policy (discussed in Chapter 8); and the growing crisis faced by the country's rulers at that time. Apart from the events surrounding the Kalahari incident, disturbances were continuing in Soweto and the war in Rhodesia was intensifying. Finally, at the end of the year, following the death in police custody of Steve Biko, the bannings of the Black Consciousness and other organisations, and the imposition of the arms embargo by the UN Security Council, a general election was called in November at which Mr Vorster and the Nationalist Party won a predictable landslide victory.

In the West, incredulity was expressed that the Soviet Union could have detected the test site without the USA having known about it.[24] Adelman and Knight drew the following conclusion about the need for improved US surveillance: 'If South Africa should reopen the Kalahari site, it would be better that the information be discovered first by the United States, rather than the Soviet Union.'[25]

Soviet motives for revealing the information about the alleged test-site in the manner she did are a matter for speculation; but there was no doubt that the timing embarrassed Western governments. The diplomatic incident came just before a United Nations Conference on Apartheid, which was held in Lagos to mobilise action against South Africa and where the four Western nations were bound to come under attack for their nuclear cooperation with South Africa.[26] As we have seen, for the most part such cooperation was a thing of the past in the case of the United States, UK and West Germany – although suspicions remained of a continuing West German role in transferring enrichment technology to South Africa. However, in the case of France, cooperation was continuing in the construction of the nuclear power stations at Koeberg. At the time, therefore, France had the greatest interest in settling the matter without jeopardising nuclear cooperation with South Africa and yet at the same time satisfying African and world opinion. The task was made the more delicate by the substantial French economic interests in black Africa.

France therefore let it be known that she would take any nuclear explosion very seriously. Not only would such an explosion result in the termination of the Koeberg reactor contract, but a full break in diplomatic and trade relations was possible. She may have been persuaded to take this stand by the United States. Despite America's rapidly diminishing nuclear leverage, relations with the United States were of more importance to South Africa than relations with France. However, the United States was engaged in delicate negotiations over Rhodesian independence, and the Americans may not have wished to jeopardise her relations with South Africa, whose cooperation was needed over these negotiations.[27]

The French Prime Minister Raymond Barre had already attempted to assuage opposition at home and abroad to the Koeberg contract by putting it in the context of South Africa's nuclear fuel cycle capacity. He pointed out that South Africa 'already had a nuclear military capability and that the reactors add nothing to it'.[28] It was pointed out that the reactors would be subject to IAEA safeguards, and the spent fuel, containing plutonium, returned to France. In an equally frank and revealing statement, the French Foreign Minister, M. de Guiringaud, when asked in a French radio interview about the Soviet allegations, said that:

> . . . we did indeed receive information that South Africa was preparing for an atomic explosion, which, according to the South African authorities, was for peaceful purposes. We know what a peaceful atomic explosion is; however, it is not possible to distinguish between a peaceful atomic explosion and an atomic explosion for purposes of military nuclear testing. We therefore warned South Africa that we would regard such testing as endangering all the peace processes under way and as having potentially serious consequences with respect to our relationship with South Africa.[29]

It is indeed possible that France was informed that South Africa was preparing for a 'peaceful' atomic explosion (which, as the French Foreign Minister correctly stated, is indistinguishable from a weapons test). South Africa's attitude to Article V of the NPT which provides for peaceful nuclear explosions (PNEs) under the guidance and supervision of the existing nuclear weapon states has been outlined above. (It should be noted however that, as a result of the 1974 Indian test, the alibi that such an explosion was intended for peaceful purposes was wearing very thin by 1977.) As early as 1972 and 1973 the Annual Reports of the South African Atomic Energy Board contained information about the Board's investigations into the peaceful applications of nuclear explosions.[30] Other evidence that South Africa was interested in conducting a nuclear explosion is as follows: (i) it was discovered that in the past South African scientists had done a literature survey in the United States on the peaceful applications of nuclear explosions;[31] (ii) the African National Congress (ANC), obtained a document, published in 1972 by the Atomic Energy Board, which assessed the seismic effect of a 10-kiloton nuclear explosion in the border areas, as well as any effect there might be on the local white population;[32] (iii) in 1979, Dr Renfrew Christie, an Oxford-based academic, was detained and accused of passing information to the ANC about possible locations for nuclear tests, and also a plan of the layout of the Koeberg power stations.[33] He was arrested and sentenced to ten years' imprisonment under the Terrorism Act in 1980.

The 1977 Kalahari incident thus provoked increased international concern about South Africa's nuclear capabilities and intentions. President Carter, in a departure from previous US policy (under the Nuclear Non-Proliferation Act) of requiring full-scope safeguards as a condition for nuclear exports, stated that the condition for South Africa receiving enriched uranium would now be her signature of the NPT. Ambassador Gerard Smith, Carter's Special Representative for Non-proliferation Matters, was sent to Pretoria in 1978 to try to persuade South Africa to sign the treaty. South Africa's conditions for signature were revealed to be substantial. As well as renewed American supply of enriched uranium and components for her enrichment plant, South Africa wanted American help in getting her reinstated on the IAEA Board of Governors.[34] South Africa must have known that the USA could not deliver on this last demand in particular. In fact South Africa seemed determined to defy the United States and prevent international controls on her nuclear programme. In April 1979 three military attachés serving at the US embassy in Pretoria were expelled for taking photographs from the ambassador's plane, of the Valindaba plant[35] (and other mainly military installations in nearby southern African countries). In return the United States expelled all but one of the South African military attachés from Washington. Then, in early 1980, Radio South Africa announced that:

> a group of American spies is reported to have arrived in South Africa in an attempt to learn the country's nuclear secrets. The Johannesburg newspaper, *The Sunday Times*, quoted top intelligence sources as saying that the spies are under surveillance but no major moves to expose them could be expected for some time. The sources said that so far the Americans have been frustrated in their efforts to discover the formula for South Africa's uranium enrichment process and other nuclear research secrets despite the use of spy planes, satellites and undercover agents.[36]

NUCLEAR EXPLOSIONS OVER THE SOUTHERN OCEANS?

If South Africa had wished to explode a nuclear device, the increased international concern and attention and the statements of her own leaders following the 1977 Kalahari incident made it extremely unlikely that she would attempt an underground explosion which would have been bound to have been detected. (The tell-tale installations in the Kalahari were in fact dismantled in 1978.) An atmospheric test could not be labelled 'peaceful' and moreover South Africa had signed the Partial Test Ban Treaty and thus agreed not to conduct such tests. It was possible, however, that such a test might not be detected, or, if it was, South Africa could have denied responsibility. Indeed, it has been pointed out that Prime Minister Vorster's statements in 1977 did not preclude such a test – possibly carried out with the help of another country.

South Africa had experience with monitoring such tests, having worked with the United States, French and British atomic energy authorities in monitoring the radioactive fall-out from their tests in the southern hemisphere during the 1950s and 1960s, and having done meteorological research on the 'Cape Town Anomaly' – an area of the South Atlantic between the Cape and Antarctic where the ionised layer of the atmosphere comes close to the earth's surface and which is normally avoided by shipping because of the high background radiation level.[37]

In October 1979 the United States government announced that on 22 September one of its satellites had detected signs of a nuclear explosion of approximately 2 to 4 kilotons yield in the atmosphere over the South Atlantic, off the Cape. The Carter administration had been forced to make the announcement before the State Department wanted to make its suspicions public because the ABC television network had got hold of the news and was preparing to report it.[38] These suspicions were based on a double flash of light detected by a Vela satellite, a type specifically designed to detect nuclear explosions in the atmosphere.

Corroborating evidence was provided by the US Central Intelligence Agency (CIA) which established that South Africa had been conducting a secret naval exercise at the same time and in the same area.[39] Also on the same night, US scientists operating a radio telescope at Arecibo in Puerto Rico detected a ripple moving through the ionosphere and coming from the right direction and at the right velocity to have been from a nuclear explosion in the South Atlantic.[40]

South Africa denied all knowledge of any nuclear explosion, and the news clearly embarrassed the American government, whose Vela satellite had detected the evidence with its optical sensors only, and not with the sensors that detect nuclear radiation and electromagnetic disturbances. Tests for radioactive fall-out in the area did not start until 25 September by which time fall-out from an explosion would have diminished considerably. The reported size of the explosion, 2–4 kT, moreover, was so small that any fall-out could have escaped detection. However the Vela satellite had detected the characteristic double flash on forty-one previous occasions, each of which were later confirmed to have been caused by nuclear explosions.[41] A physics laboratory in New Zealand did report afterwards finding traces of short-lived fission products in rainwater. This would have been consistent with a nuclear explosion in the southern hemisphere; but the report was later withdrawn.

The Carter administration was divided. The State Department had originally wanted to suppress the information about the Vela sighting. Defence Intelligence and CIA analysts, however, had concluded that a nuclear explosion had occurred and were not averse to saying so.[42] However the important point was that this time, unlike with the 1977 Kalahari incident, the United States and not the Soviet Union had been the first to detect the possible nuclear explosion. The US government could therefore to a certain extent control the ensuing course of events.

President Carter set up a panel of experts to examine the scientific evidence to see if there might not be an alternative explanation for what had occurred. The results of the inquiry were inconclusive, but it reported that the 'double flash' could have been caused by a small meteoroid striking the satellite, and the resulting debris then glinting in the sunlight.[43] The report caused further divisions amongst analysts. Many thought that the explanation given was simply not credible. However, the administration clearly felt that it had to produce some explanation other than that there had been a nuclear explosion.[44] The incident received less publicity than that given to the Kalahari incident. It was not followed by a similar international storm of protest and the issue soon died down; but it left a residue of concern about the ability of the USA to detect nuclear tests and thus verify the Partial Test Ban Treaty. Following the 22 September event, whether it was a nuclear explosion or alternatively a so-called 'zoo event', the US was reported to have increased its satellite and naval surveillance of possible South African nuclear testing.[45]

If the event had indeed been a nuclear explosion, there was speculation that it might have been an Israeli nuclear test or a joint Israeli–South African test. (It was also suggested that the installations in the Kalahari Desert in 1977 were erected for testing an Israeli weapon.) If Israel wished to test a weapon, above the oceans south of the Cape would have provided an ideal location, and an anonymous test would also have been consistent with Israel's stated intention of 'not being the first to introduce nuclear weapons into the Middle East'.[46] The speculation was fuelled by reports of visits to South Africa by Israeli nuclear scientists around the same time (September 1979), and a CBS television report to the effect that 'informed sources' had confirmed that the event had been an Israeli test 'conducted with the help and cooperation of the South African government'.[47] The 'informed sources' were apparently two Israeli journalists, Eli Teicher and Ami Dor-on, who had just finished a book, entitled *None Will Survive Us*, on the history of Israel's nuclear weapons programme. The Israeli government attempted to suppress both the book and the CBS report.[48] The CIA subsequently confirmed that, if the event was in fact a nuclear explosion, the two most likely candidates were South Africa or Israel, or perhaps both acting in cooperation.[49]

Later there were reports of more 'flashes' having been detected by the heat sensors of a Vela satellite over the same area of the oceans south of the Cape.[50] Three separate flashes were apparently detected on 15 December 1980. The heat sensors on the Vela satellites are designed to detect missile launches. The characteristic double flash of a nuclear explosion was not detected by the satellite's light sensors. This time the US government was ready with an explanation as soon as newspapers in Washington and Johannesburg had published accounts of the flashes. Unfortunately, once again there was no consensus within the American government. It was agreed that the cause was probably a 'natural event' rather than a nuclear explosion, but the fact that the most widely accepted explanation within the American government was again that the flashes were caused by meteors renewed scepticism about this explanation.

7 South Africa's Nuclear Weapons Capability

South African leaders have generally insisted that her nuclear programme is peaceful. However, leaders as far back as Prime Minister Verwoerd in the 1960s (before the announcement of the development of her enrichment technology) have frequently stated that South Africa was developing or had developed the *capability* to produce nuclear weapons.[1] Such statements have usually been followed by qualifications or denials, often by Atomic Energy Board officials wishing to preserve external nuclear cooperation, that this was South Africa's intention. (The intentions behind South Africa's nuclear programme are discussed in the next chapter.) Thus, in 1971, the head of the Board, Dr A. J. A. Roux, stated that, with her own enrichment technology, South Africa had a nuclear weapons capability, although it was her policy to use her enriched uranium for peaceful purposes. He stated that it would have been difficult to produce a plutonium bomb because material and equipment would have had to be imported and these would then have come under safeguards.[2] Similarly, the vice-chairman of the Board, Dr Louw Alberts, claimed, after the 1974 Indian nuclear explosion, that South Africa could also produce atomic weapons and that her nuclear programme was more advanced than that of India.[3]

Perhaps the most significant of such remarks was made by Prime Minister Vorster in an interview in 1976: 'We are only interested in the peaceful applications of nuclear power. But we can enrich uranium, and we have the capability. And we did not sign the nuclear non-proliferation treaty.'[4] When enquiries were made through diplomatic channels by the United States, the South African government stated that Mr Vorster had been quoted out of context. Nevertheless, later in the same year the Interior Minister made the same claim in nearly identical phraseology.[5]

Authoritative foreign observers, including the then French Prime Minister in 1977,[6] have added their weight to the general impression that South Africa has the capability to produce nuclear weapons. In 1975, the International Institute for Strategic Studies stated that South Africa could be three years away from nuclear weapons possession.[7] In 1977 a 'well-informed' US government official was reported as saying that South Africa could produce a nuclear weapon within two to four years, or within a few months if a crash programme was initiated.[8]

119

FISSILE MATERIAL

Such assessments are based on South Africa's financial and technological resources and her ability to produce weapons-grade fissile
material from her unsafeguarded enrichment plant. Estimating how
much weapons-grade enriched uranium could have been produced from
South Africa's pilot enrichment plant is a highly speculative exercise.
The plant is not subject to safeguards; its capacity is kept secret; it is not
possible to know whether, when or for how long it has been operated at
full capacity; and it is not possible to know whether, when and for how
long it has been used to produce weapons-grade high-enriched uranium
(HEU), rather than low-enriched uranium. But it is certain that the pilot
plant *can* produce HEU, because it has been used to produce 45 per cent
enriched uranium for the Safari-1 reloads. If it was designed to produce
low-enriched uranium (LEU), it could still be modified to produce HEU
by either the addition in series of more separation stages, or by stopping
the plant and recycling the product several times (batch recycling) until
the desired degree of enrichment is reached.[9]

From the information in Tables 1.1 and A.1 the following estimates
can be made concerning the number of weapons South Africa could
have made: if we consider the capacity normally quoted for the pilot
plant, 6000SWU/a, this would be large enough to produce annually one
or possibly two nuclear weapons of minimum size 15–25kg HEU. The
plant has been in operation since 1975, although full capacity was not
reached until March 1977. Nevertheless it is likely that South Africa
could have produced sufficient high-enriched uranium by the time of the
August 1977 Kalahari incident for one or two nuclear weapons of 15–
25kg HEU each.[10] Assuming the plant was operating at full capacity
continuously since March 1977, the plant could have produced 75kg of
90 per cent HEU, sufficient for three to five weapons of the same size, by
the time of the September 1979 incident over the South Atlantic, when
the US Vela satellite detected the 'double flash' sign that could have
come from a nuclear test. (These estimates are based on the assumption
that natural uranium is used as the plant's feed. If 3 per cent low-
enriched uranium was used for the feed, it would have to be free of
safeguards, but it would allow three times as much HEU to be
produced.)[11]

Depending on the sophistication of the device, such a weapon could
have a yield of 10–20 kilotons. In practice, most nuclear weapon states
have had to use twice as much fissile material to give an explosion of this
yield for their first weapons. The Hiroshima bomb used 60kg of HEU

and yielded approximately 15 kilotons. On the other hand, it is possible to construct a sophisticated nuclear device, using a beryllium reflector and compacting the fissile material for example, using less than 10kg HEU.

Assuming that the 'double flash' detected by the Vela satellite in 1979 was caused by a nuclear explosion, its reported strength of 2 to 4 kilotons puzzled observers, who concluded that either South Africa (if it was South Africa that had conducted the nuclear explosion) was able to produce a much more sophisticated 'battlefield' or 'trigger' device than had been suspected, or a larger device had given a disappointingly low yield and that South Africa had produced a *less* sophisticated device than had been suspected (and than other nuclear weapon states had achieved with their first nuclear explosions).[12]

To recap, we have concluded that since 1977 South Africa could have produced one or two nuclear weapons each year, assuming full use of 6000SWU/a pilot plant. Since 1981, South Africa has produced 45 per cent enriched uranium for the fuel reloads for the Safari-1 research reactor. For these reloads, two or three kilograms of enriched uranium may have been produced each year (on average). The separative work requirement for this would be less than a tenth of the 6000SWU/a capacity assumed for the pilot plant. Thus, spare capacity would still be left to produce one nuclear weapon a year (since 1981) if that was South Africa's intention.

From the late 1980s onwards South Africa will have a maximum of 300 000SWU/a capacity available from her semi-commercial production plant. Her stated intention is that this will be safeguarded; but difficult negotiations with the IAEA lie ahead before a safeguards agreement can be concluded, and it is quite possible that South Africa may withdraw the plant from safeguards before or after these negotiations are concluded. She will certainly use the implied threat of such withdrawal as a lever in her relations with the major Western countries trying to shape the global non-proliferation regime.

South Africa's stated intention concerning the production plant is also that it will be used to provide enrichment for the Koeberg power reactor reloads. These reloads will require approximately 200 000SWU/a, assuming a 0.3 per cent tails assay at which, it has been reported, the plant will operate.[13] Thus, assuming that the plant could be operated at a maximum capacity of 300 000SWU/a, there would remain 100 000SWU/a of capacity unutilised after Koeberg's needs have been supplied. This spare capacity could theoretically be used to produce 500 kg/a of high-enriched uranium: enough for twenty weapons, each containing 25kg of fissile material, every year. The plant would however have to be stopped and adapted every time it is used to produce low-enriched uranium for the Koeberg reactors. Aside from these practical difficulties, South Africa would not have the freedom to adapt the plant undetected if the plant is subjected to IAEA safeguards. If the plant is not safeguarded, or is withdrawn from safeguards, and South Africa is able to obtain enrichment for the Koeberg fuel from overseas, the full capacity of a 300 000SWU/a plant could be used to produce 60 to 100 weapons each year, each weapon containing 15 to 25kg HEU.

As we have said, these estimates must be considered highly speculative. They depend crucially on assumptions concerning the enrichment capacity available. If this varies, the figures for the HEU production capability of the plant(s) should be adjusted accordingly, and hence the computation for the number of weapons that could be produced from this fissile material will change. For example, as mentioned in Chapter 5, it is quite possible that South Africa may have an enrichment plant of intermediate capacity between the 6000SWU/a pilot plant and a 300 000SWU/a production plant. Such an intermediate capacity plant could have been constructed by scaling up the former or from the first separating stages of the latter. (Although it should be noted that journalists have been allowed to visit the construction site of the production plant but not the pilot plant.)[14]

The only other detailed estimates available of the number of weapons South Africa could have produced are those contained in the report of the UN Secretary-General on South Africa's nuclear capability.[15] These are similar to those given above, except that a 10 000SWU/a capacity is assumed for the pilot plant. So the estimates for the amount of fissile material and the number of weapons that could have been produced are correspondingly larger.

FINANCIAL AND MANPOWER RESOURCES

There is widespread agreement among observers that South Africa has sufficient economic resources to have produced nuclear weapons. For example, in 1981 Betts considered a nuclear weapons programme of US$100 million a year would be well within South Africa's means; it would amount to less than 5 per cent of her defence budget which, as noted in Chapter 3, could be expanded without undue financial hardship (although there would be manpower constraints).[16] This sum does not include the cost of the planes or missiles that would be needed to deliver the weapons, but as we will see in the next section, this cost would be borne by South Africa's conventional arms budget. As long ago as 1965 Dr Andries Visser, a member of the South African Atomic Energy Board, was reported as saying: ' . . . we should have such a bomb to prevent aggression from loud-mouthed Afro-Asiatic states . . . *money is no problem, the capital for such a bomb is available.*'[17]

As explained in Chapter 1, by far the largest component would be the cost of producing the fissile material. Reworking this to the metal and the design and assembly of the weapon would be much less expensive, as would any weapons-testing considered necessary. Most of the work required to obtain this fissile material would presumably have been done at the National Nuclear Research Centre at Pelindaba and UCOR's plant at the adjacent site known as Valindaba, though Adelman and Knight have suggested that, for reasons of security, the actual design and fabrication of any nuclear device would have been undertaken elsewhere.[18] Presumably much of the cost would have been borne by the budgets of UCOR and the former Atomic Energy Board (now the Nuclear Development Corporation), the funding for which comes from the Department of Mineral and Energy Affairs. For the year ending March 1983, these were R85 million and R166 million respectively.[19] The plants that may have been established for military reasons, with little or no commercial or scientific justification, are the conversion, enrichment and fabrication facilities. Certainly none of these plants has yet yielded any commercial return to South Africa. Of these fuel-cycle facilities, the enrichment capacity, present and under construction, would have been much the most costly.

The means by which South Africa has acquired the technology for the various stages of the nuclear fuel cycle have been outlined in Chapter 5. So far as South Africa's own scientific and technological resources are concerned, she has a cadre of well-qualified scientists and engineers. There are four universities in South Africa with nuclear-related programmes.[20] She has benefited from being able to recruit scientists and engineers from Western countries, in particular Britain. In addition large numbers of South African scientists and engineers have gone to the West for training.

As indicated in Chapter 1, most of the information needed for the design and construction of a nuclear weapon is available in the open literature. The technical skills needed in such areas as materials-handling, precision-machining, high-explosive technology and metallurgy could be drawn from South Africa's mining, engineering, construction, explosives, arms, chemical and uranium-processing industries, all of which are highly developed.

Many observers believe that South Africa may have obtained assistance from the 'pariah network' in this area of weapon design and fabrication.[21] In particular it is believed that an arrangement may have been made between Israel and South Africa whereby Israel has given South Africa assistance with weapon design, fabrication and testing, in return for South African assistance with some of the technological skills mentioned above, supplies of uranium and/or cooperation with testing in the remote southern oceans.[22] It should be noted, however, that there is very little evidence on which to base these beliefs. Besides occasional leaks from intelligence sources, the rumours are based on such incidents as Mr Vorster's 1976 visit to Israel[23] and the visit of the Taiwanese premier to South Africa in 1980, when he toured Pelindaba.[24]

So far as weapons-testing is concerned, as noted in Chapter 1 it is not now considered necessary to test a nuclear explosive device in order to prove it technically. Should a test be desired for political reasons, however, facilities in the Kalahari Desert would be appropriate and could be easily constructed.[25]

DELIVERY SYSTEMS

Finally, lest it be thought that South Africa has not got the sophisticated missile and command, control and communication systems necessary to deliver a nuclear warhead, it should be pointed out that, in the absence of nuclear weapons possession by the perceived enemy, combat aircraft such as the Canberras, Buccaneers and Mirages possessed by South Africa would be quite adequate for a nuclear strike on a nearby African country.[26] These could carry weapons weighing from 450kg to 1100kg, of the sort South Africa is probably capable of manufacturing (this being the total mass of the weapon, rather than the much smaller mass of the fissile material). Larger, bulkier and heavier weapons of from 2500 to 4500kg could, however, be delivered by commercial aircraft or military transporters.[27] Should South Africa have developed a smaller, more sophisticated device, this could be fitted into the Cactus or other similar missile systems developed by her in the late 1960s. This would give South Africa a short-range capability. Should a longer range be required, South Africa may be able to circumvent the UN arms embargo to obtain the technology for Israel's Jericho missile.[28] The development of further sophisticated missile systems, with or without the help of Israel, should clearly not be ruled out. In the absence of any sophisticated electronic defence systems installed in nearby African countries, command, control and communication should surely pose no problem for South Africa.

South Africa seems to have benefited from an association with West German companies in setting up a rocket research and ionosphere centre in 1963–4 at Tsumeb in Namibia with the financial support of the West German Ministry of Defence.[29] This research station may be of significance in view of the facts that (i) although it has been stated that the station is concerned only with meteorological research, it was established as a result of initial contacts concerning nuclear cooperation between West Germany and South Africa, and (ii) South Africa is known to have conducted research on the ionosphere over the South Atlantic south of the Cape – in the same region as the unexplained event in September 1979.[30]

More recently it has become clear that South Africa's capability for delivering nuclear warheads has advanced, with the admission that long-range cannon and shells for the 155mm G5 weapons system are being manufactured for the state-controlled Armscor corporation.[31] The G5 gun-howitzer system was developed by the American Space Research Corporation (SRC) based in Vermont with premises astride the US–Canadian border. South Africa learned of the success in the field of a similar system possessed by Israel and produced by SRC. There is well-documented evidence (including a 1982 congressional subcommittee report) that the US Central Intelligence Agency helped South Africa acquire the technology for the system after South Africa found during her intervention in Angola in 1975 that she needed to counter the Soviet Katyusha rocket-launchers possessed by the Cubans. In 1977 the Space Research Corporation supplied 60 000 155 mm shells and four 155 mm guns via Canada and Antigua. When the transaction was revealed, two SRC employees received minor jail sentences for evading the UN arms embargo. The chairman of Armscor stated that the G5 system was tested in Canada and Antigua. Armscor launched its own G5 system in 1982 with plans for a G6 mobile 'export version'.[32] Armed with a small nuclear warhead, the system is capable of destroying a relatively small area with a very high degree of accuracy within a 40 km range. The size and height of the 'double flash' recorded by the American Vela satellite in September 1979 suggest that it could have been produced by the explosion of a warhead fired from the G5 system.[33]

8 South Africa's Nuclear Intentions

While we have seen in the preceding chapters how South Africa has, over the years, acquired the capability for producing nuclear weapons, it is difficult to see any need for their development. We have seen in Chapter 3 that South Africa's conventional military capability far exceeds that of her African neighbours even if they combined their efforts. Black African countries have never seriously threatened South Africa with military attack.

The military threat to South Africa comes from within her borders, from revolt in the black townships and from the attempted sabotage of strategic installations and attacks on police stations by the armed wing of the African National Congress. We have seen in Chapter 3 that South Africa's external military response to this threat has been in the form of pre-emptive and punitive raids against ANC personnel and offices in neighbouring countries. Initially South Africa pursued similar tactics against the South West African People's Organisation (SWAPO) by launching raids on SWAPO camps in Angola. Subsequently South Africa resorted to continuous occupation of southern Angola in order to prevent SWAPO incursions across the border into Namibia. South Africa has also pursued a less overt policy of destabilising neighbouring countries that provide facilities or bases for the ANC and SWAPO, by also herself providing arms and logistical support to dissident groups within these countries. Whether or not these are sensible military tactics from South Africa's point of view, it is difficult to see any possible utility here for nuclear weapons. South Africa's conventional capability, in particular her air (and sea) superiority over any black African state, is more than adequate to enable her to undertake conventional raids on nearby countries without the need to threaten them with nuclear attack.[1]

BLACK AFRICA AND NUCLEAR WEAPONS

If South Africa has developed or is developing nuclear weapons, she would not be responding to the possession, development or capability for development of nuclear weapons by any possible adversaries in Africa. No black African country can be considered a likely candidate

126

for nuclear weapons development. At present, the only nuclear facility south of the Sahara, other than those in South Africa, is a research reactor in Zaire. A similar research reactor in Ghana was closed in 1966 following the overthrow of President Nkrumah. Morocco, Egypt and Libya also have research reactors; and these countries and Nigeria have announced nuclear power programmes. Gabon also has nuclear power ambitions, but has only been offered a research reactor by France. All the above countries have signed the NPT and have little prospect of acquiring the sensitive facilities (enrichment or reprocessing plants) and the nuclear self-sufficiency that would be needed, to minimise the effect of the non-proliferation sanctions of the developed countries, if they wished to develop nuclear weapons.

It is true that some front-line African states, namely Angola, Mozambique, Tanzania, Zambia and Zimbabwe, have not signed the Non-Proliferation Treaty. However their non-signature should be seen in the context of global arms-control politics rather than as an indication of a desire to acquire nuclear weapons. As non-aligned states, these countries object to the discriminatory nature of the NPT and the lack of progress made towards disarmament by the nuclear weapon states, in particular the superpowers.

Collectively, African states' first declaration of policy concerning nuclear weapons was a call by the first summit conference of the Organisation of African Unity in 1964 for the continent to be declared a nuclear weapon-free zone (NWFZ). This call was in response to earlier nuclear weapon tests by France in Algeria. It was overwhelmingly approved by the UN General Assembly the following year, and again in 1974.[2] However there has been little progress towards the establishment of an African NWFZ because of 'unfinished business' in South Africa. It is unlikely that other African states would be willing to sign a treaty with South Africa whilst she maintains the policy of apartheid. South Africa herself is not known to have stated an official position on a proposed African NWFZ (she was not present for the 1974 UN debate); but, as Betts has stated: 'agreement to a nuclear-free zone, as to the NPT, would merely reflect a South African government decision not to acquire nuclear weapons; it would not determine it.'[3]

More recently, in 1983, outgoing OAU Secretary General Edem Kodjo, in an attempt to unite a weakened and divided organisation, called on those African states with the capability, to develop nuclear weapons to counter those of South Africa. He stated that because South Africa was widely believed to possess the bomb, OAU efforts to establish a NWFZ should be abandoned.[4] However, so long as African states do not have and are unlikely to acquire the capability to develop nuclear weapons, such calls of frustration as that of Mr Kodjo are of academic interest only. Indeed a debate about the alleged racially discriminatory nature of the non-proliferation regime and the desirability of independent African nations acquiring nuclear weapons to enhance their prestige has been largely confined to African academic circles.[5]

In the real world, the practical prospects of Mr Kodjo's call being heeded are zero. The only black African country which might conceivably in the long term possess sufficient financial and technological resources to develop nuclear weapons is Nigeria. Although Nigeria has interests in uranium deposits in Niger and Guinea, her nuclear plans have not advanced significantly beyond the drawing board.[6] She would require outside help for them to be realised, and this is only likely to be provided under strict IAEA safeguards. Nigeria has however warned that she would not remain indifferent to the acquisition of nuclear weapons by South Africa; and she might consider that a nuclear programme (peaceful or otherwise) would enhance her prestige as the major black African power.[7] Under Article X, Nigeria can withdraw from the NPT after giving three months' notice. However such a step, coupled with a significant nuclear development programme, might well provoke a South African preventive strike similar to that launched by Israel on Iraq's research reactor in 1981. For the present, Nigeria's nuclear posture must be judged as empty rhetoric lacking in substance.

MILITARY MOTIVATIONS

Thus, if South Africa has a nuclear weapons programme, she is not responding to the possession of nuclear weapons by any possible African adversary. This contrasts with past cases of nuclear weapons proliferation and possible future proliferation in South Asia or South America. In every case, states acquired nuclear weapons or are developing the capability to counteract the similar capability of a potential adversary. South Africa's strategic situation in this case resembles more that of Israel. Both states possess overwhelming conventional military superiority over hostile neighbours; but both are dependent on support from the West. Both may therefore have initiated a nuclear weapons programme in order to have a weapon of last resort should Western support be withheld. South Africa is already the subject of a mandatory arms embargo imposed in 1977 by the UN Security Council. Although she has, since that time, been able to continue her acquisition of modern sophisticated armaments, South Africa may be fearful that, with the likelihood that she will become increasingly the subject of sanctions on imports of technology and equipment, she may not be able to maintain indefinitely this qualitative superiority in armaments. Moreover, despite her overwhelming quantitative as well as qualitative military superiority, South Africa retains a paranoia about the beleaguered situation of the white population at the southern tip of black Africa. She may thus have developed nuclear weapons for the same purpose as she had developed a seemingly unnecessary overwhelming conventional superiority: to convey the impression, both to her own people and the outside world, that in spite of the odds against her, the South African regime can survive indefinitely in a nuclear 'laager'.[8]

However, this psychological use of nuclear weapons may be thought to lack military credibility. Thus, South Africa will probably continue to publicise her nuclear weapons capability by such means as hints, ambiguous comments and anonymous tests, rather than make any open declaration of nuclear weapons possession which would draw a hostile response from Western nations. South Africa would probably only take the step of announcing nuclear weapons possession when her military situation had deteriorated drastically and she had lost practically all hope of Western military support.[9] Such an announcement *might* convince the West that South Africa could not be ignored and that dealings with her should be continued, but it would also indicate a changed military balance in southern Africa.

Such a changed military balance, inducing South Africa to declare nuclear weapons possession, might be caused by the increased involvement in the area of the Soviet Union or her surrogates. Possible scenarios include (i) increased military aid by Soviet-bloc countries to African front-line states subject to South African attack, or (ii) the use of the Soviet Navy to enforce United Nations sanctions.[10] However, it should be stressed that, notwithstanding South African paranoia and propaganda, and with the notable exception of the Cuban troops and Soviet-bloc advisers stationed in Angola, the involvement of the Soviet-bloc countries in southern Africa, where they have no economic interests, is at present minimal. Even in such hypothetical scenarios of increased Soviet involvement, a South African nuclear weapon would still lack military credibility so long as she continues to enjoy conventional superiority in the area; and the use of South African nuclear weapons against Soviet submarines enforcing a naval blockade is even less credible.[11]

It has been suggested that South Africa's military superiority, including her possible possession of nuclear weapons, has already deterred increased Soviet and Cuban intervention – for example, in support of SWAPO guerrillas.[12] However, whether or not this is the case, South African nuclear weapons alone might not act as a significant deterrent to any 'legitimate' action by the Soviet Union, for example: action in support of UN Security Council resolutions regarding economic sanctions or Namibian independence.

However, preceding statements have taken no account of the role played by the West, in particular the United States, in such scenarios. If the USA joined with the Soviet Union in enforcing UN Security Council resolutions, South African nuclear weapons would have no utility at all. South Africa's *fear*, which she might feel would justify her possession of nuclear weapons, would be that the USA would stand by and allow Soviet intervention to take place. South Africa's *hope* might be that her possession of nuclear weapons and/or Soviet intervention might 'trigger' United States intervention on the side of South Africa, whose nuclear weapons might thus be a 'tripwire' for an East–West conflict,[13] with South Africa unofficially incorporated into the Western alliance and the conflict over apartheid between the people of South Africa being temporarily forgotten. Whether this hope was realistic would depend on the circumstances under which South Africa's nuclear weapons were declared and the Soviet Union intervened, the sequence of those events, and US calculations of gains and losses brought by intervention in support of South Africa. However, it would seem at least equally likely that a South African declaration of nuclear weapons possession would *encourage* greater Soviet regional involvement (for example in the form of friendship treaties offered to neighbouring states threatened by South Africa)[14] and may *remove* any possibility of a United States security guarantee for South Africa. Thus South Africa is likely to continue to drop hints about rather than openly declare nuclear weapons possession. She would hope that this might bring a realisation in the USA of Western interests there, and that greater Western support might then be forthcoming.[15]

South African nuclear weapons would therefore seem to have most relevance in the context of her defence against intervention by Soviet bloc troops or what she might care to depict as the overwhelming combined forces of black Africa. In spite of South Africa's hopes and fears that such scenarios for nuclear weapons possession are realistic, they are not. The South African regime has stressed these military situations because it can gain support from her white population for defence policies which can be implemented without undue difficulty. However, as has been mentioned above, the only realistic military threat to the South African regime, and one which is far more difficult to meet, comes from the people of South Africa themselves. South Africa's rulers formerly chose to strip the majority of the population of their citizenship. It was thus easier for the white minority to perceive the threat to be an external one. However, South Africa's military policies, including her warnings about nuclear weapons possession, will, paradoxically, induce the ANC to concentrate on military attacks organised *within* the country. These will ultimately be the most difficult for South Africa to combat.

ECONOMIC AND PRESTIGE CONSIDERATIONS

We should at least briefly consider the possibility that South Africa's nuclear installations are for peaceful civil purposes and that they can be justified solely on economic grounds, as she claims.[16] The installations whose economic value is most debatable are the enrichment plants (present and planned). As recounted in Chapter 5, for a short time in the early 1970s, during the development of South Africa's enrichment process, it seemed that there might be a worldwide shortage of enrichment. However, it is now clear that the international enrichment market is oversupplied and there will be excess capacity for the foreseeable future. Moreover, costs for the South African helikon process and the related Becker nozzle process being commercially developed in Brazil have escalated.[17] There thus seems to be no prospect of South Africa competing internationally in the enrichment market.

None the less, it has also been noted elsewhere that there is an economic incentive for all major uranium producers to have their concentrate upgraded (converted and enriched) to the maximum extent possible before being exported. To be specific, if uranium concentrate is converted and enriched before export, the yield in foreign exchange receipts is approximately doubled. Thus Canada and Australia have, like South Africa, sought to ensure that uranium supply contracts with Western utilities have contained clauses providing for such upgrading when capacity exists. Moreover, given South Africa's intermediate level of technological and industrial development and her low energy costs, her choice of aerodynamic nozzle enrichment technology, rather than the more sophisticated centrifuge or diffusion technologies, could be justified on purely economic grounds, *were the technology proved.*

However, South Africa's failure to divulge sufficient details of the technology to any prospective partner in exchange for the partner's capital contribution casts doubts on South Africa's stated peaceful intentions and economic motives.[18]

Nevertheless, South Africa's nuclear programme, and in particular her enrichment plants, could still be justified on strategic but none the less peaceful grounds. Faced as she is with the prospect of an oil boycott, South Africa's development of nuclear power to ensure self-sufficiency in energy is logical. Given that her nuclear fuel imports might also be cut off by non-proliferation or other sanctions, her development of an enrichment capability to supply her own requirements is also logical.

Such demonstrations of self-sufficiency using advanced technologies, like the oil-from-coal and enrichment technologies, that are claimed to have been developed indigenously, are also thought to bring to the South African government added prestige – both at home and abroad.[19] That South Africa considers such demonstrations important for domestic political purposes was shown by the timing of the government's announcement, on the eve of the 1981 general election, that South Africa had achieved a fuel fabrication capability and was thus able partially to overcome American non-proliferation sanctions.[20] The dependence of South Africa on the transfer of advanced technology from Western industrialised countries has been noted in Chapter 3. Notwithstanding this dependence, demonstrations that South Africa can make a technological contribution to Western 'civilisation' with indigenously-developed techniques such as oil-from-coal conversion, uranium enrichment and heart transplantation, are perceived as enhancing her standing in the world.[21] Thus, soon after Mr Vorster's 1970 announcement of the development of a 'unique' enrichment process, described as an achievement 'unequalled in the history of our country',[22] the President of the Atomic Energy Board, A. J. A. Roux, stated that it was:

> a phenomenal achievement of world dimensions . . . it is an entirely new principle. And we have thought it out and worked it out ourselves every calculation and every little step in the process. . . . It is all the work of South Africans.[23]

(We have also already noted in Chapter 5 the importance, for her standing at home and abroad, that the South African government attached to the prompt and efficient construction and operation of the Koeberg power plant.)

The South African government also acquires kudos, domestically and internationally, from a demonstrated nuclear weapons capability. This respect comes without the need to announce or demonstrate her possession of nuclear weapons. Indeed, so long as there is no evident military need to have such weapons, prestige considerations would suggest that such an announcement or demonstration should not be made. (There is little prestige to be derived from developing a bomb that is seen as militarily unnecessary, or indeed by constructing an enrichment plant that cannot be justified economically.) A demonstrated nuclear weapons *capability*, periodically publicised, together with non-signature of the Non-Proliferation Treaty, are sufficient to gain international and domestic respect.[24] Thus, asked in a 1976 interview about South Africa's nuclear weapons capability, Prime Minister Vorster replied: 'We are only interested in the peaceful applications of nuclear power. But we can enrich uranium, and we have the capability. And we did not sign the nuclear non-proliferation treaty.'[25] And, as long ago as 1970, the Afrikaans newspaper, *Die Beeld*, observed that:

> Mr. Vorster has not yet said categorically that South Africa will never make an atomic bomb. In view of this fact, people will have to look at us in a new light. South Africa now becomes an altogether different proposition if you want to tackle it.[26]

South Africa may consider that one beneficial result of the events surrounding the discovery of an alleged test site in the Kalahari in 1977 and the 'double flash' over the South Atlantic in 1979 may have been the publicity that was attracted for her nuclear weapons capability. This does not necessarily mean that South Africa stage-managed the 1977 events for this purpose. She may merely have taken advantage of the publicity brought by the original Soviet allegations (whether or not the purpose of the facilities in the Kalahari was actually to conduct a nuclear test).

The time of the discovery of the alleged test site in 1977 might however have seemed to South Africa appropriate for a demonstration of nuclear strength. Following the independence of Mozambique and Angola (where South Africa suffered a diplomatic if not a military humiliation), the Soweto disturbances and, later, the death in police custody of Steve Biko, South Africa's international situation seemed to be deteriorating rapidly. According to Betts (writing of the 1977 events):

> In these circumstances a nuclear shock may have seemed the appropriate counter to mounting pressure, a way of highlighting Afrikaner power and determination, a demonstration that apartheid is here to stay and that the world must deal gingerly with Pretoria.[27]

It is difficult here to distinguish considerations of prestige from military motivations. However, as Betts has pointed out, such clear evidence of preparation for a nuclear test would be likely to increase rather than decrease South Africa's international isolation. Such a move is therefore likely only in a moment of real desperation.[28] Moreover South Africa may be considered to have suffered strategically from the 1977 Kalahari episode because of the ensuing demonstration of superpower cooperation in preventing a possible nuclear explosion. It is generally agreed that such demonstrations of shared superpower interests in southern Africa are not viewed favourably by South Africa, who feels that her supposed strategic value to the West becomes better recognised during periods of Cold War tension.[29]

THE URANIUM EXPORT WEAPON

As a major uranium-producing country South Africa possesses a diplomatic bargaining card which she can play in order to obtain favours from the West. There may be a tacit understanding that in return for her 'responsible' policy concerning uranium exports, South Africa can expect the West to strive to ease her international political isolation.[30] Although it is felt that South Africa *has* generally pursued a responsible export policy, she retains the option of unsafeguarded uranium sales and, as with nuclear weapons possession, may be content that periodic rumours of such sales may serve her purposes. Western countries, in particular the United States, may feel they have to maintain close relations with South Africa in order to prevent any such 'irresponsible' behaviour.[31]

Of the so-called 'nth' countries considered in Chapter 2 to be on the threshold of possessing nuclear weapons but unlikely to take the final step of announcing their possession, South Africa is unique in both being a major uranium producer and having been involved in the nuclear trade since its inception. At that time, during the 1950s, South Africa would have perceived the strategic significance of the uranium trade at first hand. As we saw in Chapter 4, during the 1950s and early 1960s nearly all South Africa's uranium exports were used for weapons purposes, mainly in the United States, but also in Britain and later, possibly for the same purpose, in Israel and France. These supplies were greatly appreciated and, as we saw in Chapter 5, South Africa was well rewarded for them. As a major uranium-producing nation South Africa also played an important part during the second part of this period in the Atoms for Peace era and would have appreciated the high priority attached by the great powers to the race for the 'peaceful atom', which was largely a prestige race, as economic returns were considered likely only in the long term. So, having seen the value attached to her uranium supplies for the military and prestige uses of nuclear technology, it would have been surprising if South Africa had *not* wanted to share in these evident benefits.[32]

As a uranium-exporting nation South Africa was also closely involved in Western non-proliferation policies from the beginning and would have noted the importance attached by the United States, in particular, to these policies. As American control of enrichment supply replaced joint British and American control of uranium supply as the means by which nuclear proliferation was retarded, South Africa would have been in a good position to appreciate the significance of the United States enrichment monopoly. Much more recently South Africa would have thus appreciated the significance of the breaking of that monopoly by the European producers, notably the French-led Eurodif consortium.

These matters have been discussed in previous chapters. In particular South Africa's non-proliferation policy concerning safeguards on her exports of uranium and, potentially, enriched uranium has been discussed in Chapters 4 and 6. We have seen in Chapter 2 that other uranium exporters, notably Australia and Canada, have attached stringent non-proliferation conditions, such as full-scope safeguards, to their uranium exports. South Africa may well have exploited this by selling uranium to countries unwilling to accept these conditions.[33] By so doing, South Africa may have obtained, besides a higher price for her uranium, some diplomatic leverage in her relations with these customers. She may expect favours from them in return.[34] Thus Kapur has stated that:

> One dimension of [South Africa's] nuclear policy is to engage in resources diplomacy, to make money and to influence Western buyers of much-needed uranium, particularly if these buyers face unpleasant cut-off threats or embargoes from North American and Australian sources.[35]

Examples of South African uranium diplomacy have included: (i) the 1975 contract to supply Iran with uranium for the Shah's ambitious nuclear power programme, a deal seen at the time to be related to the fact that Iran supplied most of South Africa's oil imports and, it was believed, had agreed to help fund the construction of a commercial enrichment plant in South Africa;[36] and (ii) West Germany's interest in transferring the nozzle enrichment technology to South Africa in return for obtaining a secure supply of uranium, free from the non-proliferation constraints attached by Canada and Australia.[37] Referring to South Africa's position as a major supplier of uranium to the world market, the vice-president of the Atomic Energy Board, Louw Alberts, boasted in 1975 that: 'we now have a bargaining position equal to that of any Arab oil country'.[38]

The bargaining position has become even stronger now that South Africa is able to supply enriched uranium and enrichment technology. Lodgaard has referred to 'the frightening, and perhaps not very distant prospect of South African exports of highly enriched uranium to other countries – without strings, but for a suitably high economic, political or military price'.[39] South Africa *may* already have delivered some enriched uranium from her pilot plant to fellow pariahs such as Israel or Taiwan. However the plant has only produced limited amounts of enrichment (although enough to fuel a research reactor or for several weapons). Thus it is likely that South Africa would wish to retain her present and past production for her own use. Nevertheless there are likely to be continuing rumours about actual or potential South African enrichment supplies,[40] especially when the semi-commercial production plant starts production in the late 1980s. South Africa thus possesses the capacity to sabotage the non-proliferation regime instituted by the leading nuclear suppliers, by selling enriched uranium without their stringent safeguard conditions.[41]

As we saw in Chapter 6, it is considerations such as these that have led the United States once more partially to accommodate South Africa within that non-proliferation regime. In a sense, South Africa's enrichment capacity has enabled her to rejoin the leading industrial nations determining the regime. South Africa has now stated that she will observe the spirit of the Non-Proliferation Treaty and the Nuclear Suppliers Group in her nuclear exports. In return for this declaration of responsible nuclear exporting intent, South Africa will expect the United States to treat her as a member of the Western family of nations and help ease her political and military isolation. Otherwise she will this time play the *enriched* uranium bargaining counter, by means of hints and rumours of unsafeguarded sales for example. The United States may consider the threat posed to the non-proliferation regime by the South African enriched uranium export weapon to be more real than the threat posed to black Africa by a South African nuclear explosive device.

THE POLITICS OF NUCLEAR UNCERTAINTY

In the discussion above of possible military, economic, prestige and diplomatic motivations for South Africa's nuclear capability, we have seen that she has pursued a policy of secrecy and seems deliberately to have encouraged uncertainty concerning her uranium exports, enrichment technology and general intentions.[42] If indeed South Africa has been developing a nuclear weapons capability she would have wished to keep this secret, for fear that, if she was more explicit about her capabilities and intentions, pressure of world opinion might force Western countries to reduce their economic, technological and military links with her.[43]

Several studies of the politics of nuclear weapons proliferation have shown that whilst the weapons are being developed and until there is a clear military need for such weapons, governments will maintain a policy of strict secrecy about their development.[44]

However, South Africa has been unable to keep her nuclear capability *totally* secret. Mr Vorster was forced to announce South Africa's development of enrichment technology in 1970, lest the news leak out in some other way. Details of this technology became known from her enquiries in West Germany and her import of components from the West. Inevitably such incomplete revelations provoked rumours about South Africa's nuclear capability and intentions. Although from time to time government spokesmen were forced to deny that South Africa had or intended to make nuclear weapons, at other times rumours to this effect seemed to be encouraged by government leaders. If the nuclear deterrent was seen as necessary in the last resort, then, in the interim, rumours that South Africa possessed nuclear weapons were similarly seen as having a deterrent effect on South Africa's enemies.[45] South Africa's atomic scientists and officials frequently denied such reports or 'clarified' politicians' statements, only to be followed by further ambiguous remarks by politicians or military leaders engaging in deterrence by uncertainty. One need look no further than Prime Minister Vorster's remarks on three separate occasions quoted in Chapters 6, 7 and 8. A cartoon in a South African newspaper is reported to have read 'Who needs a real bomb? Rumours are a cheaper deterrent.'[46]

As we have seen, this uncertainty is increased by South Africa's non-signature of the Non-Proliferation Treaty and evidence that she may have conducted a nuclear test over the South Atlantic in 1979, and been about to conduct a test in the Kalahari Desert in 1977. It has been noted that South Africa's leaders may have exploited the latter event (whether or not the facilities in the Kalahari were intended as a nuclear test site) with the use of deliberately ambiguous remarks to encourage such uncertainty concerning South Africa's nuclear weapons capability and intentions.[47]

It is likely that South Africa has also used the 'politics of nuclear uncertainty' to gain concessions from the West. For the West, an openly declared South African bomb would focus unwelcome attention on continuing economic, technological and strategic links with South Africa. It is therefore in the interest of Western nations that any intended possession of nuclear weapons should be kept covert. South Africa could thus have blackmailed Western nations by 'threatening' to declare such possession unless the West continues to grant her favours to ease her international isolation. Again, such a threat need not have been openly stated, at the diplomatic negotiating table or elsewhere, but could nevertheless have been established by the use of hints, rumours and non-signature of the NPT.[48] For example, Kapur considers that the Kalahari incident had the effect of easing President Carter's human rights policy of putting pressure on South Africa to reform apartheid.[49]

Whilst South Africa thus has a strong political motive for developing her nuclear weapons capability, there are similar arguments *against* openly declaring that that is what she is doing: namely that such a declaration would lead to erosion of Western economic and political support.[50] We can appropriately conclude this discussion of South Africa's use of the nuclear weapons option as a diplomatic or political bargaining tool with the words of Edouard Bustin:

> . . . since we are ultimately dealing with a problem of credibility, it might be argued that whatever bargaining advantage Pretoria might be able to spin off from the exercise of its nuclear option could be derived more effectively (and is indeed already being derived) from publicizing its capacity to 'go nuclear' – which is highly credible – rather than from the threat of subsequently using such weapons – which is demonstrably less credible.[51]

CHANGING NUCLEAR MOTIVES

It is quite possible, indeed likely, that South Africa is herself uncertain about her nuclear intentions, or rather that she now has the nuclear weapons option, but has not yet decided whether or when to announce that she has developed or is developing such weapons. Although South Africa may always have had the long-term objective of developing nuclear weapons, her short-term nuclear objectives may have altered during the 1970s. Kapur has termed a country's development of nuclear technology a 'phasal' activity. As a country gradually develops a capability over the complete nuclear fuel cycle and becomes increasingly self-sufficient in nuclear technology and material, it is able to to do more with its capability, and its intentions regarding the use of its capability may change and become more ambitious. The implication is that a nation's nuclear policy is in part determined by its scientists and technologists.[52]

Thus South Africa's nuclear intentions may have shifted gradually, becoming more military and less peaceful. This change would have coincided with South Africa's deteriorating international relations as she became increasingly isolated during the 1970s. Originally, South Africa's main intention may have been to utilise nuclear technology to obtain economic and strategic benefits of a peaceful nature. However, as it became clear that she would be unable to obtain Western backing for commercial enrichment plant, and that she would thus not become a large-scale supplier of enrichment services on whom Western nations would become dependent, her nuclear intentions changed and more hints were dropped about her nuclear weapons option (which had never been surrendered).[53] It should be noted that such a change in nuclear intentions also coincided with deteriorating prospects for nuclear energy worldwide, making South Africa's original stated intention of establishing a commercial enrichment capacity to supply both the world market *and* a network of power stations along South Africa's coastline decreasingly realistic.

After 1980, with sympathetic right-wing governments in power in both Britain and America determined to respond to Soviet actions in the Third World, South Africa's international isolation was temporarily eased. By stressing the strategic importance to the West of the Cape route and her mineral supplies, South Africa reaped certain benefits and a closer relationship with the United States, rationalised by US policymakers as a policy of 'constructive engagement'. Further overt hints about nuclear weapons possession (in the form of anonymous tests, for example) would compromise these improved relations and are thus unlikely in the near future. In the longer term, however, these improved relations with the West will probably come to be seen as but a temporary respite in South Africa's gradual and continuing isolation. South Africa's rulers no doubt understand this and are thus extremely unlikely to surrender the nuclear weapons option, for example by signing the NPT. Rather, it is likely that her weapons capability, including her delivery capability, will continue to be secretly developed to the stage that South Africa possesses undeclared 'bombs in the basement' (if she does not already possess them), ready to be assembled and deployed within hours of a decision to do so. In the meantime, as she develops her nuclear weapons capability, South Africa will continue to use her weapons option as a diplomatic bargaining counter to buy favours and time from the West.

The discussion of the possible military uses of nuclear weapons at the beginning of this chapter causes one to wonder whether they would be a credible deterrrent even in the 'last resort'. One can speculate endlessly about possible 'last resort' scenarios, but such speculation is rarely profitable. In any case, the use of nuclear weapons even then would seem, to the outsider, irrational. It would seem at least equally likely in the 'last resort', as the ANC achieves greater military success and accommodation is made to its demands, that South Africa's nuclear capability will be downplayed as its military utility is seen to be negligible. More may then be heard about Western fears concerning how an ANC government might use the capability it would inherit.

However, as several observers have pointed out, what matters would be how the South African regime would see the value of a nuclear deterrent under 'last resort' circumstances.[54] Under conditions that appear politically apocalyptic to the Afrikaner regime – the threat of the end of white control – the nuclear option might well be exercised.[55] No matter how irrational this may seem to the outside world, it could have a symbolic effect as a gesture of defiance and be viewed positively by her white population.[56]

That South Africa's rulers have always had the long-term strategic objective of acquiring nuclear weapons is suggested by two final quotations: first, as long ago as 1965 Prime Minister Verwoerd, inaugurating South Africa's first nuclear reactor, Safari-1, in the presence of foreign dignatories and atomic energy administrators, stated that: 'It is the duty of South Africa not only to consider the military uses . . . but to do all in its power to direct its uses for peaceful purposes.'[57] This may have been an accurate statement of South Africa's nuclear intentions even then, with South Africa's peaceful intentions being of secondary importance to her military intentions. South Africa's true intentions would have been known only to Dr Verwoerd and a handful of officials and politicians. However, the Prime Minister's remarks were of course later 'clarified' by officials emphasising South Africa's peaceful purposes.

Finally, in a similar promotion of nuclear uncertainty, and another demonstration of her politicians' wish to promote the prestige aspects of South Africa's nuclear capability and her (almost literally irrational) use of the nuclear option in the last resort, former Information and Interior Minister Connie Mulder stated in a 1977 interview that:

> If we are attacked, no rules apply at all if it comes to a question of our existence. We will use all means at our disposal, whatever they may be. It is true that we have just completed our own pilot plant that uses very advanced technology, and that we have major uranium resources.[58]

9 Conclusions for Western Policy

INTELLIGENCE, SECRECY AND UNCERTAINTY

In this final chapter we look at the implications of South African nuclear developments for Western, in particular United States, non-proliferation policy and for foreign policy towards South Africa. Openly acknowledged possession of nuclear weapons by South Africa would be damaging to both policies. It would gravely compromise efforts to discourage the development of nuclear weapons elsewhere and there would be considerable pressure from black African, non-aligned and Soviet bloc countries to impose further sanctions on South Africa. Such sanctions would be damaging to Western economic interests and might be felt to encourage the very forces within South Africa that have pressed for the development of nuclear weapons;[1] but failure by Western nations to take such steps would lead to further gains for Soviet influence in Africa – at the expense of the West.

To the extent that South Africa has developed a nuclear weapons capability – possibly as far as already-assembled or readily-assembled 'bombs in the basement' – the United States and the West therefore share South Africa's desire to keep such developments secret. As with Israel, the US government has viewed unfavourably the leaking of assessments by its own intelligence agencies that South Africa may have developed and even (in 1979) tested a nuclear device. The interests of both the United States and South African governments in fostering secrecy and uncertainty about the development of nuclear weapons by South Africa therefore converge. The United States is willing neither to confirm nor firmly to deny that South Africa is developing nuclear weapons. Since the 1977 Kalahari incident, the US government has tended to deny that South Africa possesses such weapons, but it has thereby left itself vulnerable to South African blackmail: South Africa could quietly threaten to reveal weapons possession if certain favours are not granted by the West. On the other hand, as mentioned, United States' confirmation that South Africa is developing nuclear weapons would gravely damage America's global non-proliferation posture, and the West would also come under severe pressure to impose costly economic sanctions on South Africa.

142

Thus, during the 1977 Kalahari and 1979 South Atlantic nuclear test incidents, *both* the United States and South Africa could be seen to be promoting uncertainty about South Africa's nuclear weapons plans. In neither case did the US government want news of a possible weapons test revealed. In the case of the alleged test site in the Kalahari, the information was revealed by the Soviet Union. News of a possible nuclear explosion over the South Atlantic in 1979 was initially suppressed in the United States, but later revealed when a television network got the information.

As we saw in Chapter 6, as a result of these incidents the United States decided that nuclear developments in South Africa should be closely monitored.[2] Such monitoring will include satellite surveillance to detect possible future tests and preparations for tests. Satellite observation would also enable the US government to make an assessment of the enrichment plants' electricity consumption. This would give an indication of the size of the plants, which would in turn enable the United States to assess how much weapons-grade enriched uranium they could have produced.

We noted in Chapter 6 that, during the Carter administration, monitoring of South African nuclear developments by US intelligence agencies extended to covert operations within the country. Again these operations centred on attempts to ascertain the state of South Africa's enrichment programme. In fact the CIA had initiated covert operations in 1974, but these were terminated a year later when they were discovered by the South African security authorities.[3] Such covert operations were a departure from the normal cooperation with South Africa concerning the sharing of intelligence; and, since the operations were discovered and the responsible US officials expelled by South Africa, and there has also subsequently been a return to a closer US–South African intergovernmental relationship, it is unlikely that they have been resumed. In any case, as we concluded in the previous chapter, further South African suggestions of nuclear weapons development are unlikely in the near future, as such suggestions would compromise this closer relationship. There has even been informed speculation in the press that South African and United States intelligence officials might reach an understanding on the secrecy of future tests.[4] Nevertheless, should there be further international incidents similar to those in 1977 and 1979, satellite surveillance would give the US authorities better intelligence about South Africa's nuclear development than they had in those years. The American government would then be able to control the release of information to the public; and, as before, its first instinct would be to try to suppress evidence of nuclear weapons development.[5]

THE EFFECT OF NON-PROLIFERATION POLICIES ON SOUTH AFRICA'S NUCLEAR PROGRAMME

We saw in Chapter 5 that South Africa has built up her nuclear capability to the extent that, with the minor exception of her continued dependence on fuel fabrication services provided for the Koeberg power reactors by France, she is now practically self-sufficient in technology and material for the front-end of the fuel cycle. There therefore remains very little leverage for Western non-proliferation policies over nuclear developments in South Africa.

As with most of the other near-nuclear weapon states discussed in Chapter 2, South Africa acquired much of her nuclear capability before such acquisition was made difficult by the Nuclear Suppliers Group trigger list policy and the subsequent US Nuclear Non-Proliferation Act. Earlier non-proliferation policies had lacked sanctions, as United States control over Western trade, first in natural uranium and then in enriched uranium, had been considered sufficient to ensure that importing nations' nuclear installations would be subject to safeguards.

Of course the significant development by South Africa was that of her enrichment technology. As explained in Chapter 5, South Africa seems to have obtained the know-how and some of the components for this from West Germany before the transfer of such technology was forbidden (except under IAEA safeguards) under the Nuclear Suppliers Group policy announced in 1978. After 1978, export of certain enrichment plant components was prohibited; but the secretive way in which some items may have been imported and the very similar way in which Pakistan has acquired enrichment technology illustrate the difficulty in enforcing embargoes of nuclear equipment, particularly dual-use equipment such as compressors which may have other uses than in nuclear plants. (South Africa is thought to have circumvented the United Nations arms embargo in a similar fashion.) South Africa's claim that her enrichment process has been developed independently and is not a variation of the West German jet nozzle process also illustrates the difficulty for technology-holders trying to exert influence to achieve non-proliferation goals *after* the technology has been transferred. As we saw in Chapter 2, this issue was raised in the case of West Germany's transfer of sensitive technology to Brazil. However, West Germany's overt transfer of enrichment technology to Brazil, with known non-proliferation conditions attached, would seem far preferable, from a non-proliferation viewpoint, to the same country's covert transfer, with no known conditions attached, of the same technology to South Africa, assuming that is what took place.

It is debatable whether South Africa has been helped in obtaining a nuclear weapons capability by the agreement with France for the construction of the power reactors at Koeberg. Certainly the French Prime Minister was correct in saying that the reactors do not provide a direct addition to South Africa's nuclear weapons capability. However it could be argued that, in helping South Africa acquire the initial fuel loads for the reactors, France may have relieved her of the need to divert resources from a programme dedicated to weapons production. Thus, anti-apartheid campaigners and non-aligned and Soviet bloc countries alike have been pressing, at the United Nations and elsewhere, for a comprehensive nuclear embargo to be imposed on South Africa in addition to the arms embargo. Western countries do not accept that they have helped South Africa acquire a nuclear weapons capability and thus resisted these demands until 1985, when, as part of their sanctions packages following the 1984–5 township unrest, the United States and the European Community stated that there would be no more significant nuclear exports to South Africa.

It should also be noted that, in the early years of her nuclear programme, South Africa obtained considerable assistance from Britain and America. This was the Atoms for Peace era, when it was the policy of those countries to export civilian nuclear technology in a liberal fashion in the hope that recipient nations would not feel it necessary to develop their own technology, which might later be used for developing weapons. Again, it is debatable how far this early scientific and technological assistance has helped South Africa to develop a nuclear weapons capability. The Safari-1 research reactor, provided by the United States, and the substantial aid, particularly in the form of training, provided by both Britain and America for South Africa's fundamental nuclear research may not have directly helped the country acquire a weapons capability; but it helped South Africa develop the essential scientific and technological skills and experience which enabled the country to develop that capability. Moreover, as pointed out in the previous chapter, South Africa's capacity, acquired with the help of Britain and America after the Second World War, for the large-scale efficient production of natural uranium, has provided that country with considerable strategic and political benefits which are not unrelated to her development of an enrichment and nuclear weapons capability.

In the 1950s, South Africa agreed to supply Britain and America with uranium for their weapons programmes in exchange for nuclear scientific and technological assistance from those countries. South Africa may wish to maintain this linkage between her export of uranium and her import of advanced technology. As explained in Chapter 2, a key concern of American non-proliferation policy in the late 1970s was to show that there was ample uranium readily available worldwide and that the 'plutonium economy' with its attendant proliferation risks could therefore be postponed indefinitely. It was therefore seen to be in the interests of US non-proliferation policy that South Africa's uranium exports be maximised;[6] and the United States may have been prepared to grant political concessions, helping to ease South Africa's further international isolation, as a reward for the efforts of South Africa's uranium mining industry. The United States may not have wished to import South African uranium; and there may have been some raising of eyebrows over the circumstances under which South Africa uranium supplies might have been made available to countries such as Iran and Taiwan, considered possible proliferation risks; but United States non-proliferation planners would have been quite satisfied with the ready availability of large quantities of South African uranium for countries not considered proliferation risks, such as Japan and West European nations.

Since the mid-1970s, American efforts to prevent South Africa getting nuclear weapons rested on her leverage over the supply of enrichment for the Safari-1 and Koeberg reactors. This was formalised with the stipulation, under the 1978 US Nuclear Non-Proliferation Act, that the United States could provide these enrichment services only if the pilot enrichment plant became subject to international safeguards. Although this plant was eventually used to provide enriched uranium to fuel the Safari-1 reactor, it was still felt that South Africa would continue to depend on United States supplies of enriched uranium for the Koeberg reactors during the early 1980s, until South Africa's own production enrichment plant came on stream in the mid-1980s. In the event, as we have seen, South Africa was able to obtain sufficient enriched uranium, to fuel the Koeberg reactors for two or three years, in Europe. So even this US leverage over South Africa's nuclear programme has practically disappeared.

In fact, over the last decade or so, South Africa can be seen to have adopted a dual strategy of depending increasingly on French and West German rather than American sources for nuclear technology and material, whilst at the same time developing her own capability to the extent that she is now practically self-sufficient over the whole of the front-end of the fuel cycle.[7] In view of the increasingly stringent non-proliferation policies adopted by the major powers led by the USA, South Africa's dual strategy may be considered to have been prudent, and is not unlike the policies adopted by other medium powers, such as

Brazil, Argentina, India and Pakistan, at whom these non-proliferation policies have been directed.

It may thus be felt that United States non-proliferation policies, in particular the 1978 US Nuclear Non-Proliferation Act (NNPA), by seeking to prevent the transfer of nuclear technology and material except under stringent safeguards conditions, actually encouraged South Africa's own development of that technology, so that she is now practically self-sufficient.[8] In the meantime South Africa obtained enrichment technology from West Germany and power reactors and fuel from France when these countries' non-proliferation policies were not as strict as America's.[9]

This points to the need for a more concerted Western approach to non-proliferation. Possible nuclear cooperation between Israel and South Africa also raises the problem of how the West can discourage unsafeguarded nuclear cooperation between second-tier countries, particularly the newly-industrialising countries of the South. In the case of South Africa, we have seen in Chapter 6 that that country has chosen to adopt the rules of the Non-Proliferation Treaty and the Nuclear Suppliers Group for her nuclear exports. By so doing she has obtained concessions to her interests from the United States. It is likely that in the future the Western non-proliferation regime will increasingly have to accommodate itself to the interests of semi-industrialised countries like South Africa that are themselves gaining a nuclear export capacity. However, formal admission of these countries into the Nuclear Suppliers Group (for example) is highly unlikely. The Suppliers Group no longer meets in any case; and, when there have been suggestions that South Africa should be admitted in the past, it became clear that the Soviet-bloc and some Western nations would oppose this, and it was therefore not pressed.[10] Future discussions between nuclear-exporting countries (including South Africa) are likely to be more informal and secretive than in the past. Although the United States will seek to orchestrate them, policy announcements by nuclear-exporting nations to the effect that all exports will be safeguarded are likely to be made individually or by groups with closely-shared interests such as the European Community nations. Suspicions of Third World nuclear-importing countries of renewed cartel-like activity by the Suppliers Group will thereby be allayed.

South Africa and other countries discussed in Chapter 2 which are at a similar stage in their nuclear development and are gaining an export potential are therefore likely to be increasingly involved in the determination of the global non-proliferation regime. Few countries are totally self-sufficient in nuclear technology and materials however, and the countries in question are no exception. They remain partially dependent on imports and therefore exposed to Western non-proliferation policies, albeit at a much lower level of vulnerability.

EFFORTS TO INDUCE SOUTH AFRICA'S SIGNATURE OF THE NPT

In South Africa's case, the Reagan administration retained its predecessor's publicly-stated conditions for the resumption of enrichment supplies, namely that South Africa should accept full-scope safeguards and sign the Non-Proliferation Treaty (NPT). This last condition went beyond the requirements of the Nuclear Non-Proliferation Act.[11]

South Africa's attitude to the NPT and moves to induce her signature have been discussed in Chapter 6. Like Israel, South Africa has sought international understanding for her refusal to sign by pointing to the discriminatory nature of the treaty; but, as with Israel, few observers have taken these stated objections at face value.[12] The negotiation of real disarmament measures by the superpowers would start to repair this discrimination, but South Africa has little interest in superpower nuclear arms control measures, especially as, in the improved East–West climate which would be necessary for their success, South Africa may fear that her supposed strategic value to the West might not be adequately recognised.

If South Africa did sign the NPT, all her nuclear facilities, including the pilot enrichment plant, would have to come under IAEA safeguards. South Africa might also be pressed to account for enriched uranium already produced by this plant. However it would be impossible to verify such accounts, and South African secrecy about her production and sales of natural uranium (the feed for the plant) is relevant here. It would thus be possible for South Africa secretly to maintain a store of high-enriched uranium (possibly already assembled into bombs). Moreover, IAEA safeguards are not perfect. In particular, as noted in the Appendix below, safeguarding techniques on enrichment plants, particularly those using aerodynamic technology, have not yet been finalised; and there may be considerable technical and political problems in agreeing a safeguards arrangement between the IAEA and South Africa. It may thus be possible, albeit politically highly risky, for South Africa to circumvent safeguards and keep a stock of weapons-grade enriched uranium or divert such fissile material from an enrichment plant undetected.[13] The point is not that such evasion of the NPT by South Africa is likely, but that international anti-apartheid opposition to the regime would have some grounds for doubting the value of a South African signature.

At various times during the 1970s it appeared that South Africa might be about to sign the NPT.[14] However, these faint signals were always followed by inexplicable delay and further objections to signature being found by South Africa.[15] In this respect her dealings with the United States over the NPT have resembled similar tactics employed by South Africa in negotiations over Namibian independence. In both sets of negotiations, the South African regime faced domestic Afrikaner opposition to any agreement; and she held out for concessions, including possibly a security guarantee, to ease her international isolation, which the West was unable to provide. Moreover, as we have argued in the previous chapter, South Africa's failure to sign the NPT is partly designed to promote uncertainty about her nuclear capabilities and intentions. Several observers have pointed out that she has little to gain from signature, international opposition to the regime being caused by apartheid rather than her nuclear policies.[16]

However it may be worth making a few qualifying and speculative remarks here concerning the policy of a future South African regime. As with foreign affairs in general, there is at present little public discussion and a general consensus exists among the white population in support of the government's stance on nuclear matters. However, as South Africa gets progressively weaker in relative terms, the irrelevance of nuclear weapons to her strategic situation may be recognised and Afrikanerdom may become less united and self-confident in utilising the bargaining power of both a potential 'bomb in the basement' and her capacity for unsafeguarded nuclear exports. A weakened or essentially different South African government (of whatever description), with policies that may be more difficult to label as 'apartheid', may then find it expedient to alleviate its international isolation and mistrust of its intentions by signing the NPT.

If such a hypothetical government did discover that the Nationalist regime had produced nuclear weapons and if that government wished to publicise this fact, a unique exercise in nuclear disarmament would necessarily ensue. From a non-proliferation viewpoint it might be preferable if the new government were quietly to dismantle the weapons and possibly also one or both of the enrichment plants. If it needed assistance or wished the IAEA to supervise this process in order to allay international suspicion, the superpowers might become concerned that

IAEA inspectors could acquire sensitive information concerning weapon assembly and the enrichment technique, and then pass this information to their own national governments. Considerations of wider international security may therefore lead a future South African government to ask either superpower (depending on the political complexion of that new government) to supervise the disassembly of any weapons and possibly the pilot enrichment plant. Any know-how gained in the process would be of less significance to a superpower; but there would still be some suspicion on the part of the other superpower and neighbouring African countries concerning the thoroughness with which the task was accomplished. Another problem which could arise is that a handful of former government employees may possess nuclear 'secrets' (of the bomb assembly and enrichment techniques) which they may be willing to pass on or sell to other governments.

Whilst it may be intriguing to speculate about such future eventualities, for the present, as we have argued, it is far from certain that signature of the NPT by the current regime would be welcomed unreservedly by significant sections of the international community, such as the non-aligned and Soviet-bloc nations which are pressing for South Africa's increased isolation,[17] although the IAEA would be bound to recognise South Africa's signature if deposited in London or Washington. For example, these countries would be embarrassed by their guarantee, under Article IV, that NPT signatories should have unimpeded access to peaceful nuclear technology.[18] South Africa has already served notice that she considers this clause important; and doubts about it being honoured are given as another important reason for withholding her signature.[19] Similarly she has stated that she does not feel the United States has honoured her obligation under their bilateral agreement for nuclear cooperation to supply enriched uranium. South Africa's government feels that it may continue to be similarly deprived, contrary to the spirit of Article IV, even if it were to sign the NPT.[20]

So one may conclude that, although the Carter administration appeared to have been adopting a tough stance in 1977 when, following the international alarm over the possibility of an imminent test of a nuclear explosive device in the Kalahari Desert, it demanded NPT signature as a condition of further nuclear supplies, and then made another determined effort to persuade South Africa to sign the treaty, with hindsight this stance looks more like a fruitless gesture (although it was successful in diverting moves for nuclear sanctions against South Africa). The Carter administration must have known that there was very little prospect of the Nationalist government signing the NPT, and that the United States did not have the necessary influence to force it to do so. It would seem preferable and more acceptable to international opinion that Western efforts should be focused on persuading South Africa to accept full-scope safeguards.[21]

NUCLEAR RELATIONS AND WESTERN FOREIGN POLICY TOWARDS SOUTH AFRICA

In fact, United States non-proliferation policy towards South Africa, which has seemed to be clutching at the straws of America's rapidly vanishing influence over South Africa's nuclear programme, can only be understood if viewed in the context of America's overall foreign policy towards the region. Indeed, as explained in Chapter 2, the trend in United States non-proliferation thinking since the end of the Carter presidency has been that policy should be integrated into strategic policy towards different geopolitical regions.[22]

If past universalist policies for curbing the global spread of weapons-related nuclear technology have failed to prevent South Africa acquiring such technology, or rather if these policies were adopted too late and then only by some supplier nations, what then are the prospects for success of this new bilateral non-proliferation policy which seeks to integrate non-proliferation goals into general foreign policy towards southern Africa and which seeks to address South Africa's motivations for acquiring nuclear weapons rather than the means by which such weapons are acquired? South Africa would certainly welcome a policy which puts more emphasis on 'dialogue', linkage with other bilateral foreign policy issues, and seeks to address her 'legitimate security concerns'.[23] Overt concessions such as arms transfers and security guarantees are politically impossible for the West to grant and would encourage South African aggression against neighbouring states; but there are other more modest and less public measures which could be adopted and which would be greatly appreciated by the South African regime. These include: cooperation in her acquisition of dual-purpose items (which can have both military and civilian applications), exchange of intelligence and other information between South Africa and those Western countries perceiving shared security interests and, in general, a more sympathetic understanding of South Africa's desire to ease her beleaguered situation. These requirements of the South African government have been substantially met by the Reagan and Thatcher governments and, as argued in the previous chapter, this has helped to minimise South Africa's incentives for announcing nuclear weapons possession for the time being.

However, although incentives of a nation like South Africa for possessing nuclear weapons may have been reduced and a possible announcement of their possession indefinitely postponed, such a nation may consider it prudent to continue to develop the technology, possibly to the extent of having readily-assembled bombs. Such a course is particularly likely to be followed if, like Israel or South Africa, the nation is an international pariah and may feel that, even if Western concessions are granted, they could later be withdrawn under pressure of world opinion,[24] as happened to South Africa in 1985.

Thus the West's continuing, though now minor, nuclear relations with South Africa, should be seen in the context of overall foreign policy which seeks to preserve links with the country. Although breaking these nuclear relations might seem a relatively inexpensive gesture which would bring the benefit of largely satisfying international concern over Western nuclear collaboration with South Africa, such a gesture would be inconsistent with this policy. Policy-makers have rationalised these continuing relations by arguing that, by this dialogue or 'constructive engagement', as it is now called, the West may still be able to influence South African policy, whether over apartheid, Namibian independence of nuclear developments.[25]

During President Carter's administration, this emphasis on dialogue, rationalised on non-proliferation grounds, seemed to some observers to conflict with the President's policy of maintaining close relations only with those nations with good human rights records.[26] However, as we observed in Chapter 3 above, President Carter's human rights stance over apartheid amounted mainly to rhetoric. Dialogue has remained the dominant theme of Western policy towards South Africa, as it was even during the Carter administration.

South Africa's policy-makers well understand and share the West's perception that dialogue must be maintained. Her attitude concerning signature of the Non-Proliferation Treaty – making no move towards signature yet not ruling it out – is partly designed to maintain a dialogue with the West.[27] Yet in this dialogue, the West feels unable to offer carrots *or* sticks to induce NPT signature or acceptance of full-scope safeguards. If the West were to adopt a more bullying approach, there could be further South African hints of nuclear weapons possession and unsafeguarded nuclear exports, and she may become more obstructive over Namibia. This would cause the West to back off again. On the other hand, if inducements of a nuclear or military nature were offered, South

Africa might seem to be being rewarded for her nuclear achievements, liberal Western and Third World opinion would be offended and Western non-proliferation policy might appear inconsistent in its application. So Western policy-makers face a dilemma over nuclear relations, as they do over relations generally with South Africa.[28]

Thus continued dialogue on nuclear questions hides American indecisiveness: a policy of letting things drift. It also reflects a more 'laissez-faire' approach to proliferation generally, due partly to a feeling that the near-nuclear weapon states have few incentives for announcing weapons possession, and partly to an impression that there is little the West can do about proliferation anyway. In the case of South Africa, one result of this downgrading in the priority attached to non-proliferation, compared with other Western foreign policy goals, has been a reduction in the level of her leaders' rhetoric, as the bargaining and prestige value of her nuclear achievements appears diminished.[29]

SOUTH AFRICAN OR WESTERN LEVERAGE?

We saw in the previous chapter that South Africa has few military incentives for possessing nuclear weapons. Her intentions are rather to use her nuclear capability together with the politics of nuclear uncertainty (hints about possible weapons tests, etc.) as a diplomatic lever to extract concessions of a military, strategic or economic nature from the West or, at worst, prevent relations from deteriorating too far. Thus South Africa is able to use her nuclear weapons *option* but has no military incentive for taking the option and announcing that she has such weapons. Indeed there are disincentives, as such an announcement would probably bring further international isolation. Thus, Richard Betts has suggested that, rather than succumb to South African blackmail, the United States should call her bluff and downgrade nuclear relations,[30] which, in any case, now amount to no more than discussions over safeguards on the enrichment plants, together with the supply of relatively insignificant or dual-use items, such as radioisotopes and health and safety equipment, some of which were embargoed in any case under the further package of sanctions announced by President Reagan in the summer of 1985. Thus, according to Betts, America's attitude to the South African nuclear weapons option should be that

studied nonchalance about the matter, coupled with vague low-key statements (to the effect that the South African government could not rationally see any benefits in proliferation and would invite un-specified but severe problems and sanctions if it did develop a nuclear force) would be a reasonable form of calculated ambiguity. Such ambiguity might well be the proper reply to South Africa's own calculated ambiguity, stabilizing rhetorical deterrence between Washington and Pretoria.[31]

In fact 'studied nonchalance' would seem to be a good description of the Reagan administration's subsequent non-proliferation policy in general. In the case of South Africa it would mark a return to the pre-1974 situation when, according to Spence, there may have been

> a calculation by the Western powers that the Republic [of South Africa] has little to gain in either political or military terms from opting for nuclear power status. And if this means a diminution in its bargaining power with the West, South Africa will probably have little choice but to maintain its present noncommital policy, if only on the grounds that a bird in the hand may be of some yet unforeseen advantage when all others have flown.[32]

However, before concluding, we should note that, although South African nuclear armaments may not be militarily credible, her capacity to undermine the Western non-proliferation regime by inadequately safeguarded nuclear exports is highly credible. It may be this unmentioned threat which, in the last analysis, ensures that the West continues to maintain nuclear and other contacts. The now infamous National Security Council study, which provided the rationale for United States policy towards southern Africa during most of President Nixon's term of office, considered that the bilateral US–South African agreement for nuclear cooperation was

> . . . important in influencing South Africa to continue its policy of doing nothing in the marketing of its large production of uranium oxide which would have the effect of increasing the number of nuclear weapon powers.[33]

It is likely that there has been an unwritten understanding that a condition for South Africa remaining an ex-officio member of the Western world, at least so far as commercial and trading relations are concerned, is that she should continue to behave responsibly by requiring adequate safeguards on her nuclear exports. This would have to be a gentlemen's agreement as it would be difficult to verify compliance by South Africa. This presupposes trust on both sides; and it may be the reason why, rather than see her become increasingly isolated and unpredictable in her behaviour, the West has chosen to maintain nuclear relations with South Africa. In 1977, the US ambassador to the United Nations, Andrew Young, in a reversal of the stance he took before joining the Carter administration, suggested that ending nuclear cooperation

> would only encourage separate development [*sic*!] of South Africa's own nuclear potential . . . If you break the relationship altogether there is no way to monitor and it is almost because you can't trust them that you have to stay close to them.[34]

As well as South Africa's nuclear weapons capability, Mr Young may well have been thinking of her nuclear export capability.

It is due to considerations such as these that the USA has opposed moves to expel South Africa from the IAEA and particularly regretted South Africa's removal from the agency's Committee on the Assurances of Supply.[35] Similarly, having initially, for political reasons, omitted to invite South Africa to participate in the inaugural organising session of the International Nuclear Fuel Cycle Evaluation (INFCE), the Carter administration later found it necessary to bring South Africa into these discussions, because of her status as a substantial exporter of uranium.[36]

We saw in the previous chapter that South Africa has used her uranium export capacity to gain friends and influence overseas customers and the major Western powers responsible for the non-proliferation regime. It would be surprising if she did not entertain similar ambitions for exploiting her enrichment capacity. Admittedly this is much more modest than South Africa had originally hoped to achieve and there will be little if any spare enrichment capacity for export; but South Africa's style has been to use the capability rather than the actual sales, by such means as hints and leaked rumours of inadequately safeguarded sales, to make the major powers, in particular the United States, take the nuclear export possibility seriously. South Africa's hope, then, has been that the West will make concessions to South Africa in return for her adopting a responsible nuclear export policy with adequate safeguards attached to sales. The key importance for a successful non-proliferation regime of uranium *and* enrichment exporting nations having such a responsible policy has been clearly shown in Chapter 2; and, as we noted in Chapter 6, the response of the United States government to South Africa's 1984 declaration clarifying her non-proliferation policy concerning safeguards on her nuclear exports was one of almost visible relief.

Throughout the post-war period the United States has sought to prevent other Western nations from getting nuclear weapons. However, once these weapons had been developed by Britain and France, the USA changed her strategic and nuclear policy towards these countries, as she sought their cooperation in trying to prevent additional countries getting the bomb. South Africa may now have reached a similar stage in her bilateral nuclear relations with the United States. In this context it does not matter whether or not South Africa has nuclear weapons. The point is that, like Britain and France, she has the *capability* for manufacturing them, and therefore, if she chooses, for disseminating them elsewhere. It is likely that the emphasis in United States–South African discussions concerning proliferation has switched from trying to prevent South Africa getting nuclear weapons to trying to prevent third countries getting them with South Africa's help. It may be felt by United States non-proliferation planners that this change of emphasis has been made necessary by South Africa's enhanced nuclear capability (to be further strengthened when the larger enrichment plant comes on stream around 1987). In this context one may wonder which country has the greater leverage over the other.

At the height of the crisis in 1977 concerning a possibly imminent South African nuclear test in the Kalahari Desert, an editorial in a pro-government Afrikaans newspaper stated:

> One would have thought that it would have been tactically more profitable for (the great powers) to draw closer a potential member of the nuclear club, which South Africa is. Their bullying attitude could result in making us a maverick bull in the nuclear herd, and that is surely not a sound situation from their point of view.[37]

This advice would appear to have been heeded. The West's 'bullying attitude', if it ever existed, was soon abandoned, and the 'dialogue' resumed, although the West has seemed unable to exert any significant influence over South Africa's nuclear development. In this respect nuclear relations reflect the overall relationship between South Africa and the West; and it was considerations such as those we have been discussing that led Adelman and Knight to conclude that: 'How to prevent nuclear proliferation and how to deal with South Africa are baffling questions. Together the two problems become even more perplexing.'[38] One can therefore predict, with a fair degree of confidence, that Western policy concerning South African nuclear questions is likely to remain characterised by secrecy, nervous and distrustful watchfulness and a feeling of being powerless to do anything decisive.

Appendix: Uranium Enrichment

THE PRINCIPLES OF URANIUM ENRICHMENT

Uranium 'enrichment' means the partial separation of the two isotopes, uranium-235 (U235) and uranium-238 (U238), found in natural uranium, in order to obtain uranium with a higher concentration of the fissile isotope U235.[1] As explained in Chapter 1, natural uranium, as found in uranium ore and concentrates, consists of only 0.7 per cent U235, the remaining 99.3 per cent being U238. To produce fuel for most thermal power reactors, natural uranium must be enriched to between 2 and 4 per cent U235. This is known as low-enriched uranium or LEU.[2] Enrichment accounts for a small portion – about 5 per cent – of the total cost of nuclear-generated electricity although it amounts to between one-quarter and one-half of the relatively low fuel costs.

If U235 is to be used for a nuclear weapon, natural uranium must be more enriched than this. Typically 90 per cent U235 is used for nuclear weapons although, as explained in Chapter 1, it is possible to produce a nuclear weapon with uranium enriched as low as 10 per cent U235. For purposes of safeguards, uranium enriched to more than 20 per cent U235 is known as high-enriched uranium (HEU) or 'weapons-grade' uranium. The technology for the production of high-enriched uranium is broadly the same as that for the production of low-enriched uranium.

Isotopes of chemical elements (in this case, uranium) are chemically identical, and differ only in their physical properties, these differences being due to slight differences in mass. Enrichment is therefore a physical rather than a chemical process, although it calls for considerable skills in chemical engineering. The U235 and U238 isotopes differ in mass by only 1.3 per cent. A great deal of energy must therefore be expended in separating them. Whilst it is relatively easy scientifically to devise conceptually new enrichment (or 'separation') techniques,[3] devising new techniques which are cheaper than those already developed is very much harder. In general, the sophistication of enrichment technologies derives from the precision and materials engineering skills required for producing the separation elements and/or the high-speed moving parts.[4] Enrichment processes are typically capital and energy intensive; and a nation proposing to establish a uranium enrichment capability faces a very large energy requirement and the need for an established industrial infrastructure.

To date, only two technologies, gaseous diffusion and gas centrifuge, are used in commercial enrichment plants. Aerodynamic technology, conceived of in West Germany, is being developed in Brazil and South Africa. Theoretical work continues on other techniques, laser enrichment being worthy of mention (at the end of this Appendix) because of its implications for weapons proliferation.

The three technologies mentioned which are being or have been developed for commercial use all utilise a volatile compound of uranium: uranium hexafluoride (UF_6), or 'hex', in the gaseous form. Although 'hex' has the advantage of being readily vaporised, it has the disadvantage of being highly toxic and corrosive. Each stage of the enrichment process will only separate or enrich the uranium (in the 'hex') by a very slight amount. The uranium hexafluoride feed must therefore be passed through many identical stages, typically connected in a cascade arrangement.

An enrichment plant separates the natural uranium 'feed' into the enriched uranium 'product' and the depleted uranium 'tails'. Typical values for the feed, product and tail streams are shown in Figure A.1. The waste 'tails' consist of 'depleted' uranium: uranium with a U235 concentration less than that of the natural uranium feed. Typically the concentration of U235 in the tails is 0.2 to 0.3 per cent. This is known as the 'tails assay'. In enrichment plants the tails assay can in practice be adjusted in response to changes in the relative costs of enrichment work (energy) and the natural uranium feed. Additional cycles of depleted uranium through the separation process will produce 3 per cent enriched product in greater quantity, and the assay of U235 in the tails will be further reduced; but this would require more work per unit of product, and so be more costly. Conversely, raising the tails assay from 0.2 to 0.3 per cent will result in a saving of 20 per cent in enrichment work capacity (SWUs) but will *raise* the natural uranium feed requirements (per unit of product) by 20 per cent. The choice of tails assay thus has considerable implications for the cost of enrichment and nuclear fuel supply in general.[5]

The energy required to separate the U235 and U238 isotopes is measured in separative work units (SWUs). The production of 1kg of 3 per cent enriched uranium from natural uranium feed, in a plant

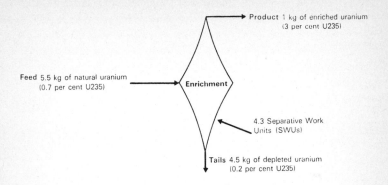

Figure A.1 Typical Relationship between Feed, Tail and Product Streams in an Enrichment Plant

operating a 0.3 per cent tails assay, requires 3.42SWU, for example. The same quantity of separative work could also be used, in the same plant (with the same tails assay), to produce 2kg of 2 per cent enriched uranium or 0.65kg of 4 per cent product. Thus, for example, the SWU can be used to compare plant capacities or enrichment demand regardless of the U235 concentrations involved. It should be noted that the separative work unit has the dimensions of mass. References in the literature to 'metric tons of separative work' when describing the size of an enrichment plant are thus to thousands of separative work units (and *not* the quantities of feed or product).

With a tails assay of 0.2 per cent, a 1000MW(e) light water power reactor needs 366t of natural uranium feed and 257 000SWU to produce the 85t of 2.4 per cent enriched uranium required for its initial fuel load. Thereafter between one-quarter and one-third of the reactor fuel core is removed and replaced on an annual basis. Each annual reload requires 33.9t of 3.15 per cent enriched uranium which is equivalent to 196t natural uranium feed and 157 200SWU at the same 0.2 per cent tails assay. With a 0.3 per cent tails assay, however, the natural uranium requirements increase to 235t, whereas the separative work requirements fall to 125 000SWU.[6] This information is summarised in Table A.1. (In practice less feed and separative work capacity is required annually because reactors typically operate only at load factors of about two-thirds.)

In principle, it is possible to convert an enrichment plant used for producing low-enriched uranium for power reactors into one for producing weapons-grade high-enriched uranium, either by batch recycling of the product or by adding more separation stages in series (possibly by rearranging cascades previously operating in parallel). Once a nation has acquired an enrichment plant for civil purposes, in connection with a nuclear power programme, it is therefore relatively

Table A.1   SWU and Natural Uranium Requirement for Enriched Uranium Products

Product	Tails assay per cent U235	Natural uranium feed tonnes U	Separative work SWU
First fuel load for 1000MW(e) Pressurised water reactor (PWR):			
85t of 2.4 per cent U235	0.2	370	260 000
	0.3	440	n.a.
Annual fuel reload for 1000MW(e) PWR:			
(i) Assuming 100 per cent load factor:			
34t of 3.1 per cent U235	0.2	200	150 000
	0.3	240	120 000
(ii) Assuming 65 per cent load factor:			
23t of 3.1 per cent U235	0.2	130	100 000
	0.3	160	80 000
Fissile material for small nuclear explosive device:			
15kg of 90 per cent U235	0.2	2.7	3 400
	0.3	3.4	3 000
25kg of 90 per cent U235	0.2	4.5	5 700
	0.3	5.6	4 800
50kg of 90 per cent U235	0.2	9.0	11 400
	0.3	11.2	9 700

n.a. not available

Sources: Adapted or computed from: Ted Greenwood, George W. Rathjens and Jack Ruina, *Nuclear Power and Weapons Proliferation*, Adelphi Papers no. 130 (London: IISS, 1976) p. 43; International Nuclear Fuel Cycle Evaluation, *Enrichment Availability*, Report of INFCE Working Group 2 (Vienna: IAEA, 1980) pp. 73, 78; The Uranium Institute, *The Uranium Equation: The Balance of Supply and Demand 1980–1995* (London: Mining Journal Books, 1981) p. 41.

easy to adapt the plant in order to produce weapons-grade uranium. Producing high-enriched uranium from a given amount of natural uranium feed would of course be more expensive than producing low-enriched uranium; but if one compares the SWUs needed to produce a given quantity of 90 per cent enriched uranium from 3 per cent enriched uranium with that required to produce the 90 per cent enriched uranium from natural uranium, it is found that about three times less separative work is required along with a five-fold reduction in the amount of feed material required.[7]

The minimum amount of high-enriched uranium required to produce a nuclear weapon is 15–25 kg.[8] Such a weapon could give an explosion yielding the same as the explosion of 20 kilotons of TNT. The Hiroshima bomb, the first enriched uranium explosive device, contained 60 kg HEU. Table A.1 shows that the minimum separative work requirements to produce explosive devices of these sizes would be in the range 3000–12 000SWU.

From the point of view of international safeguards on plants to prevent the diversion of weapons-grade uranium, or rather to deter and give 'timely warning' of such diversion, the material in the feed, product and tails streams must be continuously monitored. Otherwise it would be possible readily to convert an enrichment plant designed to produce low-enriched uranium into one producing high-enriched uranium, and then to reconvert it back again without detection. It is considered easier to perform this conversion (and reconversion) without detection for aerodynamic and centrifuge enrichment plants than for gaseous diffusion plants.

Current safeguards techniques for nuclear fuel-cycle facilities rely mainly on occasional on-site inspections by teams of IAEA experts and their perusal of materials accounts. Safeguards agreements between nations and the IAEA provide for 'material balance areas' for which such accounts are prepared. For some installations, inspections are supplemented by containment and surveillance measures, such as the use of special locks and seals, radiation sensors and television cameras. Countries are required to provide detailed design information of nuclear facilities to be safeguarded, so that these safeguards may be adequate.

In order to protect commercially sensitive information, IAEA safeguards agreements also provide for 'non-access' or 'special' material balance areas, into which IAEA inspectors are not allowed. For enrichment plants it is expected that the cascade area would be a special material balance area, design information about which the IAEA would keep confidential, and into which IAEA inspectors would not be allowed. For safeguards purposes then, the cascade area would be treated as a 'black box' with containment (for example by special seals on fire and safety exits) and surveillance of the perimeter, but no access by IAEA inspectors.[9] The purpose of inspections would be to obtain precise information about the quantity and composition of the feed, product and tails streams, by weighing, sampling and sealing of the cylinders of uranium hexafluoride used for all three streams.[10] The International Nuclear Fuel Cycle Evaluation (INFCE) considered that, for special material balance areas in enrichment plants,

> more extensive safeguards procedures could need to be applied to maintain completeness and continuity of knowledge. For example additional emphasis might need to be placed on containment and surveillance measures.[11]

At the time of INFCE (1980), the only enrichment plants to be covered by safeguards were centrifuge facilities in the Netherlands, West Germany and Japan, of which the commercial URENCO plant in the Netherlands (see below) was the only plant of significant size.[12] In fact the centrifuge technology holders are still negotiating safeguards arrangements with the IAEA (as are the South Africans over safeguards on their helikon process production plant[13]) and doubts have been raised concerning the cost of surveillance measures for the large centrifuge plant that was due to be constructed in the United States and voluntarily submitted to IAEA safeguards. An alternative to surveillance of 'limited frequency unannounced access' by inspectors has therefore been suggested.[14]

GLOBAL DEVELOPMENT OF COMMERCIAL ENRICHMENT CAPACITY

As with other stages in the nuclear fuel cycle, commercial enrichment capacity developed from that constructed for nuclear weapons manufacture. Because the barriers to entry into the industry are primarily technological, and because possession of the technology is a major step towards acquiring a weapons capability, considerable secrecy has always surrounded enrichment technologies. Nevertheless the principles of the various technologies are relatively simple and well established. They are briefly reviewed in the next section.

When nuclear technology was progressively declassified by the United States in the Atoms for Peace era following 1954, enrichment technology was the only major technology to remain classified. Nevertheless the Soviet Union, the United Kingdom and France all managed independently to develop diffusion technology. China developed her diffusion plant with the help of the Soviet Union in the late 1950s.

Thus enrichment plants based on diffusion technology were initially established in the nuclear weapon states. Because of the size of their nuclear weapons arsenals the largest plants were in the United States and the Soviet Union. Until recently, the United States government had a monopoly over the sale of commercial enrichment services in the West, from three plants now owned by the US Department of Energy at Oak Ridge (Tennessee), Paducah (Kentucky) and Portsmouth (Ohio). The Americans used this dependence of other Western nations on United States enrichment capacity both to further their non-proliferation objectives and to promote the sale of American light water reactors fuelled by low-enriched uranium (as distinct from natural uranium reactors being developed by other countries). In effect, the sale of enrichment services and light water reactors was subsidised and safeguarded, and during the 1960s and early 1970s the United States totally dominated the world market for enrichment and power reactors. (This was despite an unsuccessful attempt by France in the 1950s to get her neighbours to cooperate in building a jointly-owned European plant. Military motivations were suspected and the plan was eventually considered to be commercially unviable.[15])

At the end of the 1960s, the Soviet Union began offering enrichment in the West on attractive commercial terms through her state trading organisation Techsnabexport. Beginning in 1970, this offer was accepted by several European countries including Belgium, Finland, France, Spain, Sweden and West Germany. Neither the location nor the capacity of the Soviet enrichment facilities has ever been officially published although it is believed that her capacity is approximately 10 million SWU/a.[16] The assessment of the US Central Intelligence Agency in 1977 was that 3 million SWU a year had been allocated for export to the West.[17]

In 1970–1, prompted by this Soviet initiative and realising that her enrichment monopoly was becoming unacceptable to other nations, who might be driven to develop their own enrichment technologies, the United States initiated discussions with ten selected countries on the establishment of a joint European commercial enrichment capacity based on US diffusion technology. However the US offer was subject to stringent conditions, with the Americans retaining control of the plant and the technology, and it proved unacceptable to the other nations.[18]

Meanwhile, centrifuge technology, work on which had been under-taken in the United States and Germany during the Second World War, was being developed in several countries, and in 1968 the British, Netherlands and West German governments agreed to pool their efforts. Under the Treaty of Almelo, signed by the three countries in 1970, two companies, URENCO Limited and CENTEC GmbH were established with shareholdings by the three participating countries. URENCO was to provide central marketing and management services; CENTEC was to coordinate research and development. Pilot plants were to be established in each country. These have since been followed by larger production plants in Capenhurst in England and Almelo in the Netherlands. A third plant with a capacity of 0.4 million SWU/a is being built at Gronau in West Germany. With centrifuge technology, unlike diffusion technology, it is possible to expand production capacity in small increments; and there are plans to increase total joint capacity to 2 million SWU/a by the late 1980s, and further thereafter in response to market demand and as enrichment supply contracts are signed.[19] (Western world planned enrichment capacity and production for the period 1978–90 are shown in Table A.2.)

In 1973, the United States government raised the price and stiffened the contract terms offered for her sale of enrichment services.[20] Partly in response to this, France formed the Societé Européene d'Usines de Diffusion Gazeuse, or Eurodif, in the same year, with minor sharehold-ings by Italy, Belgium, Spain and Iran, to establish a commercial plant, based on French diffusion technology, at Tricastin in southern France. Full capacity (though not full production) of 10.8 million SWU/a was reached in 1982. Shareholders receive an enrichment supply propor-tional to their holdings (although since the Islamic revolution Iran has not taken her share for which she now has no need since her nuclear power programme has been suspended). The same countries, though with different shareholdings, also formed another consortium, Coredif, to establish another diffusion plant, but in view of the subsequent oversupply of the enrichment market, plans for a plant owned by Coredif were suspended in the 1980s.

In the wake of the 1973 Middle East War and the Arab oil embargo to certain consumers and the ensuing oil price explosion, plans for expanded nuclear power programmes were announced in several Western countries. Demand for enrichment rose rapidly; and the rush by consumers to sign contracts was hastened by concern that insufficient capacity would be available, concern that was heightened by the

Table A.2   Western World Commercial Enrichment Production and Capacity – 10^6 SWU/a

Owner (Technology holder in brackets)	Technology	Production[a] 1978	1980	1982	Capacity[b] 1984	1990
United States	diffusion	12.7	10.5	9.8	27.3	27.3
	centrifuge	—	—	—	—	2.2
Eurodif (France)	diffusion	—	6.0	6.4	10.8	10.8
URENCO (UK, Netherlands, FR Germany)	centrifuge	0.3	0.5	0.7	1.4	3.0
South Africa	aerodynamic	—	—	—	—	0.3
Brazil	aerodynamic	—	—	—	—	0.3
Japan	centrifuge	—	—	—	0.1	0.2
Techsnabexport (USSR)	diffusion	2.4	3.9	2.1	2.7(e)	2.7(e)
Total		15.4	20.9	19.0	42.3	46.8

[a] In addition to the production/capacity shown, the United Kingdom and France each have 0.4×10^6 SWU/a capacity based on diffusion technology available for military purposes (see: *SIPRI Yearbook 1978*, pp. 30–1). China has offered minor amounts on the world market, from 0.2×10^6 SWU/a capacity based on diffusion technology constructed for military purposes. (see: SIPRI, *Uranium Enrichment and Nuclear Weapon Proliferation*, 1983, p. 224).
[b] Much of the capacity is unlikely to be fully utilised or realised by date shown (see below).
(e) = Estimated capacity available for export from USSR to West: subject to variation. Actual plant capacity thought to be 10 million SWU/a (see text).
Sources: 1978, 1980 Production: INFCE, *Enrichment Availability* (Vienna: IAEA, 1980) pp. 12–13; 1982 Production: Thomas L. Neff, *The International Uranium Market* (Cambridge, Mass.: Ballinger, 1984) pp. 20–1; 1984, 1990 Capacity: Uranium Institute, *Uranium Supply and Demand: Perspectives to 1995* (London: Uranium Institute, 1984) p. 31 (existing and under construction in 1984). (In 1985, the US Department of Energy announced that it was no longer proceeding with the construction of a centrifuge plant at Portsmouth, Ohio and that the Oak Ridge diffusion plant was to be closed indefinitely. The United States is therefore likely to have only 20 million SWU/a capacity available in 1990: see text at end of Appendix.)

alteration by the United States government of her contracting terms in 1973.[21] Eurodif's projected capacity for the early 1980s was soon fully booked and, in 1974, the USA announced that her enrichment plants were fully committed and she could accept no further orders for enrichment. Plans were announced for an expansion in US capacity by means of 'cascade improvement' (CIP) and 'cascade uprating' (CUP) programmes, and for the eventual construction of plants based on centrifuge technology (the first one to be at Portsmouth, Ohio). However the implementation of these plans was delayed by budgetary constraints, political disputes within the United States concerning the relative degree of private and government control over the plants, and uncertainty about the future size of the enrichment market and the share that would be available to the United States industry.[22]

According to one observer, the 1974 American announcement that her capacity was fully booked and no more orders could be accepted

> caught many consumers by surprise, and the removal of the US as a 'reliable' supplier sent a shock wave through the international nuclear industry. Several European countries were already involved in enrichment schemes; the US action gave them greater impetus. More important, nations other than the participants in European projects sensed an insecurity in the supply of enrichment services.[23]

Argentine and Brazilian plans for enrichment capacity to serve their own requirements and those of their Latin American partners are noted in Chapter 2. According to Brenner, concern about security of enrichment supply following the 1974 US announcement was a factor which influenced Brazil's decision to establish her own enrichment plant with West German help.[24] However, the main foreign customer for United States enrichment services was Japan, and the 1974 announcement also undoubtedly accelerated Japanese development of centrifuge technology.[25]

Besides enrichment consumers, other countries with a strong incentive for establishing an enrichment capacity are the uranium-producing countries. By exporting enriched uranium rather than natural uranium concentrate (or 'yellowcake') these countries could roughly double their foreign exchange earnings. The major uranium exporters which have sufficient industrial bases to establish commercial enrichment plants are South Africa, Australia and Canada. Uranium supply contracts between electric utilities and these countries now provide that, if the producers have facilities for it, their uranium production should be upgraded, by conversion to hexafluoride and possibly enrichment, before being exported.[26] Canada already has a conversion capacity and has exported most of her uranium as hexafluoride for some time. Although the establishment of an enrichment capacity has been discussed in the past, her incentives are reduced by her desire to sell CANDU power reactors which are fuelled by natural uranium. South

Africa's plans and motivations for establishing an enrichment capacity are discussed in Chapters 5 and 8. In the mid-1970s there were discussions between Australia and Japan over the joint construction of an enrichment plant using Japanese centrifuge technology with Japan receiving a guaranteed supply of enriched uranium fuel.[27] Subsequently, Australia turned to URENCO for technology; but Australian enrichment plans have since been suspended by her Labour government.

There are substantial economic and technological barriers to the further spread of commercial enrichment capacity. It is mainly because of the economies of scale and huge capital requirements for such plants that European countries have combined in the Eurodif and URENCO arrangements. Now, with the establishment of these multinational ventures and the increased competition they have provided to the enrichment market, consumer nations' concerns about the security of supply have been alleviated. This has helped to reduce the incentives for establishing further enrichment plants. Concern about nuclear weapons proliferation dangers has thereby been allayed.[28] Moreover, the supply and demand prospects for uranium enrichment have completely changed in the last decade. With the growth of planned capacity, particularly in Europe, and the decline in demand due to the slowdown in the growth of the nuclear power industry, the American and Eurodif diffusion plants are only producing at half capacity and there is now the prospect of considerable excess enrichment capacity well into the 1990s. The already large stockpiles of low-enriched uranium have grown; and a secondary market has developed in enriched uranium supplied by electric utilities which had contracted for more enrichment than they subsequently needed. These factors all increase consumers' security of supply and reduce incentives to construct additional capacity.[29]

A COMPARISON OF ENRICHMENT TECHNOLOGIES

The discussion in the previous section of the development of commercial enrichment capacity has concentrated on diffusion and centrifuge plants. It is necessary in this final section to compare these technologies with the nozzle or aerodynamic enrichment process (or processes), from both economic and weapons-proliferation points of view. The important technical parameters, such as the number of separation stages and the energy consumption, are shown for each process in Table A.3. Finally other technologies which have prospects for development will be briefly mentioned. Some of these give cause for some concern about their implications for weapons proliferation.

Diffusion Technology

Considering first, briefly, the *gaseous diffusion* process, the principle of which is the preferential diffusion of lighter molecules of gas through a thin porous membrane or 'barrier' to a region of lower temperature and pressure: the process depends on the difference in molecular weight between the two isotopic forms of gaseous uranium hexafluoride. The key to the acquisition of diffusion technology is the development of a suitable barrier. Details of the materials used for barriers and their manufacture are strictly classified.[30] The main disadvantage of the process is the huge electric power consumption (accounting for up to three-quarters of the total operating costs for the older American plants) required mainly for the compression and cooling of the hexafluoride gas, at each stage of a process which typically has many stages.[31] There are substantial economies of scale and, because of the large capital cost of a competitively-size plant and because of the nature of the technology, considerable resources of industrial infrastructure are called for.[32]

Centrifuge Technology

The *gas centrifuge* enrichment process is based on the difference in centrifugal force experienced by molecules of different mass when rotating at high velocities in a cylinder. The process has long been considered an attractive method of enrichment and the development of stronger and lighter materials has now made rotational velocities of up to 700m/s possible.[33] The energy consumption is relatively small (less than a tenth that of diffusion plants) due to the operation of the centrifuges in a vacuum and low friction losses in the bearings.

The inherent advantage of the technology is that the plants can be built in relatively small units on a modular basis, and then expanded, by adding other stages in parallel, according to market demands. Although there are economies of scale for the centrifuge process, they are much less than for other enrichment processes. (The economies of scale tend to be in the production of the thousands of centrifuges needed for a commercial plant rather than in the operation of the plant itself.) The small unit size and low power consumption of the centrifuge process are worrying aspects from the point of view of nuclear proliferation, as they would make detection of an unsafeguarded plant difficult. Moreover, several cascades operated in parallel to produce low-enriched uranium could be rearranged in series to produce high-enriched uranium simply by 'altering the plumbing'.[34]

Aerodynamic Technology

The *aerodynamic* process which has been most developed, and about which there is most information available, is the *separation nozzle* process, developed by E. W. Becker at the Karlsruhe Nuclear Research Centre (Gesellschaft für Kernforschung (GfK)) in West Germany.[35] Becker published his first papers in the mid-1950s, and a 2000SWU/a pilot plant was started at Karlsruhe in 1967. This plant was shut down in 1972. In 1970 the Essen-based electric utility Essener Steinkohlen Elektrizitäts AG (STEAG) obtained from GfK world rights for the commercial exploitation of the separation nozzle process. Both GfK and STEAG are controlled by the West German government.

Figure A.2 shows a cross-section of the slit-shaped separation element. By means of pressure changes and the configuration of the slit arrangement, the feed, in the form of a sheet of a gas, is given a centrifugal acceleration to a supersonic speed. Dilution of the uranium hexafluoride with hydrogen (or, alternatively, helium) enables a higher velocity to be realised. The centrifugal force field sets up a concentration gradient in the gas mixture, with the gas adjacent to the outside wall enriched in U238 relative to U235. This enables a fraction enriched in U238 to be separated from a fraction enriched in U235 and accounts for the process being alternatively named the 'stationary-walled centrifuge' in South Africa. A knife-edge downstream from the slit divides the stream into a more deflected inside stream enriched in U235 and a less deflected outside stream enriched in U238 (i.e. depleted in U235). The position of the knife-edge or paring blade is known as the 'cut'. If the cut is decreased, less enriched material is obtained, but the degree of enrichment, known as the separation factor, is raised. The blades and grooves have to be machined to tolerances of one micron (10^{-4} cm). According to one expert: 'Practical construction is feasible only for highly industrialised nations with a broad technical base and a substantial, skilled labour pool.'[36]

Nevertheless, it seems to be generally accepted that nozzle technology is less demanding in terms of manufacturing capability than diffusion or centrifuge technologies.[37] Its great disadvantage is the large amount of electric power it consumes in compressing the gas mixture. Experience with developing the technology in Brazil has caused estimates for both

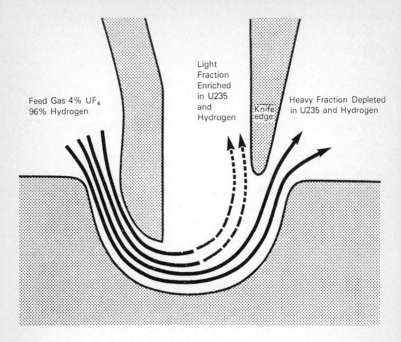

Figure A.2   Cross-section of Tubular Separation Element for Becker Nozzle Process

capital and energy costs for commercial-sized nozzle plants to be raised substantially. (When the production plant is eventually built in Brazil the separation elements used may provide a double deflection of the depleted stream with another knife-edge separating an intermediate fraction which is recycled to the feed stream in a sort of internal reflux.[38])

The demonstration plant being built by the Uranium Enrichment Corporation (UCOR) in South Africa is based on the same principle as the Becker process. Although the name sometimes used to describe it, the Advanced Vortex Tube process, has led some observers to suspect that the feed gas is accelerated in a vortex, a concept that originated in the United States, this is not certain.[39] According to the standard text on enrichment technology, features of the South African process, in particular the separation element, are surrounded by 'considerable industrial secrecy'.[40]

The South African plants employ a much lower cut (one-twentieth) than the original Becker process. This increases the separation factor, as the enriched stream is only one-twentieth of the volume of the feed stream, but it means that many more stages (separating elements) are required. This could have made the energy consumption prohibitively expensive; but the problem was overcome to a large extent by adopting a 'helikon' cascade system using an axial flow compressor that could handle several streams of different isotopic composition simultaneously without mixing. This helikon technique made possible the design of a module containing between ten and twenty separating elements and using only two compressors.[41] The energy consumption is nevertheless still large and comparable to that of the Becker process.

Comparison of Enrichment Technologies

Technical features of the diffusion, centrifuge and aerodynamic processes are compared in Table A.3 and explained below briefly and at the risk of oversimplification. Quantitative values for the different parameters vary from plant to plant and according to the way plants are operated. The ranges of values shown in Table A.3 reflect this and the fact that the table is based on information extracted from a number of sources. The data shown should be treated with some caution, because reliable information is difficult to obtain, many of the technical features of the enrichment processes being closely guarded secrets. For example, the minimum number of stages required for the production of high-enriched uranium, the material inventory and the equilibrium time of a plant all relate to its proliferation potential, and technology holders may therefore be reluctant to disclose this information. As there has been no experience with operating aerodynamic plants of greater than pilot plant size (6000 SWU/a), information regarding power consumption for these plants should be treated with particular caution.

The *separation factor* is a measure of the degree of enrichment per stage. The greater the separation factor, the fewer stages are required. It would seem that, in their UCOR plant, the South Africans have been able to improve on Becker's value (1.015) for the separation factor and that the aerodynamic processes compare favourably with diffusion enrichment, with regard to the number of stages required. However, because the UCOR process uses a cut of only one-twentieth, compared with a cut of one-quarter used in the Becker process, many more stages are required for the South African process. Nevertheless, UCOR has found that it is possible to assemble this large number of stages in a relatively small number of 'modules' using the helikon cascade technique.

It should be noted, of course, that the minimum number of stages

172

Table A.3 Comparison of Enrichment Technologies

Technical parameter	Centrifuge	Diffusion	Aerodynamic Nozzle	Aerodynamic Helikon
Separation factor	1.200–1.500	1.002–1.004	1.015	1.025–1.030
Stage cut	about 0.50	0.50	0.25	0.05
Number of stages*				
for 3% enrichment	10–13	1000–1700	550–750	1800–1900
for 90% enrichment	35	3500–4000	2000	n.a.
Power consumption (KWh/SWU)	100–400	2100–3000	3000–4000	3000–3500
Material inventory	very low	very high	intermediate	intermediate
Equilibrium time (approx) (for 3% enriched product)	few minutes	3 weeks	1 day	16 hours

n.a. not available

* minimum requirement with 0.3 per cent tails assay and no batch recycling. (For helikon process, 1848 stages are assembled in about 100 modules, to produce a 3 per cent enriched uranium product, with 0.25 per cent tails assay).

172

Sources: Benedict *et al.*, *Nuclear Chemical Engineering* (New York: McGraw-Hill, 1979) p. 895; Greenwood *et al.*, *Nuclear Power and Weapons Proliferation* (London: IISS, 1976) pp. 22–3, 25, 47; INFCE, *Enrichment Availability* (Vienna: IAEA, 1980) pp. 10, 38–44, 60, 62; SIPRI, *Uranium Enrichment and Nuclear Weapon Proliferation* (London: Taylor & Francis, 1983) pp. 20, 125–7, 134, 140–5, 188; *Nuclear Engineering International*, November 1976, p. 51.

required, as shown in Table A.3, takes no account of the size of each stage. For example, for enrichment plants of similar capacity, a centrifuge plant would in fact use more centrifuges (arranged in several parallel cascades) than the number of large-sized stages (arranged in a single cascade) required in a diffusion plant for the same feed, product and tails assays. However because of the smaller *minimum* number of stages required and the relative ease with which cascades arranged in parallel (to produce low-enriched uranium) can be rearranged in series (to produce high-enriched uranium), centrifuge technology poses more potential for nuclear weapons proliferation than diffusion technology.

Likewise jet nozzle technology is more proliferation-prone than diffusion technology because the technological requirements for producing the separating elements are less, and fewer stages (separating elements) need to be added in series to convert a plant producing low-enriched uranium into one producing high-enriched uranium.[42]

The *material inventory* of an enrichment plant is the amount of material (in the form of hexafluoride gas) contained within the plant at any time during the normal operation of the plant. This determines the *equilibrium time*: the time elapsing before the production by the cascades is in equilibrium with the product and tails assays desired. If an enrichment process has a small uranium hold-up (or inventory) and a short equilibrium time it may be easier to evade international safeguards and use the plant to produce HEU (weapons-grade uranium), by 'sneak' batch recycling of the product stream.[43] The equilibrium time for the helikon process is sixteen hours compared with an equilibrium time of a few weeks for a diffusion plant of similar separative work capacity, operating with the same feed, product and tails assays. Note that the values shown in Table A.3 are for a low-enriched uranium product. For a 90 per cent enriched uranium (HEU) product, the equilibrium times would be much greater.

The *specific power consumption* of an enrichment process relates more to the economic viability of the technology than to its proliferation potential. Electric power consumption would be only of minor concern if the separative work requirement was for only a few small explosive devices (see Table A.1 above). In this case, cost would not be a major consideration.[44] If however an enrichment plant is to be justified economically as providing a commercial service for fuel production, energy consumption becomes a crucial consideration. It can be seen from Table A.3 that aerodynamic enrichment methods consume more power (for compression of the gas mixture) than the other methods. Moreover, whilst the values given for the specific power consumption of the centrifuge and diffusion technologies are reliable, those given for the aerodynamic methods are only based on experience with the small plants currently being operated or constructed. As the Becker nozzle technology is being developed in Brazil, estimates for the power consumption have since been raised substantially.

Other Enrichment Techniques

Finally, mention should be made of other enrichment methods, most of which, like the various ion-exchange processes, are still being investigated on a laboratory-scale and have not yet been developed further. Electromagnetic enrichment, whereby an electromagnetic field is used to produce a rotating plasma, and ions of differing mass then experience differing centrifugal forces (rather like the centrifuge enrichment method), is one such technique that has not gone far beyond the laboratory stage, although it was used at great expense by the Americans, in a device known as the calutron, to produce some of the enrichment for the Hiroshima bomb. (It was closed down soon afterwards when it was realised that the diffusion method was cheaper.)[45] A chemical exchange process, which is alleged to confer non-proliferation advantages because of its large inventory and hence its long lead time (an equilibrium time of over a year for a low-enriched uranium product), has been developed as far as the pilot plant stage in France and Japan.[46] However, because of the current and projected global overcapacity in the enrichment market, none of these processes is likely to have significant impact this century. The exception is laser isotope separation (LIS), which could become commercially competitive with the established enrichment technologies and which has grave implications for weapons proliferation.

It may become possible to achieve enrichment to either reactor-grade low-enriched uranium or weapons-grade high-enriched uranium by selective laser excitation of either uranium atoms in vapour form (AVLIS) or uranium hexafluoride molecules (MLIS) using only *one* enrichment stage, with negligible tails assay and relatively low power consumption. Laser enrichment may also be used to 'strip' depleted uranium, stockpiled at existing enrichment plants, to extract the remaining 0.2 to 0.3 per cent of uranium-235 in the tails. If done on a large scale this would have the effect of extending uranium resources and delaying the advent of the breeder reactor and the plutonium economy (see Chapter 2). The possibility that, because of the very small material inventory and equilibrium time for the laser technique, the production of HEU (weapons-grade uranium) may be relatively easy and a plant could be readily concealed makes development of this technology worrying for those concerned about weapons proliferation.[47] Moreover research into the AVLIS uranium enrichment technique in the United States (and possibly elsewhere) is being undertaken in conjunction with research into its use for separating the fissile plutonium-239 from the other plutonium isotopes found in spent fuel from power reactors.[48] This research is being conducted primarily for military purposes, thus blurring the distinction, first drawn by President Eisenhower in his Atoms for Peace speech, between 'the peaceful atom' and 'the military atom'. It has been the assumption that such a distinction can be made which has underlied IAEA safeguards and most other non-proliferation measures since 1953.

A small plant to demonstrate the AVLIS process developed by the Lawrence Livermore National Laboratory in California is due to be completed in 1987. Larger-scale production is possible in the mid-1990s if, as now seems likely, the process proves commercially viable. The construction of the centrifuge plant at Portsmouth, Ohio, has now been abandoned and the diffusion plant at Oak Ridge has been closed down indefinitely, in order that more money is available to develop the AVLIS process. Besides this work in the USA, experimental work on laser enrichment is being carried out in several other countries, including Israel, Japan, the Soviet Union and several European countries. France in particular has suggested that she may also build a commercial laser enrichment plant by the late 1990s.[49]

Notes and References

Introduction

1. See, for example, Leonard Beaton and John Maddox, *The Spread of Nuclear Weapons* (London: Chatto & Windus, 1962) p. 187.
2. A. R. Newby-Fraser, *Chain Reaction: Twenty Years of Nuclear Research and Development in South Africa* (Pretoria: Atomic Energy Board, 1979).
3. Zdenek Červenka and Barbara Rogers, *The Nuclear Axis: Secret Collaboration between West Germany and South Africa* (London: Julian Friedmann, 1978).
4. *Fact v. Fiction: Rebuttal of the Charges of Alleged Cooperation between the Federal Republic of Germany and South Africa in the Nuclear and Military Fields* (Bonn: Press and Information Office of the Government of the Federal Republic of Germany, 1978).
5. See, for example, the review of *Nuclear Axis* by S. J. Warnecke in *Survival*, 21 (May/June 1979) 141–2.
6. Červenka and Rogers, *The Nuclear Axis*, pp. 54–8.
7. The various sources, too numerous to mention here, are detailed in the notes to Chapter 5 and the bibliography at the end of the book.
8. UN Centre for Disarmament, Department of Political and Security Council Affairs, *South Africa's Plan and Capability in the Nuclear Field*, Report of the Secretary-General, Document A/35/402 (New York: United Nations, 1981).

Chapter 1

1. For an introduction to the technology of nuclear weapons and nuclear power, see: Ted Greenwood, George W. Rathjens and Jack Ruina, *Nuclear Power and Weapons Proliferation*, Adelphi Papers no. 130 (London: International Institute for Strategic Studies, 1976); or J. Rotblat, 'Nuclear Energy and Nuclear Weapon Proliferation', in Stockholm International Peace Research Institute, *Nuclear Energy and Nuclear Weapons Proliferation* (London: Taylor & Francis, 1979).
2. International Atomic Energy Agency, *IAEA Safeguards Glossary* (Vienna: IAEA, 1980) p. 21, para 89.
3. Under the Non-Proliferation Treaty (NPT), the following are recognised as nuclear weapon states (the year when a nuclear device was first detonated being given in brackets): the United States of America (1945), the Soviet Union (1949), the United Kingdom (1952), France (1960) and the People's Republic of China (1964). The NPT and IAEA are further discussed in the next chapter.
4. *Isotopes* of elements have the same number of protons and are therefore chemically identical; but they have different numbers of neutrons in their nuclei. For example, atoms of uranium-233 (U233), uranium-235 (U235) and uranium-238 (U238) have the same number of protons (92), but they

have different numbers of neutrons (141, 143 and 146, respectively), and so have different physical properties. In particular, isotopes have slightly different masses.

5. Heavy water contains deuterium, an isotope of hydrogen, the normal constituent of water ('light water').

6. Greenwood *et al.*, *Nuclear Power and Weapons Proliferation*, pp. 3, 5. This section is based on this work.

7. Albert Wohlstetter, Thomas Brown, Gregory Jones, David McGarvey, Henry Rowan, Vincent Taylor and Roberta Wohlstetter, *Moving Towards Life in a Nuclear Armed Crowd?*, Final Report, ACDA/PAB-263 (Los Angeles: Pan Heuristics, 1976) pp. 22–45. See also a summary of this report by the same authors in 'The Military Potential of Civilian Nuclear Energy: Moving Towards Life in a Nuclear Armed Crowd', *Minerva*, XV (1977) 431–2; and a comparison of similar estimates in Thomas W. Graham, 'The Economics of Producing Nuclear Weapons in "Nth" countries', in Dagobert L. Brito, Michael D. Intriligator and Adele E. Wick (eds), *Strategies for Managing Nuclear Proliferation* (Lexington, Mass: D.C. Heath and Co., 1983) pp. 12–14.

8. Stephen M. Meyer, *The Dynamics of Nuclear Proliferation* (University of Chicago Press, 1984) p. 27; George H. Quester, 'The Politics of Twenty Nuclear Powers', in Richard Rosecrance (ed.), *The Future of the International Strategic System* (San Francisco: Chandler, 1972) pp. 73–4; Kenneth N. Waltz, *The Spread of Nuclear Weapons: More May Be Better*, Adelphi Papers no. 171 (London: International Institute for Strategic Studies, 1981) pp. 14–15.

9. See note 7 above. Greenwood *et al.* suggest a figure of US $195 million for a plant big enough to produce enriched uranium for 100 weapons a year (Greenwood *et al.*, *Nuclear Power and Weapons Proliferation*, p. 25).

10. See note 7 above. Greenwood *et al.* suggest the cost might be US $10–25 million, the plant taking three to seven years to build (ibid., p. 18).

11. Ibid., p. 6.

12. Rotblat, 'Nuclear Energy and Nuclear Weapon Proliferation', p. 402.

13. J. C. Hopkins, 'Nuclear Weapon Technology', in Stockholm International Peace Research Institute, *Nuclear Proliferation Problems* (Cambridge, Mass: The MIT Press, 1974) p. 114.

14. See: Lewis A. Dunn, 'Half Past India's Bang', *Foreign Policy*, no. 36 (1979) 79–80; Greenwood *et al.*, *Nuclear Power and Weapons Proliferation*, p. 29.

Chapter 2

1. For a dissenting opinion to this otherwise generally accepted conventional wisdom see: Kenneth N. Waltz, *The Spread of Nuclear Weapons: More May Be Better*, Adelphi Papers no. 171 (London: International Institute for Strategic Studies, 1981).

2. See Chapter 4, Table 4.2. below.

3. Margaret Gowing, *Britain and Atomic Energy, 1939–1945* (London: Macmillan, 1964) pp. 307–19; Margaret Gowing, *Independence and*

Deterrence: Britain and Atomic Energy, 1945–1952, Vol. 1, 'Policy-making' (London: Macmillan, 1974) p. 355.

4. Arnold Kramish, 'Four Decades of Living with the Genie: United States Nuclear Export Policy', in Robert Boardman and James F. Keeley (eds), *Nuclear Exports and World Politics* (New York: St Martin's Press, 1983) pp. 18–19.

5. Peter Pringle and James Spigelman, *The Nuclear Barons* (New York: Holt, Rinehart & Winston, 1981) pp. 202–4, 506–7, 526.

6. H. L. Nieburg, *Nuclear Secrecy and Foreign Policy* (Washington DC: Public Affairs Press, 1964) pp. 40–3.

7. Stockholm International Peace Research Institute, *Uranium Enrichment and Nuclear Weapon Proliferation* (London: Taylor & Francis, 1983) pp. 196–7. See also the Appendix below.

8. Nieburg, *Nuclear Secrecy and Foreign Policy*, pp. 66–7, 89–101.

9. John G. Stoessinger, 'Atoms for Peace: The International Atomic Energy Agency', in: Commission to Study the Organization of Peace, *Organizing Peace in the Nuclear Age* (New York University Press, 1959) pp. 121–4; Bernhard G. Bechhoefer, 'Negotiating the Statute of the International Atomic Energy Agency', *International Organization*, 13 (1959) 42–3, 45–6.

10. The choice of nations to join the Soviet Union and the eight Western nations in negotiating the IAEA statute was rationalised in terms of their resources of 'source material': Czechoslovakia was a uranium producer; India and Brazil both possessed large thorium deposits. (See Stoessinger, 'Atoms for Peace: The International Atomic Energy Agency', p. 119.) The notion that the few nations considered able to produce uranium (or thorium) could control nuclear commerce in the interests of non-proliferation persisted.

11. Bertrand Goldschmidt, *The Atomic Complex: A Worldwide Political History of Nuclear Energy* (La Grange Park, Ill.: American Nuclear Society, 1982) pp. 119, 279–81; Bertrand Goldschmidt, 'The Origins of the International Atomic Energy Agency', *IAEA Bulletin*, 19 (August 1977) 17–18; Stoessinger, 'Atoms for Peace: The International Atomic Energy Agency,' pp. 142, 157–8. See also Chapter 4 below.

12. See also Chapter 4 below.

13. David Fischer, *International Safeguards 1979* (London: International Consultative Group on Nuclear Energy (Rockefeller Foundation/Royal Institute of International Affairs), 1979) p. 29 (emphasis in original).

14. International Atomic Energy Agency, *The Structure and Content of Agreements between the Agency and States Required in Connection with the Treaty on the Non-proliferation of Nuclear Weapons*, INFCIRC/153 (Vienna: IAEA, 1972) paragraph 128.

15. L. W. Herron, 'A Lawyer's View of Safeguards and Non-proliferation', *IAEA Bulletin*, 24 (September 1982) 36, 38.

16. The text of the Non-Proliferation Treaty is reproduced in a number of works, including: Michael J. Brenner, *Nuclear Power and Non-proliferation: The Remaking of US Policy* (Cambridge University Press, 1981) pp. 256–66; William C. Potter, *Nuclear Power and Nonproliferation: An Interdisciplinary Perspective* (Cambridge, Mass.:

Oelgeschlager, Gunn and Hain, 1982) pp. 243–6.

17.　George Quester, *The Politics of Nuclear Proliferation* (Baltimore, Md.: Johns Hopkins University Press, 1973) pp. 199, 201, 204.

18.　Potter, *Nuclear Power and Nonproliferation*, pp. 158, 160; International Institute for Strategic Studies, *Strategic Survey 1979* (London: IISS, 1980) p. 16; B. Sanders, 'Nuclear Exporting Policies', in Stockholm International Peace Research Institute, *Nuclear Energy and Nuclear Weapons Proliferation* (London: Taylor & Francis, 1979) pp. 246–7.

19.　International Institute for Strategic Studies, *Strategic Survey 1981–1982* (London: IISS, 1982) pp. 21–2.

20.　IISS, *Strategic Survey 1979*, p. 16; IISS, *Strategic Survey 1981–1982*, p. 21; Lewis A. Dunn, *Controlling the Bomb: Nuclear Proliferation in the 1980s* (New Haven: Yale University Press, 1982) p. 37; Stockholm International Peace Research Institute, *World Armaments and Disarmament, SIPRI Yearbook 1981* (London: Taylor & Francis, 1981) p. 300. See the Appendix for a discussion of the URENCO enrichment consortium and centrifuge enrichment technology.

21.　International Institute for Strategic Studies, *Strategic Survey 1976* (London: IISS, 1977) p. 115; William Perry and Sheila Kern, 'The Brazilian Nuclear Program in A Foreign Policy Context', *Comparative Strategy*, 1 (1978) 62–3; Jozef Goldblat and Victor Millan, 'Militarization and Arms Control in Latin America', in Stockholm International Peace Research Institute, *World Armaments and Disarmament, SIPRI Yearbook 1982* (London: Taylor & Francis, 1982) p. 418; Judith Perera, 'Brazil Struggles with Nuclear Power', *New Scientist*, 17 May 1984, p. 31.

22.　Goldblat and Millan, 'Militarization and Arms Control in Latin America', p. 418; Perry and Kern, 'The Brazilian Nuclear Program in A Foreign Policy Context', p. 62; Dunn, *Controlling the Bomb*, p. 33. These matters are further discussed below and in Chapters 4, 5 and 8.

23.　See: P. Boskma, 'Jet Nozzle and Vortex Tube Enrichment Technologies', in SIPRI, *Nuclear Energy and Nuclear Weapons Proliferation*, p. 68; Goldblat and Millan, 'Militarization and Arms Control in Latin America', p. 419; *Science*, 30 May 1975, pp. 913–14.

24.　The jet nozzle enrichment technology is discussed in the Appendix. The possible role of STEAG in developing the same or similar enrichment technology in South Africa is recounted in Chapter 5.

25.　Hartmut Krugmann, 'The German–Brazilian Nuclear Deal', *Bulletin of the Atomic Scientists*, 37 (February 1981) 34; James J. Glackin, 'The Dangerous Drift in Uranium Enrichment', *Bulletin of the Atomic Scientists*, 32 (February 1976) 22; International Nuclear Fuel Cycle Evaluation, *Enrichment Availability*, Report of INFCE Working Group 2 (Vienna: IAEA, 1980) pp. 11, 70–2; *Nuclear Fuel*, 26 April 1982.

26.　See: Dunn, *Controlling the Bomb*, p. 33; Potter, *Nuclear Power and Nonproliferation*, pp. 107–9; Ted Greenwood, George W. Rathjens and Jack Ruina, *Nuclear Power and Weapons Proliferation*, Adelphi Papers no. 130 (London: International Institute for Strategic Studies, 1976) p. 29.

27.　Pringle and Spigelman, *The Nuclear Barons*, pp. 380–1, 545–6; Brenner,

Nuclear Power and Non-proliferation, pp. 94–6, 182–6.

28. Dunn, *Controlling the Bomb*, p. 34; Sanders, 'Nuclear Exporting Policies', pp. 242–3; Brenner, *Nuclear Power and Non-proliferation*, pp. 94–6; Potter, *Nuclear Power and Nonproliferation*, p. 45.

29. The NSG trigger list is contained in IAEA document INFCIRC/254, published in 1978. The Zangger Committee trigger list is contained in IAEA document INFCIRC/209, first published in 1974. The details and significance of the NSG guidelines are discussed in: Stockholm International Peace Research Institute, *World Armaments and Disarmament, SIPRI Yearbook 1977* (Cambridge, Mass.: The MIT Press, 1977) pp. 20–3.

30. Ibid., p. 21. For the significance of these items for the various enrichment technologies, see the Appendix below.

31. *Nucleonics Week*, 2 February 1984.

32. See also: Greenwood *et al.*, *Nuclear Power and Weapons Proliferation*, p. 29; Dunn, *Controlling the Bomb*, p. 42.

33. Sanders, 'Nuclear Exporting Policies', p. 247. We may note here that, at the time of the London Club deliberations, France was concerned to obtain the contract for the construction of the Koeberg power reactors in South Africa (see: Chapter 5 below; and William Walker and Måns Lönnroth, *Nuclear Power Struggles: Industrial Competition and Proliferation Control* (London: George Allen & Unwin, 1983) p. 145).

34. Potter, *Nuclear Power and Nonproliferation*, p. 217; Dunn, *Controlling the Bomb*, pp. 41–3; Sanders, 'Nuclear Exporting Policies,' p. 247; *SIPRI Yearbook 1977*, p. 23.

35. *Nucleonics Week*, 1 March 1984; 8 March 1984; 19 July 1984. *Nuclear Engineering International*, September 1984, p. 11. South Africa's agreement in 1984 to conduct her nuclear exports 'in line with the spirit, principles and goals' of the London Club guidelines is discussed in Chapter 6 below.

36. Brenner, *Nuclear Power and Non-proliferation*, pp. 103–4, 113–14; Potter, *Nuclear Power and Nonproliferation*, pp. 46–7.

37. A good analysis of the domestic United States political situation leading to the passage of the Nuclear Non-Proliferation Act is found in: Brenner, *Nuclear Power and Non-proliferation*, pp. 186–92.

38. Sverre Lodgaard, 'Nuclear Power and Nuclear Proliferation: Export Policies and Proliferation Resistance', in Stockholm International Peace Research Institute, *World Armaments and Disarmament, SIPRI Yearbook 1979* (London: Taylor & Francis, 1979) p. 323. See also the next section of this chapter and the Appendix below.

39. *SIPRI Yearbook 1977*, p. 361; IISS, *Strategic Survey 1981–1982*, p. 23; Bertrand Goldschmidt, 'A Historical Survey of Nonproliferation Policies,' *International Security*, 2 (1977) 214; *Nucleonics Week*, 30 September 1982; 16 December 1982.

40. Joseph A. Yager, 'Influencing Incentives and Capabilities', in Joseph A. Yager (ed.), *Nonproliferation and US Foreign Policy* (Washington DC: The Brookings Institution, 1980) p. 420.

41. See Chapter 4, Tables 4.1 and 4.2 below.

42. Henry D. Jacoby, 'Uranium Dependence and the Proliferation Problem', *Technology Review*, June 1977, p. 19; Potter, *Nuclear Power and Nonproliferation*, pp. 49–50, 120–1; Lodgaard, 'Nuclear Power and Nuclear Proliferation: Export Policies and Proliferation Resistance', p. 322.

43. See Chapter 4 below.

44. The following two paragraphs are based on the following sources: Steven J. Warnecke, *Uranium, Nonproliferation and Energy Security*, Atlantic Paper no. 37 (Paris: Atlantic Institute for International Affairs, 1979) pp. 96–7; The Uranium Institute, *The Uranium Equation: The Balance of Supply and Demand 1980–1995* (London: Mining Journal Books, 1981) p. 32; Marian Radetzki, *Uranium: A Strategic Source of Energy* (London: Croom Helm, 1981) p. 132; Dr A. vonKienlin, 'Commercial Effects of Current Non-proliferation Policies', in Mining Journal Books Ltd (ed.), *Uranium Supply and Demand* (London: Mining Journal Books, 1978) p. 308. Historic figures for world uranium production are shown in Chapter 4, Table 4.2 below.

45. IISS, *Strategic Survey 1981–1982*, pp. 20–2.

46. Potter, *Nuclear Power and Nonproliferation*, pp. 115–16; Yager 'Influencing Incentives and Capabilities,' p. 421; Gerard Smith and George Rathjens, 'Reassessing Nuclear Nonproliferation Policy', *Foreign Affairs*, 59 (1981) 887. Developments in the enrichment market during the 1970s are described in more detail in the Appendix below.

47. Brenner, *Nuclear Power and Non-proliferation*, pp. 54–5.

48. Thomas L. Neff and Henry D. Jacoby, 'Nonproliferation Strategy in a Changing Nuclear Fuel Market,' *Foreign Affairs*, 57 (1979) 1136–7.

49. Lodgaard, 'Nuclear Power and Nuclear Proliferation: Export Policies and Proliferation Resistance', p. 321.

50. Neff and Jacoby, 'Nonproliferation Strategy in a Changing Nuclear Fuel Market', p. 1137.

51. Ibid., pp. 1137–8. See also: Lodgaard, 'Nuclear Power and Nuclear Proliferation: Export and Proliferation Resistance,' p. 322; Warnecke, *Uranium, Nonproliferation and Energy Security*, p. 96.

52. This description of Argentina's announcement of an enrichment plant and the reasons for its development is based on a number of sources including: Daniel Poneman, 'Nuclear Proliferation Prospects for Argentina', *Orbis*, 27 (1984) 857–8, 876–7; Judith Perera, 'Argentina's Nuclear Red Herring', *New Scientist*, 8 December 1983, pp. 726–7; and editorial in ibid., p. 718; *Nucleonics Week*, 24 November 1983; 14 February 1985; *Nuclear News*, January 1984, p. 60. Brazilian nuclear developments have been described above. Diffusion enrichment technology is described in the Appendix.

53. The arrangement whereby South Africa obtained enrichment for the first fuel loads for her Koeberg reactors is described in Chapter 5 below. For details and background to the arrangements whereby Brazil and India were able to obtain enriched uranium from European suppliers, see the following: *The Energy Daily*, 19 October 1981; *Nature*, 29 October 1981, p. 695; 9 December 1982, p. 475; *Nuclear Engineering International*,

September 1982, p. 9; January 1983, p. 7; *Nuclear Fuel*, 2 August 1982; 6 December 1982; *Nucleonics Week*, 5 August 1982; 26 August 1982; 2 September 1982; 16 September 1982; 14 October 1982; 18 November 1982; 2 December 1982; *Science*, 13 August 1982, pp. 614–15.

54. Stockholm International Peace Research Institute, *World Armaments and Disarmament, SIPRI Yearbook 1983* (London: Taylor & Francis, 1983) pp. 71, 88, 90; Thomas L. Neff, *The International Uranium Market* (Cambridge, Mass.:Ballinger, 1984) pp. 66–8; IISS, *Strategic Survey 1981–1982*, p. 19; *The Energy Daily*, 17 July 1981; 9 September 1981; *Nuclear Fuel*, 20 July 1981; *Nucleonics Week*, 17 June 1982; 10 March 1983; *Science*, 31 July 1981, pp. 522–3; 25 June 1982, p. 1388.

55. International Nuclear Fuel Cycle Evaluation, *INFCE Summary Volume* (Vienna:IAEA, 1980) pp. 18–19, 24, 51; Potter, *Nuclear Power and Nonproliferation*, pp. 50–1.

56. U. Farinelli, 'A Preliminary Evaluation of the Technical Aspects of INFCE', in SIPRI, *Nuclear Energy and Nuclear Weapons Proliferation*, p. 266. See also Potter, *Nuclear power and Nonproliferation*, pp. 114–15.

57. See Chapter 4 below.

58. The above account of recent developments in the markets for natural and enriched uranium is based on the following sources: Thomas L. Neff and Henry D. Jacoby, 'World Uranium: Softening Markets and Rising Security,' *Technology Review*, January 1981, pp. 20–30; The Uranium Institute, *The Uranium Equation*, pp. 18, 21, 40; The Uranium Institute, *Uranium Supply and Demand: Perspectives to 1995* (London: The Uranium Institute, 1984) pp. 4, 58, 65, 73; Neff, *The International Uranium Market*, pp. 284, 297–8; *Mining Journal*, 24 July 1981; 11 September 1981; 19 February 1982.

59. Neff and Jacoby, 'World Uranium: Softening Markets and Rising Security', p. 29; Smith and Rathjens, 'Reassessing Nuclear Nonproliferation Policy', p. 893.

60. Potter, *Nuclear Power and Nonproliferation*, pp. 53, 109–10; Dunn, *Controlling the Bomb*, pp. 35–6, 39–40.

61. United States military and economic aid to Pakistan had previously been cut off by Act of Congress, because of that nation's continuing development of its enrichment and reprocessing plants.

62. Succinct summaries of 'nth' countries' possible motivations for acquiring nuclear weapons can be found in the following: Waltz, *The Spread of Nuclear Weapons*, pp. 7–8; Dunn, *Controlling the Bomb*, p. 68; Potter, *Nuclear Power and Nonproliferation*, pp. 131–44; Yager, 'Influencing Incentives and Capabilities', p. 408; Richard K. Betts, 'Paranoids, Pygmies, Pariahs and Nonproliferation', *Foreign Policy*, no. 26 (1977) 163–4.

63. J. Goldblat, 'Implementation of the Non-Proliferation Treaty', in SIPRI, *Nuclear Energy and Nuclear Weapons Proliferation*, p. 347.

64. Text of President Reagan's July 16 statement on proliferation, reproduced in *Nuclear Fuel*, 20 July 1981. See also: IISS, *Strategic Survey 1981–1982*, pp. 22–3.

65. See Yager, 'Influencing Incentives and Capabilities', pp. 409–13; Potter, *Nuclear Power and Nonproliferation*, pp. 199–209.

Chapter 3

1. This is admittedly a crude and debatable generalisation of what characterises the pariah powers; but space does not permit a thorough discussion, and for our purposes it will suffice.
2. Relations between South Africa and other African states are further discussed below.
3. Chester A. Crocker, *South Africa's Defense Posture: Coping with Vulnerability*, The Washington Papers, vol. 9, no. 8 (Beverly Hills: Sage Publications, 1981) pp. 71–3.
4. See, for example: Kenneth L. Adelman, 'The Strategy of Defiance: South Africa', *Comparative Strategy*, 1 (1978) 35; International Institute for Strategic Studies, *Strategic Survey 1981–1982* (London: IISS, 1982) pp. 111, 113.
5. See: Crocker *South Africa's Defense Posture*, pp. 93–4.
6. Manpower estimates in this paragraph are taken from: International Institute for Strategic Studies, *The Military Balance 1985–1986* (London: IISS, 1985) pp. 106–7.
7. This paragraph is based, *inter alia*, on: Chester A. Crocker, 'Current and Projected Military Balances in Southern Africa', in Richard E. Bissell and Chester A. Crocker (eds), *South Africa into the 1980s* (Boulder: Westview Press, 1979) pp. 71, 82–5, 88.
8. Ibid., pp. 88–90; Colin Legum (ed.), *Africa Contemporary Record*, Annual Survey and Documents, XV, 1983–1984 (New York: Africana Publishing Co., 1985) p. B 718.
9. The remainder of this paragraph is based, *inter alia*, on ibid.; and William Gutteridge, *South Africa: Strategy for Survival?*, Conflict Studies no. 131. (London: Institute for the Study of Conflict, 1981) p. 16.
10. Adelman, 'The Strategy of Defiance', p. 36; Crocker, *South Africa's Defense Posture*, pp. 45–6; Peter L. Bunce, 'The Growth of South Africa's Defence Industry and its Israeli Connection', *Journal of the Royal United Services Institute for Defence Studies*, 129 (1984) 46.
11. Crocker, *South Africa's Defense Posture*, pp. 42, 48–9; Robert S. Jaster, *South Africa's Narrowing Security Options*, Adelphi Papers no. 159 (London: International Institute for Strategic Studies, 1980) pp. 16, 40.
12. Ibid., pp. 27–8; John de St Jorre, *A House Divided: South Africa's Uncertain Future* (Washington DC: Carnegie Endowment for International Peace, 1977) pp. 81–2.
13. IISS, *Strategic Survey 1981–1982*, pp. 110–12.
14. These matters are discussed in: Robert M. Price, 'Pretoria's Southern African Strategy', *African Affairs*, 83 (1984) 27–30.
15. See: Gutteridge, *South Africa: Strategy for Survival?*, p. 14.
16. Foreign Minister Muller, quoted in Jaster, *South Africa's Narrowing Security Options*, p. 18.
17. See: Barry Cohen and Mohamed A. El-Khawas (eds), *The Kissinger Study on Southern Africa* (Nottingham: Spokesman Books, 1975).
18. Larry W. Bowman, 'The Strategic Importance of South Africa to the United States: An Appraisal and Policy Analysis', *African Affairs*, 81 (1982) 161. See also: Adelman, 'The Strategy of Defiance', pp. 34–5.

19. Jaster, *South Africa's Narrowing Security Options*, p. 12; Richard E. Bissell, *South Africa and the United States: The Erosion of an Influence Relationship* (New York: Praeger, 1982) p. 69.

20. Christopher Coker, 'South Africa and the Western Alliance 1949–81: A History of Illusions', *Journal of the Royal United Services Institute for Defence Studies*, 127 (1982) 34–8; Bowman, 'The Strategic Importance of South Africa to the United States', pp. 176–7; Adelman, 'The Strategy of Defiance', p. 35.

21. Crocker, *South Africa's Defense Posture*, pp. 9–11.

22. Coker, 'South Africa and the Western Alliance', p. 39; Bowman 'The Strategic Importance of South Africa to the United States', p. 175; Bissell, *South Africa and the United States*, p. 64.

23. Bissell, *South Africa and the United States*, p. 67; Jaster, *South Africa's Narrowing Security Options*, pp. 20, 33; Gutteridge, *South Africa: Strategy for Survival?*, p. 20; Bowman, 'The Strategic Importance of South Africa to the United States', pp. 167, 175–80; de St Jorre, *A House Divided: South Africa's Uncertain Future*, p. 89.

24. Bissell, *South Africa and the United States*, p. 68.

25. Ibid., p. 70; James Dingeman, 'Covert Operations in Central and Southern Africa', in Western Massachusetts Association of Concerned African Scholars (ed.), *US Military Involvement in Southern Africa* (Boston: South End Press, 1978) p. 90.

26. Bowman, 'The Strategic Importance of South Africa to the United States', pp. 167, 175; Bissell, *South Africa and the United States*, p. 68.

27. Crocker. *South Africa's Defense Posture*, pp. 74–6; Jaster, *South Africa's Narrowing Security Options*, p. 40; de St Jorre, *A House Divided: South Africa's Uncertain Future*, pp. 98–9; Gutteridge, *South Africa: Strategy for Survival?*, p. 23. Estimates of South Africa's oil consumption and production are approximate, as official figures are classified. South Africa's energy situation is further discussed in Chapter 5.

28. Jaster, *South Africa's Narrowing Security Options*, p. 29.

29. Adelman, 'The Strategy of Defiance', pp. 47–8.

30. de St Jorre, *A House Divided: South Africa's Uncertain Future*, p. 105. Much of the last section of this chapter is based on this source (pp. 105–7).

31. Ibid., p. 106; James Adams, *The Unnatural Alliance* (London: Quartet Books, 1984) p. 7. Pre-revolutionary Iran also had a personal link with South Africa: the Shah's father was exiled to South Africa by the British during the Second World War.

32. *The Economist*, 17 April 1976.

33. de St Jorre, *A House Divided: South Africa's Uncertain Future*, p. 107; Adams, *The Unnatural Alliance*, pp. 20, 23–6, 111.

34. Bissell, *South Africa and the United States*, p. 64. See also: Adelman, 'The Strategy of Defiance', p. 48.

35. Robert E. Harkavy, 'Pariah States and Nuclear Proliferation', *International Organisation*, 35 (1981) 155. See also: Bunce, 'The Growth of South Africa's Defence Industry and its Israeli Connection', pp. 45–6; Adams, *The Unnatural Alliance*, pp. 32, 93.

36. Harkavy, 'Pariah States and Nuclear Proliferation', p. 157; Edouard

Bustin, 'South Africa's Foreign Policy Alternatives and Deterrence Needs', in Onkar Marwah and Ann Schulz (eds) *Nuclear Proliferation and the Near-Nuclear Countries* (Cambridge, Mass.: Ballinger, 1975) p. 206.

37. de St Jorre, *A House Divided: South Africa's Uncertain Future*, p. 113.

Chapter 4

1. The first two paragraphs of this chapter are based on: Marian Radetzki, *Uranium: A Strategic Source of Energy* (London: Croom Helm, 1981) pp. 37, 39; Margaret Gowing, *Independence and Deterrence: Britain and Atomic Energy, 1945–1952*, vol. 1, 'Policy-making' (London: Macmillan, 1974) pp. 146, 383, 391; Zdenek Červenka and Barbara Rogers, *The Nuclear Axis: Secret Collaboration between West Germany and South Africa* (London: Julian Friedmann, 1978) pp. 110–11, 240.

2. Gowing, *Independence and Deterrence*, p. 355.

3. Geoff Berridge, *Economic Power in Anglo-South African Diplomacy: Simonstown, Sharpeville and After* (London: Macmillan, 1981) pp. 52–7.

4. C. S. McLean and T. K. Prentice, 'The South African Uranium Industry', paper submitted to the First International Conference on the Peaceful Uses of Atomic Energy, Geneva, 1956, quoted in Červenka and Rogers, *The Nuclear Axis*, p. 111.

5. A. R. Newby-Fraser, *Chain Reaction: Twenty Years of Nuclear Research and Development in South Africa* (Pretoria: Atomic Energy Board, 1979) p. 65; European Nuclear Energy Agency and International Atomic Energy Agency, *Uranium Production and Short Term Demand* (Paris: OECD, 1969) p. 11; US Congress, House, Committee on International Relations, Subcommittee on International Resources, Food and Energy, *Resource Development in South Africa and US Policy*, Hearings, 94th Congress, 2nd Session, 8 June 1976, Appendix 6, Responses by the Energy Research and Development Administration to Additional Questions submitted in Writing by Congressman Diggs (Washington DC: US Government Printing Office, 1976) p. 297.

6. See Table 4.2 and Radetzki, *Uranium: A Strategic Source of Energy*, pp. 37, 39–40.

7. Manfred Stephany, 'Influence of Stockpiles on the Market for Natural Uranium', in: The Uranium Institute, *Uranium and Nuclear Energy: 1981* (London: Butterworth, 1982) p. 107.

8. *Nuclear Fuel*, 21 May 1984.

9. Radetzki, *Uranium: A Strategic Source of Energy*, p. 44; Nancy Stauffer, 'Uranium Exporters: Who They Are and How They Work', *Technology Review*, January 1981, p. 28.

10. Berridge, *Economic Power in Anglo-South African Diplomacy*, p. 58.

11. Robert I. Rotberg and Norma Kriger, 'Uranium and the Nuclear Industry', in Robert I. Rotberg, *Suffer the Future: Policy Choices in Southern Africa* (Cambridge, Mass.: Harvard University Press, 1980) p. 143.

12. Radetzki, *Uranium: A Strategic Source of Energy*, pp. 44–5.

13. See Chapter 2 and Appendix.

14. The usual source for uranium spot market quotations (in the units stated)

is the California-based Nuclear Exchange Corporation's *Nuexco Monthly Report*. This price rise was later followed by an equally dramatic fall in 1980 from US$40/lb to US$27/lb U_3O_8.

15.   The best analysis of the cartel affair can be found in: Radetzki, *Uranium: A Strategic Source of Energy*. See, in particular, pp. 117–22, 137. See also: Thomas L. Neff, *The International Uranium Market* (Cambridge, Mass.: Ballinger, 1984) pp. 45, 48–52.

16.   *Nuclear Fuel*, 6 July 1981.

17.   Aldo Cassuto, 'Can Uranium Enrichment Enrich South Africa?', *The World Today*, 26 (1970) 424; Rotberg and Kriger, 'Uranium and the Nuclear Industry', p. 147; Stauffer, 'Uranium Exporters: Who They Are and How They Work', p. 28. Colin Legum (ed.), *Africa Contemporary Record*, Annual Survey and Documents, XV, 1982–3 (New York: Africana Publishing Co., 1984) p. B769.

18.   The most authoritative estimates of international uranium trading statistics, which cannot be gleaned from official figures, are provided by the International Energy Studies Program of the Massachusetts Institute of Technology Energy Laboratory. Its director is Thomas Neff. See: *Africa Confidential*, 19 January 1983; and Neff, *The International Uranium Market*, pp. 183–4, 234–5, 247.

19.   *Le Monde*, 23 July 1977, cited in Richard E. Bissell, *South Africa and the United States: The Erosion of an Influence Relationship* (New York: Praeger, 1982) p. 115.

20.   US Bureau of Mines, *The Mineral Industry of the Republic of South Africa*, preprint from the 1977 Bureau of Mines Minerals Yearbook (Washington DC: US Government Printing Office, 1981) p. 18. COGEMA is a major international trader in uranium, and the yellowcake obtained from South Africa may in fact be re-exported.

21.   William M. Raiford, *The European Role in Africa and US Interests*, Congressional Research Service Report no. 81–202F (Washington DC: The Library of Congress, 1981) p. 71; *Nuclear Engineering International*, February 1979, p. 7.

22.   *Mining Annual Review 1981*, p. 474; International Institute for Strategic Studies, *Strategic Survey 1981–1982* (London: IISS, 1982) p. 21.

23.   The Uranium Institute, *Uranium Supply and Demand: Perspectives to 1995* (London: The Uranium Institute, 1984) p. 7; Neff, *The International Uranium Market*, pp. 262–5; *Nuclear News*, October 1984, pp. 59–60. It should be noted however that the instrument used in the 1960s and 1970s to impose the uranium embargo, namely its enrichment monopoly, is no longer available to the US government.

24.   *Nuclear Engineering International*, July 1978, p. 11; Steven J. Warnecke, *Uranium, Nonproliferation and Energy Security*, Atlantic Paper no. 37 (Paris: Atlantic Institute for International Affairs, 1979) pp. 87–8.

25.   Peter Pringle and James Spigelman, *The Nuclear Barons* (New York: Holt, Rinehart & Winston, 1981) pp. 294, 526. South Africa's sales of uranium to Israel are also discussed in: William Epstein, *The Last Chance: Nuclear Proliferation and Arms Control*. (New York: Macmillan, 1976) p. 156; George Quester, *The Politics of Nuclear Proliferation* (Baltimore, Md.: Johns Hopkins University Press, 1973) p. 98.

26. The evolution of the non-proliferation regime from a unilateral one (the American-led Western Suppliers Group) to a multilateral one (the NPT and IAEA safeguards), and then back to a unilateral one (the American-led Nuclear Suppliers Group) is described in Chapter 2. See also: Pringle and Spigelman, *The Nuclear Barons*, pp. 380, 545–6.

27. Bertrand Goldschmidt, *The Atomic Complex: A Worldwide Political History of Nuclear Energy* (La Grange Park, Ill.: American Nuclear Society, 1982) p. 287.

28. See Chapter 6 and the discussion in Chapters 8 and 9 for the reasons for South Africa's refusal to sign the NPT.

29. See: Ashok Kapur, *International Nuclear Proliferation: Multilateral Diplomacy and Regional Aspects* (London: Praeger, 1979) pp. 234, 240; J. E. Spence, 'The Republic of South Africa: Proliferation and the Politics of "Outward Movement" ', in Robert M. Lawrence and Joel Larus (eds), *Nuclear Proliferation PHASE II* (Lawrence: University of Kansas, 1974) p. 221n; Denis Venter, 'South Africa and the International Controversy surrounding its Nuclear Capability', *Politikon*, 5 (1978) 24–5.

30. Mason Willrich, 'A Workable International Nuclear Energy Regime', *The Washington Quarterly*, 2 (1979) p. 29n; Venter, 'South Africa and the International Controversy surrounding its Nuclear Capability', p. 25; The Uranium Institute, *The Uranium Equation: The Balance of Supply and Demand 1980–1995* (London: Mining Journal Books, 1981) p. 32.

31. *Africa Confidential*, 19 January 1983. Actually RTZ signed the contract with the UK Atomic Energy Authority, but after BNFL was formed in 1970 the contract was transferred.

32. Ibid.

33. The other major mining activity in Namibia is diamond mining by a subsidiary of the South African De Beers mining company (part of the Anglo American group of companies). At the 1982 annual General Conference of the IAEA, the UN Council for Namibia was voted into full membership of that organisation.

34. Warnecke, *Uranium, Nonproliferation and Energy Security*, p. 102; *Africa Confidential*, 19 September 1979; 19 January 1983.

35. *Observer*, 30 January 1983; *Guardian*, 3 February 1983.

36. Once again the MIT Energy Laboratory provides the most authoritative data. See note 18 above and: Neff, *The International Uranium Market*, pp. 189–91.

37. Ibid., pp. 190–1. According to the MIT, West German consumers have contracted to buy 6140t U between 1975 and 1986. See: *Africa Confidential*, 19 January 1983.

38. Ibid.

39. Ibid.; Neff, *The International Uranium Market*, p. 190.

40. *Nuclear Fuel*, 26 April 1982.

41. Ibid., 2 January 1984.

42. *Mining Annual Review*, 1981, p. 486; Neff, *The International Uranium Market*, p. 189.

43. Nor is there any information available on what would be the uranium exporting policy of a likely SWAPO government in a future independent Namibia, although it may be intriguing to speculate on this.

44.   In 1985, policy control over Rössing Uranium Limited was transferred from the South African parastatal, the Industrial Development Corporation, to the 'transitional' Namibian government, which has not been recognised by any country other than South Africa (*Mining Journal*, 21 June 1985). See also Chapter 3.

Chapter 5

1.   *Washington Post*, 16 February 1977, cited in Zdenek Červenka and Barbara Rogers, *The Nuclear Axis: Secret Collaboration between West Germany and South Africa* (London: Julian Friedmann, 1978) p. 159. See also: ibid., p. 249; Margaret Gowing, *Independence and Deterrence: Britain and Atomic Energy, 1945–1952*, vol. 1, 'Policy-making' (London: Macmillan, 1974) pp. 334–5; Warren H. Donnelly and William N. Raiford, *US Foreign Policy Towards South Africa: The Case of Nuclear Cooperation*, Congressional Research Service Report no. 82-24S-F (Washington DC: Library of Congress, 1981) pp. 4–5.

2.   For example, see the speech given by the British Foreign Secretary to the Royal Commonwealth Society shortly before the 1983 Commonwealth conference reported in: *Africa Research Bulletin*, Political Social and Cultural Series, 15 December 1983, p. 7047C; *Guardian*, 15 November 1983. See also: *New Scientist*, 28 February 1980, p. 636; A. R. Newby-Fraser, *Chain Reaction: Twenty Years of Nuclear Research and Development in South Africa* (Pretoria: Atomic Energy Board, 1979) p. 9.

3.   Dan Smith, *South Africa's Nuclear Capability* (London: World Campaign against Military and Nuclear Collaboration with South Africa, 1980) p. 14.

4.   Ibid. See also the comments of A. J. A. Roux quoted in Červenka and Rogers, *The Nuclear Axis*, p. 162.

5.   Details may be found in: ibid., p. 163; Newby-Fraser, *Chain Reaction*, pp. 178–84; D. S. Greenberg, 'South Africa: Booming Nation's Research and Industry Benefit from Close Ties with the United States', *Science*, 10 July 1970, p. 162.

6.   Newby-Fraser, *Chain Reaction*, pp. 58, 116, 118, 124.

7.   Ibid, pp. 92–4, 104.

8.   Ibid., pp. 96–9. What is known about the South African enrichment process is briefly described in the Appendix.

9.   Ibid., p. 92.

10.   Ibid., pp. 59, 103.

11.   J. E. Spence, 'Nuclear Weapons and the Obstacles to World Order', *Optima*, 24 (1974) 112; Aldo Cassuto, 'Can Uranium Enrichment Enrich South Africa?', *The World Today*, 26 (1970) 420. South Africa's attitude to the Non-Proliferation Treaty is discussed in Chapter 6. IAEA safeguarding of enrichment plants (which has hitherto been minimal, as nearly all the plants have been in nuclear weapon states) is discussed in the Appendix.

12.   See, for example: Červenka and Rogers, *The Nuclear Axis*, pp. 175–6; Cassuto, 'Can Uranium Enrichment Enrich South Africa?', pp. 423–4; Dr Gerald Wick, 'New Vistas for Isotope Separation', *New Scientist*, 23

September 1971, p. 694; Mike Muller, 'The Enriching Politics of South Africa's Uranium', *New Scientist*, 2 May 1974, pp. 252–4.

13. *Financial Times*, 22 October 1970, quoted in J. E. Spence, 'The Republic of South Africa: Proliferation and the Politics of "Outward Movement" ' in, Robert M. Lawrence and Joel Larus (eds), *Nuclear Proliferation PHASE II* (Lawrence: University Press of Kansas, 1974) p. 217.

14. See below, and: Cassuto, 'Can Uranium Enrichment Enrich South Africa?', p. 425.

15. Dr A. J. A. Roux, 'South Africa's Position in the World Nuclear Energy Picture', paper presented at the Sectoral Industrial Congress of the Afrikaanse Handelsinstituut, Johannesburg, on 1 May 1973, and reproduced in Ashok Kapur, *International Nuclear Proliferation: Multilateral Diplomacy and Regional Aspects* (London: Praeger, 1979) pp. 265–6. The significant developments in the global enrichment market during the early 1970s are described in the Appendix.

16. International Institute for Strategic Studies, *Strategic Survey 1981–1982* (London: IISS, 1982) pp. 21–2; US Congress, House, Committee on International Relations, Subcommittee on Africa, *United States–South Africa Relations: Nuclear Cooperation*, Hearings, 95th Congress, 2nd Session, 30 June 1977, Testimony by Ronald H. Siegel (Washington DC: US Government Printing Office, 1977) pp. 2–3; Červenka and Rogers, *The Nuclear Axis*, pp. 62–3, 160, 177–8.

17. Červenka and Rogers, *The Nuclear Axis*, p. 190.

18. J. E. Spence, 'Nuclear Weapons and South Africa – The Incentives and Constraints on Policy', in Timothy M. Shaw and Kenneth A. Heard (eds), *Cooperation and Conflict in Southern Africa: Papers on a Regional Subsystem* (Washington DC: University Press of America, 1976) p. 411.

19. Cassuto, 'Can Uranium Enrichment Enrich South Africa?', pp. 420, 426–7.

20. *Nuclear Engineering International*, September 1973, p. 667; April 1974, p. 255; July 1974, p. 582; *Science*, 29 March 1974, p. 1271.

21. *Westdeutsche Allgemaine Zeitung*, 6 September 1975; and *Frankfurter Rundschau*, 9 September 1975, both cited in Anti-Apartheid Movement (AAB) in the Federal Republic of Germany and West Berlin, *Reply: Answer to a Denial of the Government of the Federal Republic of Germany concerning the Military–Nuclear Collaboration between the Federal Republic of Germany and South Africa* (Bonn: AAB, 1979) p. 7.

22. Robert Gillette, 'Uranium Enrichment: With Help, South Africa is Progressing', *Science*, 13 June 1975, pp. 1190–2; Červenka and Rogers, *The Nuclear Axis*, pp. 75–6.

23. Červenka and Rogers, *The Nuclear Axis*, p. 180; Newby-Fraser, *Chain Reaction*, pp. 99, 106–11.

24. The official history of the South African Atomic Energy Board gives an account of Dr Grant's alleged invention of the vortex tube technique. See: Newby-Fraser, *Chain Reaction*, pp. 95–6.

25. Gillette, 'Uranium Enrichment: With Help, South Africa is Progressing', p. 1092; *Science*, 29 March 1974, p. 1271; 30 May 1975, p. 912.

26. African National Congress of South Africa, *The Nuclear Conspiracy: FRG Collaborates to Strengthen Apartheid* (Bonn: ANC, 1975). The

documents were reprinted in: African National Congress of South Africa, *Conspiracy to Arm Apartheid Continues: FRG–SA Collaboration* (Bonn: ANC, 1977); Červenka and Rogers, *The Nuclear Axis;* Anti-Apartheid Movement, *Reply.* All four publications assess the evidence of West German–South African collaboration, official and unofficial, revealed by the stolen documents. However, perhaps the best summary of this is found in: Smith, *South Africa's Nuclear Capability.*

27.   *Fact v. Fiction: Rebuttal of the Charges of Alleged Co-operation between the Federal Republic of Germany and South Africa in the Nuclear and Military Fields* (Bonn: Press and Information Office of the Government of the Federal Republic of Germany, 1978).

28.   ANC, *Conspiracy to Arm Apartheid Continues*, pp. 34–7, 57, 65, 86.

29.   *Fact v. Fiction*, p. 21.

30.   See: Anti-Apartheid Movement, *Reply*, pp. 13–14, and the Appendix below.

31.   *Fact v. Fiction*, pp. 16–17; ANC, *Conspiracy to Arm Apartheid Continues*, p. 29.

32.   STEAG press release, Essen, 9 April 1974, reproduced in Anti-Apartheid Movement, *Reply*, pp. 52–3. See also: *Rand Daily Mail*, 23 April 1974, quoted in ibid., p. 78; *Fact v. Fiction*, p. 16.

33.   South Africa's motivations for her cooperation with STEAG are further discussed in Chapter 8.

34.   *Science*, 30 May 1975, p. 912.

35.   Kapur, *International Nuclear Proliferation*, p. 238.

36.   See Chapter 2 and the Appendix. See also: Stockholm International Peace Research Institute, *Uranium Enrichment and Nuclear Weapon Proliferation* (London: Taylor & Francis, 1983) pp. 221–2.

37.   Quoted in Anti-Apartheid Movement, *Reply*, p. 9.

38.   Červenka and Rogers, *The Nuclear Axis*, p. 183; Kenneth Adelman and Albion Knight, 'Can South Africa go Nuclear?', *Orbis*, 23 (1979) 637; *Nuclear News*, May 1975, p. 38.

39.   Newby-Fraser, *Chain Reaction*, p. 111.

40.   *Nuclear Engineering International*, November 1976, p. 50; Manson Benedict, Thomas H. Pigford and Hans Wolfgang-Levi, *Nuclear Chemical Engineering* (New York: McGraw Hill, 1981) pp. 817, 889; International Nuclear Fuel Cycle Evaluation, *Enrichment Availability*, Report of INFCE Working Group 2 (Vienna: IAEA, 1980) p. 72.

41.   UN Centre for Disarmament, Department of Political and Security Council Affairs, *South Africa's Plan and Capability in the Nuclear Field*, Report of the Secretary-General, Document A/35/402 (New York: United Nations, 1981) pp. 10, 20.

42.   Benedict *et al.*, *Nuclear Chemical Engineering*, p. 889.

43.   *The Energy Daily*, 4 May 1981; Robert I. Rotberg and Norma Kriger, 'Uranium and the Nuclear Industry', in Robert I. Rotberg, *Suffer the Future: Policy Choices in Southern Africa* (Cambridge, Mass.: Harvard University Press, 1980) p. 152.

44.   Some of the confusion surrounding discussion of South Africa's enrichment capacity stems from the units of measurement used (see Appendix). For example, commentators have confused tonnes of

separative work ('000SWU) with tonnes of uranium feed or enriched uranium product. To avoid such confusion we have quoted enrichment capacities in separative work units per annum (SWU/a) *and* in tonnes ('000kg) of separative work per annum (t SWU/a). These units are explained in the Appendix.

45. Kapur, *International Nuclear Proliferation*, p. 237.
46. See Chapter 2 and Appendix. See also: Allen K. Hammond, 'Uranium: Will There be a Shortage or an Embarrassment of Enrichment?', *Science*, 28 May 1976, pp. 866–7.
47. Červenka and Rogers, *The Nuclear Axis*, pp. 186, 190; Newby-Fraser, *Chain Reaction*, pp. 105, 112; *The Economist*, 25 February 1978, p. 80.
48. Rotberg and Kriger, 'Uranium and the Nuclear Industry', pp. 153–4; Richard K. Betts, 'A Diplomatic Bomb? South Africa's Nuclear Potential', in Joseph A. Yager (ed.), *Nonproliferation and US Foreign Policy* (Washington DC: The Brookings Institution, 1980) p. 289; *Nuclear Engineering International*, August 1977, p. 12.
49. *International Herald Tribune*, 13 October 1975, cited in Červenka and Rogers, *The Nuclear Axis*, pp. 78, 183.
50. See Chapter 4 and Appendix for details of the Rössing mine and developments in the markets for natural uranium and enrichment during the 1970s.
51. Roux, 'South Africa's Position in the World Nuclear Energy Picture', p. 268.
52. US Congress, *United States–South Africa Relations: Nuclear Cooperation*, p. 18.
53. *Nuclear Engineering International*, August 1977, pp. 12–13; testimony by Nelson F. Sievering, Jr, Assistant Administrator for International Affairs, Energy Research and Development Administration, in US Congress, *United States–South Africa Relations: Nuclear Cooperation*, p. 27.
54. *The Economist*, 25 February 1978, pp. 79–80; Červenka and Rogers, *The Nuclear Axis*, pp. 191–2; Newby-Fraser, *Chain Reaction*, pp. 112–13.
55. Betts, 'A Diplomatic Bomb? South Africa's Nuclear Potential', p. 290n. The Koeberg reactors and South Africa's difficulties in obtaining their enriched uranium fuel loads are discussed below.
56. See Appendix, Table A.1.
57. Cassuto, 'Can Uranium Enrichment Enrich South Africa?'.
58. Adelman and Knight, 'Can South Africa go Nuclear?', p. 167.
59. See: Newby-Fraser, *Chain Reaction*, pp. 79, 81, 98.
60. Ibid., p. 79.
61. Spence, 'Nuclear Weapons and South Africa', p. 412.
62. *Rand Daily Mail*, 24 October 1970, and other sources cited in Červenka and Rogers, *The Nuclear Axis*, p. 185.
63. *Rand Daily Mail*, 2 March 1970, cited in ibid.; *Mining Annual Review* 1970, p. 313.
64. *Nucleonics Week*, 8 April 1982.
65. Newby-Fraser, *Chain Reaction*, p. 92.
66. Červenka and Rogers, *The Nuclear Axis*, pp. 164, 170–2; Newby-Fraser, *Chain Reaction*, pp. 127–9; Cassuto, 'Can Uranium Enrichment Enrich

South Africa?', pp. 421–2.

67.   Červenka and Rogers, *The Nuclear Axis*, pp. 165, 167; Newby-Fraser, *Chain Reaction*, pp. 131–2; Donnelly and Raiford, *US Foreign Policy Towards South Africa*, pp. 12, 16.

68.   Richard E. Bissell, *South Africa and the United States: The Erosion of an Influence Relationship* (New York: Praeger, 1982) p. 108; Červenka and Rogers, *The Nuclear Axis*, pp. 166–9, 246, 286–7, 307. Peter Pringle and James Spigelman, *The Nuclear Barons* (New York: Holt, Rinehart & Winston, 1981) pp. 347, 352; *The Times*, 13 July 1976.

69.   *Africa Confidential*, 20 October 1982; *Nucleonics Week*, 16 December 1982; Červenka and Rogers, *The Nuclear Axis*, p. 169; Richard K. Betts, 'A Diplomatic Bomb for South Africa?', *International Security*, 4 (1979) 102–3.

70.   *Nucleonics Week*, 8 April 1982; 22 April 1982.

71.   *Africa Research Bulletin*, Political, Social and Cultural Series, 15 January 1983, p. 6682; *Nucleonics Week*, 23 December 1982; 6 January 1983; 27 January 1983.

72.   Donnelly and Raiford, *US Foreign Policy Towards South Africa*, p. 8; Newby-Fraser, *Chain Reaction*, pp. 196–7; *Nucleonics Week*, 29 April 1982; 16 December 1982; 22 December 1983; 29 March 1984; 12 September 1985.

73.   See: Chapter 4; Bertrand Goldschmidt, *The Atomic Complex: A Worldwide Political History of Nuclear Energy* (La Grange Park, Ill.: American Nuclear Society, 1982) p. 287; Červenka and Rogers, *The Nuclear Axis*, p. 197.

74.   Bissell, *South Africa and the United States*, p. 116; Donnelly and Raiford, *US Foreign Policy Towards South Africa*, p. 13; Richard K. Betts, 'Preventing the Development of South African Nuclear Weapons', in Joseph A. Yager (ed.), *Nonproliferation and US Foreign Policy*, pp. 402–3; Červenka and Rogers, *The Nuclear Axis*, p. 245; *African Research Bulletin*, Economic, Financial and Technical Series, 30 November 1978, p. 4900; *Africa Confidential*, 12 November 1980.

75.   Newby-Fraser, *Chain Reaction*, p. 55; *The Times*, 15 August 1980.

76.   *Financial Times*, 30 April 1981; *The Times*, 30 April 1981; Rotberg and Kriger, 'Uranium and the Nuclear Industry', p. 148.

77.   See, for example: Rotberg and Kriger, 'Uranium and the Nuclear Industry', p. 148; Newby-Fraser, *Chain Reaction*, pp. 66, 196, 201.

78.   See: *Nucleonics Week*, 4 June 1981; and Table A.1, in the Appendix below.

79.   *Nucleonics Week*, 13 August 1981; *The Energy Daily*, 18 September 1981; *Nuclear News*, October 1981, p. 135.

80.   *The Energy Daily*, 10 December 1981; *Nucleonics Week*, 18 February 1982; *Nuclear Engineering International*, June 1982, p. 9.

81.   *Africa Confidential*, 6 January 1982. As Koeberg was to be submitted to IAEA safeguards there was no need for South Africa to pay the heavy premium for unsafeguarded fuel. *Washington Post* (13, 18 and 19 November 1981) had reported that the enriched uranium had been supplied by China through third parties, possibly in Switzerland or West Germany (the 'Chinese laundry'). Chinese officials responded that nations importing nuclear material from China were prohibited from

retransferring it, in particular to Israel or South Africa. According to James Malone, the Assistant Secretary in the US State Department with responsibility for matters pertaining to nuclear commerce, China had made the mistake of dealing with companies rather than countries. She had not got good end-use guarantees and so had been deceived about the ultimate destination. He believed that some uranium enriched in China *had* got to South Africa. See: *Nucleonics Week*, 19 August 1982; *Nuclear News*, October 1982, p. 23; *The Energy Daily*, 18 November 1981; *Africa Report*, January–February 1982, p. 23.

82. Donnelly and Raiford, *US Foreign Policy Towards South Africa*, pp. 16n, 39n.

83. *Nucleonics Week*, 8 April 1982.

84. *Nucleonics Week*, 17 March 1983; *Nuclear Fuel*, 17 January 1983; 18 July 1983; 27 February 1984.

85. See: Kapur, *International Nuclear Proliferation*, p. 243; Bissell, *South Africa and the United States*, p. 114.

86. *Nuclear Europe*, May 1984. See also: *Nuclear Fuel*, 8 October 1984.

87. Newby-Fraser, *Chain Reaction*, p. 196. For suggestions that South Africa has a reprocessing plant, see: Červenka and Rogers, *The Nuclear Axis*, pp. 193, 198–9.

88. *Nuclear Fuel*, 8 October 1984.

89. *Nucleonics Week*, 26 July 1984; 2 August 1984.

90. Newby-Fraser, *Chain Reaction*, pp. 35, 96.

91. Colin Legum (ed.), *Africa Contemporary Record*, Annual Survey and Documents, XV, 1982–3 (New York: Africana Publishing Co., 1984) pp. B766, B769; *Nucleonics Week*, 30 June 1983.

Chapter 6

1. Zdenek Červenka and Barbara Rogers, *The Nuclear Axis: Secret Collaboration between West Germany and South Africa* (London: Julian Friedmann, 1978) pp. 42, 59; A. R. Newby-Fraser, *Chain Reaction: Twenty Years of Nuclear Research and Development in South Africa* (Pretoria: Atomic Energy Board, 1979) p. 193.

2. J. E. Spence, 'The Republic of South Africa: Proliferation and the Politics of "Outward Movement" ', in Robert M. Lawrence and Joel Larus (eds), *Nuclear Proliferation PHASE II* (Lawrence: University Press of Kansas, 1974) p. 221.

3. George Quester, *The Politics of Nuclear Proliferation* (Baltimore: Johns Hopkins University Press, 1973) p. 200.

4. Ashok Kapur, *International Nuclear Proliferation: Multilateral Diplomacy and Regional Aspects* (London: Praeger, 1979) p. 241.

5. Richard K. Betts, 'Preventing the Development of South African Nuclear Weapons', in Joseph A. Yager (ed.), *Nonproliferation and US Foreign Policy* (Washington DC: The Brookings Institution, 1980) p. 399. At the 1982 General Conference of the IAEA, the UN Council for Namibia was admitted to membership of the IAEA to represent the interests of Namibia (see Chapter 4).

6. See Chapter 2.

7. It could be argued that, as South Africa already has a nuclear weapons capability by virtue of her unsafeguarded enrichment plant, safeguarding the Safari-1 and Koeberg reactors provides little assurance to the international community. However, in the absence of safeguards, South Africa might feel free to separate plutonium from the spent fuel from the reactors, and thus enhance the size and sophistication of her weapons capability. There would also be fears about the transfer of plutonium or spent fuel to other pariah nations such as Israel or Taiwan.

8. See Chapter 2.

9. Quester, *The Politics of Nuclear Proliferation*, pp. 98, 201.

10. See: United Nations, General Assembly, 22nd Session, *UN Document A/C.1/PV.1571*, 20 May 1968, pp. 52–60, as cited and discussed in, for example: Kapur, *International Nuclear Proliferation*, p. 240; Spence, 'The Republic of South Africa', pp. 222–3, 227.

11. See Chapter 5, and the discussion of safeguards on enrichment plants in the Appendix.

12. See: International Atomic Energy Agency, *The Structure and Content of Agreements between the Agency and States Required in Connection with the Treaty on the Non-proliferation of Nuclear Weapons*, INFCIRC/153 (Vienna: IAEA, 1972); L. W. Herron, 'A Lawyer's View of Safeguards and Non-proliferation', *IAEA Bulletin*, 24 (September 1982) 36.

13. Quester, *The Politics of Nuclear Proliferation*, p. 198; Spence, 'The Republic of South Africa', p. 221.

14. See: Chapters 8 and 9 for further discussion of South Africa's attitude to the NPT and prospects for her eventual signature. See also: Kapur, *International Nuclear Proliferation*, p. 262.

15. See Chapter 5 and: *Nuclear Fuel*, 27 February 1984; *Nucleonics Week*, 9 February 1984. The South African announcement was reported in the *Department of State Bulletin*, 84 (March 1984) 57.

16. See: *Nucleonics Week*, 19 July 1984; *Nuclear Engineering International*, September 1984.

17. Questor, *The Politics of Nuclear Proliferation*, p. 203.

18. Quoted in: UN Centre for Disarmament, Department of Political and Security Council Affairs, *South Africa's Plan and Capability in the Nuclear Field*, Report of the Secretary General, Document A/35/402 (New York: United Nations, 1981) p. 28.

19. Ibid.

20. See: Ibid., p. 37.

21. Quoted in *Africa Research Bulletin*, Political, Social, and Cultural Series, 15 September 1977, p. 4546.

22. Statement of the South African Department of Foreign Affairs, 25 October 1977, quoted in Richard E. Bissell, *South Africa and the United States: The Erosion of an Influence Relationship* (New York: Praeger, 1982) p. 109 (emphasis in the original).

23. Quoted in *Africa Research Bulletin*, Political, Social and Cultural Series, 15 September 1977, p. 4546.

24. See: Bissell, *South Africa and the United States*, p. 111; Červenka and Rogers, *The Nuclear Axis*, p. 282.

25. Kenneth Adelman and Albion Knight, 'Can South Africa go Nuclear?',

Orbis, 23 (1979) 646.

26. The African National Congress had issued its second publication, *Conspiracy to Arm Apartheid Continues* (Bonn: ANC, 1977), giving details and allegations about nuclear cooperation between South Africa and West Germany, to coincide with the conference.

27. Bissell, *South Africa and the United States*, pp. 110–11; Denis Venter, 'South Africa and the International Controversy surrounding its Nuclear Capability', *Politikon*, 5 (1978) 21.

28. Quoted in Bissell, *South Africa and the United States*, p. 109.

29. Statement made by the French Minister for Foreign Affairs, M. de Guiringaud, on French radio, 22 August 1977, reproduced in UN Centre for Disarmament, *South Africa's Plan and Capability in the Nuclear Field*, p. 40.

30. Robert I. Rotberg and Norma Kriger, 'Uranium and the Nuclear Industry', in Robert I. Rotberg, *Suffer the Future: Policy Choices in Southern Africa* (Cambridge, Mass.: Harvard University Press, 1980) p. 155. See also: Červenka and Rogers, *The Nuclear Axis*, pp. 207–8.

31. Warren H. Donnelly and William N. Raiford, *US Foreign Policy Towards South Africa: The Case of Nuclear Cooperation*, Congressional Research Service Report no. 82–24S-F (Washington DC: The Library of Congress, 1981) p. 10. See also: Richard K. Betts, 'A Diplomatic Bomb? South Africa's Nuclear Potential' in Joseph A. Yager (ed.), *Nonproliferation and US Foreign Policy* (Washington DC: The Brookings Institution, 1980) p. 304.

32. *Observer*, 25 February 1979; *New Statesman*, 16 March 1979.

33. *Nature*, 17 April 1980, p. 587; *Facts on File*, 20 June 1980, p. 466.

34. Robert. S. Jaster, *South Africa's Narrowing Security Options*, Adelphi Papers no. 159 (London: International Institute for Strategic Studies, 1980) p. 46.

35. Colin Legum (ed.), *Africa Contemporary Record*, Annual Survey and Documents, XII, 1979–80 (New York: Africana Publising Co., 1981) p. A75.

36. Bissell, *South Africa and the United States*, pp. 65, 109; *Facts and Reports from Southern Africa*, 1980, p. I 101.

37. Newby-Fraser, *Chain Reaction*, p. 157; Červenka and Rogers, *The Nuclear Axis*, pp. 207–9, 252–3.

38. Stockholm International Peace Research Institute, *World Armaments and Disarmament; SIPRI Yearbook 1980* (London: Taylor & Francis, 1980) p. 198; *The Economist*, 3 November 1979, p. 54.

39. International Institute for Strategic Studies, *Strategic Survey 1980–1981* (London: IISS, 1981) p. 115; *Keesings Contemporary Archives*, XXVI (1980) p. 30196. The double flash was in fact detected near the South African-owned Prince Edward Islands in the remote southern seas, where the Atlantic Ocean meets the Indian Ocean.

40. *Science*, 1 February 1980, p. 504.

41. Betts, 'A Diplomatic Bomb? South Africa's Nuclear Potential', p. 303; *Keesings Contemporary Archives*, XXVI (1980) p. 30196; IISS, *Strategic Survey 1980–1981*, p. 115.

42. Bissell, *South Africa and the United States*, p. 113; *Facts on File*, 40 (1980)

p. 548.
43. *Nature*, 24 July 1980, p. 325.
44. *Science*, 1 February 1980, pp. 505–6; 14 March 1980; p. 1185; 29 August 1980.
45. Colin Legum (ed.), *Africa Contemporary Record*, Annual Survey and Documents, XII, 1979–80 (London: Africana Publishing Co, 1981) pp. A75, B832.
46. Betts, 'A Diplomatic Bomb? South Africa's Nuclear Potential', p. 298; James Adams, *The Unnatural Alliance* (London: Quartet Books, 1984) p. 180.
47. *Guardian*, 2 October 1980; *Facts on File*, 40 (1980) p. 141.
48. Adams, *The Unnatural Alliance*, p. 195; *The Times*, 14 August 1980; *Nature*, 28 February 1980, p. 807; *Science*, 14 March 1980, p. 1185.
49. *New Scientist*, 24 July 1980, p. 268. The CIA later added, in congressional testimony, that Taiwan may have helped the two countries (See: *Daily Telegraph*, 19 February 1981). The suggestion by Kramish that the 1979 event was an Indian nuclear test is much less conventional (see: Arnold Kramish, 'Nuclear Flashes in the Night', *The Washington Quarterly*, 3 (1980) 4–10).
50. IISS, *Strategic Survey 1980–1981*, p. 115; *Daily Telegraph*, 19 February 1981; *Science*, 6 March 1981, p. 1020.

Chapter 7

1. Examples of such statements are quoted in African National Congress, *Conspiracy to Arm Apartheid Continues* (Bonn: ANC, 1977) pp. 70–1.
2. *The Star* (Johannesburg), 17 April 1971, cited in ibid., p. 71.
3. *The Times*, 12 July 1974, cited in ibid.
4. *Newsweek*, 17 March 1976, cited in Zdenek Červenka and Barbara Rogers, *The Nuclear Axis: Secret Collaboration between West Germany and South Africa* (London: Julian Friedmann, 1978) p. 213.
5. Ibid.
6. See Chapter 6 above.
7. International Institute for Strategic Studies, *Strategic Survey 1974* (London: IISS, 1975) p. 35.
8. *Washington Post*, 16 February 1977.
9. See Appendix.
10. UN Centre for Disarmament, Department of Political and Security Council Affairs, *South Africa's Plan and Capability in the Nuclear Field*, Report of the Secretary-General, Document A/35/402 (New York: United Nations, 1981) p. 20.
11. See Appendix. Reports that South Africa may have obtained unsafeguarded low-enriched uranium from China in 1981 are relevant here (see Chapter 5, note 81).
12. See Richard K. Betts, 'A Diplomatic Bomb? South Africa's Nuclear Potential' in Joseph A. Yager (ed.), *Nonproliferation and US Foreign Policy* (Washington DC: The Brookings Institution, 1980) p. 304. One may note that Adelman and Knight had already foreseen that South Africa's objective may have been to develop such a battlefield weapon.

See Kenneth Adelman and Albion Knight, 'Can South Africa go Nuclear?', *Orbis*, 23 (1979) 643.

13. *Nucleonics Week*, 8 April 1982. The term 'tails assay' is explained in the Appendix.

14. Ibid.

15. UN Centre for Disarmament, *South Africa's Plan and Capability in the Nuclear Field*, pp. 19–21.

16. See Table 3.1 and Betts, 'A Diplomatic Bomb? South Africa's Nuclear Potential?', p. 291. See also: Adelman and Knight, 'Can South Africa go Nuclear?', p. 639.

17. *New York Times*, 28 February 1965, cited in J. E. Spence, 'The Republic of South Africa: Proliferation and the Politics of "Outward Movement"', in Robert M. Lawrence and Joel Larus (eds), *Nuclear Proliferation PHASE II* (Lawrence: University Press of Kansas 1974) p. 215 (emphasis added).

18. Adelman and Knight, 'Can South Africa go Nuclear?', p. 636.

19. Colin Legum (ed.), *Africa Contemporary Record*, Annual Survey and Documents, XV, 1982–3 (New York: Africana Publishing Co., 1984) p. B767.

20. Adelman and Knight, 'Can South Africa go Nuclear?', p. 635.

21. See, for example: ibid.; Richard K. Betts, 'A Diplomatic Bomb for South Africa?', *International Security*, 4 (1979) 103–4; Robert S. Jaster, 'Politics and the "Afrikaner Bomb"', *Orbis*, 27 (1984) 830.

22. See: Lewis A. Dunn, 'Nuclear "Gray Marketeering"', *International Security*, 1 (1977) 112; George Quester, *The Politics of Nuclear Proliferation* (Baltimore: Johns Hopkins University Press, 1973) pp. 98, 199; Robert E. Harkavy, 'Pariah States and Nuclear Proliferation', *International Organization*, 35 (1981) 157; International Institute for Strategic Studies, *Strategic Survey 1981–1982* (London: IISS, 1982) pp. 21–2.

23. See Chapter 3.

24. Richard E. Bissell, *South Africa and the United States: The Erosion of an Influence Relationship* (New York: Praeger, 1982) p. 116.

25. Adelman and Knight, 'Can South Africa go Nuclear?', pp. 638–9.

26. J. E. Spence, 'South Africa: The Nuclear Option', *African Affairs*, 80 (1981) 442; Červenka and Rogers, *The Nuclear Axis*, p. 230; Gene I. Rochlin, 'The Development and Deployment of Nuclear Weapons Systems in a Proliferating World', in John Kerry King (ed.), *International Political Effects of the Spread of Nuclear Weapons* (Washington DC: US Government Printing Office, 1979) p. 14; Stephen M. Meyer, *The Dynamics of Nuclear Proliferation* (University of Chicago Press, 1984) p. 29.

27. UN Centre for Disarmament, *South Africa's Plan and Capability in the Nuclear Field*, pp. 22–3; Červenka and Rogers, *The Nuclear Axis*, p. 229; George H. Quester, 'The Politics of Twenty Nuclear Powers', in Richard Rosecrance (ed.), *The Future of the International Strategic System* (San Francisco: Chandler, 1972) p. 56.

28. Harkavy, 'Pariah States and Nuclear Proliferation', p. 157.

29. Červenka and Rogers, *The Nuclear Axis*, pp. 234–5; Ashok Kapur, *International Nuclear Proliferation: Multilateral Diplomacy and Regional*

Aspects (London: Praeger, 1979) p. 235; Stockholm International Peace Research Institute, *Southern Africa: The Escalation of a Conflict* (New York: Praeger, 1976) p. 142.

30.   See Chapter 6 above.
31.   *Africa Research Bulletin*, Political, Social and Cultural Series, 15 April 1982, p. 6394.
32.   Ibid.; Barbara Rogers, 'The Nuclear Threat from South Africa', *Africa*, January 1981, p. 45; Colin Legum (ed.), *Africa Contemporary Record*, Annual Survey and Documents, XIII, 1980–1 (London: Africana Publishing Co., 1981). pp. B809–10; James Adams, *The Unnatural Alliance* (London: Quartet Books, 1984) pp: 38–71; *Guardian*, 18 November 1982; *Newsweek*, 29 September 1980.
33.   Legum (ed.), *Africa Contemporary Record*, p. B809; *Guardian*, 2 October 1980.

Chapter 8

1.   On this point, see, for example: Richard K. Betts, 'A Diplomatic Bomb for South Africa?', *International Security*, 4 (1979) 97, 100; J. E. Spence, 'South Africa: The Nuclear Option', *African Affairs*, 80 (1981) 445–6; Denis Venter, 'South Africa and the International Controversy surrounding its Nuclear Capability', *Politikon*, 5 (1978) 25–6.
2.   William Epstein, *The Last Chance: Nuclear Proliferation and Arms Control* (New York: Macmillan, 1976) p. 210.
3.   Richard K. Betts, 'Preventing the Development of South African Nuclear Weapons', in Joseph A. Yager (ed.), *Nonproliferation and US Foreign Policy* (Washington DC: The Brookings Institution, 1980) p. 400.
4.   Oye Ogunbadejo, 'Africa's Nuclear Capability', *The Journal of Modern African Studies*, 22 (1984) 25.
5.   Ibid., pp. 25, 38; Tunde Adeniram, 'Black Africa Reacts', *Bulletin of the Atomic Scientists*, 38 (August/September 1982) 37. See, in particular: Ali Mazrui, 'Africa's Nuclear Future', *Survival*, 22 (1980) 76–9, and the reply by P.A. Towle in ibid., pp. 219–21.
6.   Robert D'A. Henderson, 'Nigeria: Future Nuclear Power?', *Orbis*, 25 (1981) 413–15; Ogunbadejo, 'Africa's Nuclear Capability', p. 38; J'Bayo Adekanye, 'Nigeria's Investment in Nuclear Power: A Research Note', *Arms Control*, 4 (1983) 49–60; Oye Ogunbadejo, 'Nuclear Capabilility and Nigeria's Foreign Policy', in Colin Legum (ed.), *Africa Contemporary Record*, Annual Survey and Documents, XVI, 1983–4 (New York: Africana Publishing Co., 1985) pp. A140–1.
7.   See: ibid., pp. A141–3; Julius Emeka Okolo, 'Nuclearization of Nigeria', *Comparative Strategy*, 5 (1985) 138, 143, 150, 152; Stockholm International Peace Research Institute, *World Armaments and Disarmament, SIPRI Yearbook 1981* (London: Taylor & Francis, 1981) p. 309; International Institute for Strategic Studies, *Strategic Survey 1981–1982* (London: IISS, 1982) p. 21; Henderson, 'Nigeria: Future Nuclear Power?', pp. 416–17, 421–2; Tunde Adeniran, 'Nuclear Proliferation and Black Africa: The Coming Crisis of Choice,' *Third World Quarterly*, 3 (1981) 682.

8.   Agrippah T. Mugomba, 'The Militarisation of the Indian Ocean and the Liberation of Southern Africa', *Journal of Southern African Affairs*, 4 (1979) 272–3; Ashok Kapur, *International Nuclear Proliferation: Multilateral Diplomacy and Regional Aspects* (London: Praeger, 1979) pp. 254, 259; Kenneth Adelman and Albion Knight, 'Can South Africa go Nuclear?', *Orbis*, 23 (1979) 642–3; J. E. Spence, 'The Republic of South Africa: Proliferation and the Politics of "Outward Movement" ', in Robert M. Lawrence and Joel Larus (eds), *Nuclear Proliferation PHASE II* (Lawrence: University Press of Kansas, 1974) p. 210.

9.   Richard K. Betts, 'A Diplomatic Bomb for South Africa?', *International Security*, 4 (1979) 104–5, 107; Edouard Bustin, 'South Africa's Foreign Policy Alternatives and Deterrence Needs', in Onkar Marwah and Ann Schulz (eds), *Nuclear Proliferation and the Near-Nuclear Countries* (Cambridge, Mass.: Ballinger, 1975) pp. 223–4; Spence, 'South Africa: The Nuclear Option', pp. 447–8; Robert S. Jaster, *South Africa's Narrowing Security Options*, Adelphi Papers no. 159 (London: International Institute for Strategic Studies, 1980) p. 44; Robert S. Jaster, 'Politics and the "Afrikaner Bomb" ', *Orbis*, 27 (1984) 846–7.

10. Richard K. Betts, 'A Diplomatic Bomb? South Africa's Nuclear Potential', in Joseph A. Yager (ed.), *Nonproliferation and US Foreign Policy* (Washington DC: The Brookings Institution, 1980) p. 295; L. H. Gann and Peter Duignan, *South Africa: War, Revolution, or Peace?* (Stanford: Hoover Institution Press, 1978) p. 40.

11. Betts, 'A Diplomatic Bomb for South Africa?', p. 101.

12. George H. Quester, *The Politics of Nuclear Proliferation* (Baltimore: Johns Hopkins University Press, 1973) p. 202.

13. Betts, 'A Diplomatic Bomb for South Africa?' p. 108; Bustin, 'South Africa's Foreign Policy Alternatives and Deterrence Needs', p. 223; Spence, 'South Africa: The Nuclear Option', p. 448; Chester A. Crocker, *South Africa's Defense Posture: Coping with Vulnerability*, The Washington Papers, vol. 9, no. 8 (Beverley Hills: Sage Publications, 1981) p. 63.

14. Betts, 'A Diplomatic Bomb for South Africa?', p. 104; J. E. Spence, 'Nuclear Weapons and South Africa – The Incentives and Constraints on Policy', in Timothy M. Shaw and Kenneth A. Heard (eds), *Cooperation and Conflict in Southern Africa: Papers on a Regional Subsystem* (Washington DC: University Press of America, 1976) pp. 419–20.

15. Bustin, 'South Africa's Foreign Policy Alternatives and Deterrence Needs', p. 224; Betts, 'A Diplomatic Bomb? South Africa's Nuclear Potential', p. 299.

16. See: A. R. Newby-Fraser, *Chain Reaction: Twenty Years of Nuclear Research and Development in South Africa* (Pretoria: Atomic Energy Board, 1979) pp. 92–4; Spence, 'The Republic of South Africa', pp. 215–16.

17. See Chapter 5 and Appendix.

18. P. Boskma, 'Jet Nozzle and Vortex Tube Enrichment Technologies', in Stockholm International Peace Research Institute, *Nuclear Energy and Nuclear Weapons Proliferation* (London: Taylor & Francis, 1979) pp. 66–7; Aldo Cassuto, 'Can Uranium Enrichment Enrich South Africa?', *The*

World Today, 26 (1970) 419–27.

19. Spence, 'The Republic of South Africa', p. 224.
20. Spence, 'South Africa: The Nuclear Option', p. 442n.
21. Betts, 'A Diplomatic Bomb? South Africa's Nuclear Potential', p. 287.
22. See Chapter 5 and Newby-Fraser, *Chain Reaction*, pp. 92–4.
23. Quoted in *Science*, 13 June 1975, p. 1090.
24. K. Subrahmanyam, 'The Nuclear Issue and International Security', *Bulletin of the Atomic Scientists*, 33 (February 1977) 17–18; Kapur, *International Nuclear Proliferation*, p. 254.
25. Quoted in Kapur, *International Nuclear Proliferation*, p. 259.
26. *Die Beeld*, 26 July 1980, quoted in Zdenek Červenka and Barbara Rogers, *The Nuclear Axis: Secret Collaboration between West Germany and South Africa* (London: Julian Friedmann, 1978) p. 222.
27. Betts, 'A Diplomatic Bomb? South Africa's Nuclear Potential', p. 302. See also: Richard E. Bissell, *South Africa and the United States: The Erosion of an Influence Relationship* (New York: Praeger, 1982) pp. 110, 119n; J. E. Spence, *International Problems of Nuclear Proliferation and the South African Position*, SAIIA Occasional Paper (Braamfontein: South African Institute of International Affairs, 1980) p. 9. It will be recalled that, soon after the 1977 Kalahari test incident, Prime Minister Vorster called a general election and won a massive vote of confidence from the white electorate (see Chapter 6).
28. Betts, 'A Diplomatic Bomb? South Africa's Nuclear Potential', pp. 302, 305.
29. See: Betts, 'A Diplomatic Bomb for South Africa?', p. 106; Spence, 'The Republic of South Africa', p. 225.
30. Kapur, *International Nuclear Proliferation*, pp. 234–5; Mugomba, 'The Militarization of the Indian Ocean and the Liberation of Southern Africa', p. 270; Jaster, *South Africa's Narrowing Security Options*, p. 40.
31. *Africa Confidential*, 8 July 1977; 4 August 1978; Betts, 'A Diplomatic Bomb for South Africa?', p. 103; Spence, 'Nuclear Weapons and South Africa', p. 414; Kenneth Adelman, 'The Club of Pariahs', *Africa Report*, November–December 1980, p. 10; Quester, *The Politics of Nuclear Proliferation*, pp. 98, 198.
32. She would have received encouragement in this desire from an article in *Optima* by Jacob Bronowski: J. Bronowski, 'Nuclear Power – A Great Opportunity for Southern Africa', *Optima*, 4 (1954).
33. Stockholm International Peace Research Institute, *World Armaments and Disarmament, SIPRI Yearbook 1979* (London: Taylor & Francis, 1979) p. 321; International Institute for Strategic Studies, *Strategic Survey 1977* (London: IISS, 1978) p. 111; Thomas L. Neff and Henry D. Jacoby, 'Nonproliferation Strategy in a Changing Nuclear Fuel Market', *Foreign Affairs*, 57 (1979) 1136; *The Economist*, 25 February 1977.
34. Robert I. Rotberg and Norma Kriger, 'Uranium and the Nuclear Industry', in Robert I. Rotberg, *Suffer the Future: Policy Choices in Southern Africa* (Cambridge, Mass.: Harvard University Press, 1980) pp. 156–7; *Africa Confidential*, 8 July 1977.
35. Kapur, *International Nuclear Proliferation*, p. 238.
36. See Chapter 5, and Stockholm International Peace Research Institute,

World Armaments and Disarmament, SIPRI Yearbook 1976 (London: The MIT Press, 1976) pp. 389–90; Mugomba, 'The Militarization of the Indian Ocean and the Liberation of Southern Africa', p. 278n; *Africa Confidential*, 4 August 1978; *The Economist*, 6 December 1975, p. 75.

37. See Chapter 5.

38. Quoted in *Africa Confidential*, 8 July 1977.

39. Sverre Lodgaard, 'Prospects for Non-proliferation', *Survival*, 22 (1980) 166.

40. Note for example the Brazilian Navy Minister's reported interest in a supply of South African enriched uranium for nuclear submarines. See: Judith Perera, 'Brazil Struggles with Nuclear Power', *New Scientist*, 17 May 1984, p. 33.

41. Betts, 'A Diplomatic Bomb for South Africa?', p. 103; Warren H. Donnelly and William N. Raiford, *US Foreign Policy Toward South Africa: The Case of Nuclear Cooperation*, Congressional Research Service Report no. 82–24S-F (Washington DC: The Library of Congress, 1981) p. 7; Crocker, *South Africa's Defense Posture*, p. 58.

42. See also: Spence, 'South Africa: The Nuclear Option', p. 443; Cassuto, 'Can Uranium Enrichment Enrich South Africa?', pp. 420, 424, 426.

43. Jaster, *South Africa's Narrowing Security Options*, p. 45; Spence, 'The Republic of South Africa' pp. 229–32; Bustin, 'South Africa's Foreign Policy Alternatives and Deterrence Needs', p. 222.

44. See, for example: Avigdor Haselkorn, 'Israel: From an Option to a Bomb in the Basement?', in Lawrence and Larus (eds), *Nuclear Proliferation PHASE II*, pp. 151, 170, 173; J. Rotblat, 'Nuclear Energy and Nuclear Weapon Proliferation', in Stockholm International Peace Research Institute, *Nuclear Energy and Nuclear Weapons Proliferation*, p. 402.

45. Kapur, *International Nuclear Proliferation*, pp. 253, 258–9; Bustin, 'South Africa's Foreign Policy Alternatives and Deterrence Needs', p. 221; Betts, 'A Diplomatic Bomb for South Africa?', p. 104; Jaster, *South Africa's Narrowing Security Options*, p. 46.

46. *The Times*, 15 August 1980. See also: Betts, 'A Diplomatic Bomb? South Africa's Nuclear Potential', pp. 291, 301; Spence, 'South Africa: The Nuclear Option', pp. 443–4; Bissell, *South Africa and the United States*, pp. 105, 111, 117n; Kapur, *International Nuclear Proliferation*, pp. 262–3; Jaster, 'Politics and the "Afrikaner Bomb"', p. 842.

47. Betts, 'A Diplomatic Bomb? South Africa's Nuclear Potential', pp. 291, 300; Donnelly and Raiford, *US Foreign Policy Toward South Africa*, p. 27; Bissell, *South Africa and the United States*, pp. 104, 110; Stockholm International Peace Research Institute, *World Armaments and Disarmament, SIPRI Yearbook 1978* (London: Taylor & Francis, 1978) p. 73; Crocker, *South Africa's Defense Posture*, pp. 59, 67; Jaster, 'Politics and the "Afrikaner Bomb"', p. 844.

48. Spence, 'Nuclear Weapons and South Africa', pp. 413, 420–1; Kapur, *International Nuclear Proliferation*, p. 122; Betts, 'A Diplomatic Bomb? South Africa's Nuclear Potential', pp. 302–3, 305; Bissell, *South Africa and the United States*, pp. 104–5; Robert E. Harkavy, 'Pariah States and Nuclear Proliferation', *International Organization*, 35 (1981)155.

49. Kapur, *International Nuclear Proliferation*, p. 122. See also: Spence,

'South Africa: The Nuclear Option', p. 450.

50. Spence, *International Problems of Nuclear Proliferation and the South African Position*, p. 9; Jaster, *South Africa's Narrowing Security Options*, p. 45; Crocker, *South Africa's Defense Posture*, p. 67.

51. Bustin, 'South Africa's Foreign Policy Alternatives and Deterrence Needs', pp. 223–4.

52. Kapur, *International Nuclear Proliferation*, p. 238. See also: ibid., pp. 253–4, 361; Crocker, *South Africa's Defense Posture*, p. 61.

53. Cassuto, 'Can Uranium Enrichment Enrich South Africa?', p. 426; Jaster, *South Africa's Narrowing Security Options*, p. 46; Kapur, *International Nuclear Proliferation*, p. 255; Spence, 'South Africa: The Nuclear Option', p. 450.

54. See, for example: Betts, 'A Diplomatic Bomb for South Africa?', p. 91; Jaster, 'Politics and the "Afrikaner Bomb" ', pp. 847–8; Spence, 'South Africa: The Nuclear Option', p. 451.

55. Betts, 'A Diplomatic Bomb for South Africa?', p. 108.

56. Spence, 'South Africa: The Nuclear Option', pp. 447, 451; Betts, 'A Diplomatic Bomb? South Africa's Nuclear Potential', p. 304.

57. Quoted in Červenka and Rogers, *The Nuclear Axis*, pp. 211–12.

58. *Washington Post*, 16 February 1977.

Chapter 9

1. See: Richard K. Betts, 'Preventing the Development of South African Nuclear Weapons', in Joseph A. Yager (ed.), *Nonproliferation and US Foreign Policy* (Washington DC: The Brookings Institution, 1980) p. 401; Robert S. Jaster, 'Politics and the "Afrikaner Bomb" ', *Orbis*, 27 (1984) 850.

2. See also: Robert S. Jaster, *South Africa's Narrowing Security Options*, Adelphi Papers no. 159 (London, International Institute for Strategic Studies, 1980) p. 45.

3. James Dingeman, 'Covert Operations in Central and Southern Africa', in Western Massachusetts Association of Concerned African Scholars (ed.), *US Military Involvement in Southern Africa* (Boston: South End Press, 1978) p. 90.

4. *Daily Telegraph*, 18 March 1981.

5. For suggestions and the reason that the true cause of the 1979 'double flash' over the South Atlantic was covered up by the American government, see: *Science*, 1 February 1980, p. 505; 14 March 1980, p. 1185.

6. George W. Rathjens, Deputy US Representative for Non-proliferation, US Department of State, during the 1976–80 Carter administration: interview with author, 4 September 1981.

7. It may be noted incidentally that South Africa also adopted a very similar dual strategy for her arms needs. Faced with the voluntary ban on arms exports to South Africa imposed by Britain and the United States in 1963–4, South Africa obtained arms from other West European countries, notably France, and then Israel, until the mandatory United Nations arms embargo prohibited all sales in 1977. At the same time

South Africa had built up her own armaments industry so that by the late 1970s she was practically self-sufficient.

8. Kenneth Adelman and Albion Knight, 'Can South Africa go Nuclear?', *Orbis*, 23 (1979) 646; Richard E. Bissell, *South Africa and the United States: The Erosion of an Influence Relationship* (New York: Praeger, 1982) p. 116.

9. Ashok Kapur, *International Nuclear Proliferation: Multilateral Diplomacy and Regional Aspects* (London: Praeger, 1979) pp. 242–3.

10. Ibid., p. 242.

11. Warren H. Donnelly and William N. Raiford, *US Foreign Policy Toward South Africa: The Case of Nuclear Cooperation*, Congressional Research Service Report no. 82–24S-F (Washington DC: The Library of Congress, 1981) pp. 1, 13, 18.

12. See: Avigdor Haselkorn, 'Israel: From an Option to a Bomb in the Basement?', in Robert M. Lawrence and Joel Larus (eds), *Nuclear Proliferation PHASE II* (Lawrence: University Press of Kansas, 1974) p. 155n; J. E. Spence, 'Nuclear Weapons and South Africa – The Incentives and Constraints on Policy', in Timothy M. Shaw and Kenneth A. Heard (eds), *Cooperation and Conflict in Southern Africa: Papers on a Regional Subsystem* (Washington DC: University Press of America, 1976) pp. 413–16; Kapur, *International Nuclear Proliferation*, p. 262.

13. Kapur, *International Nuclear Proliferation*, p. 263.

14. Stockholm International Peace Research Institute, *World Armaments and Disarmament, SIPRI Yearbook 1972* (London: Paul Elek, 1972) p. 317; Colin Legum (ed.), *Africa Contemporary Record*, Annual Survey and Documents, XI, 1978–9 (New York: Africana Publishing Co., 1980) p. B887; Kapur, *International Nuclear Proliferation*, pp. 76, 112, 262, 264.

15. Richard K. Betts, 'A Diplomatic Bomb for South Africa?', *International Security*, 4 (1979) 109–10; George W. Rathjens, Deputy US Representative for Non-proliferation, US Department of State during the 1976–80 Carter administration: interview with author, 4 September 1981.

16. Kapur, *International Nuclear Proliferation*, pp. 263–4; Betts, 'A Diplomatic Bomb for South Africa?', p. 109; Spence, 'Nuclear Weapons and South Africa', pp. 413–14.

17. Joseph L. Nogee, 'Soviet Nuclear Proliferation Policy: Dilemmas and Contradictions', *Orbis*, 24 (1981) 760; Dr Frank Barnaby, 'Nuclear South Africa', *New Scientist*, 19 October 1978, p. 170.

18. On this point, see: Sverre Lodgaard, 'Prospects for Non-proliferation', *Survival*, 22 (1980) 165–6.

19. Spence, 'Nuclear Weapons and South Africa', p. 415.

20. Betts, 'Preventing the Development of South African Nuclear Weapons', p. 399.

21. Lodgaard, 'Prospects for Non-proliferation' pp. 165–6.

22. See also: International Institute for Strategic Studies, *Strategic Survey 1979* (London: IISS, 1980) p. 20; Richard K. Betts, 'Paranoids, Pygmies, Pariahs and Nonproliferation', *Foreign Policy*, no. 26 (1977) 178.

23. For this trend in non-proliferation policy, and South Africa's reaction to the trend, see Chapter 2 and: Kapur, *International Nuclear Proliferation*, p. 358; Joseph A. Yager, 'Influencing Incentives and Capabilities', in

Yager (ed.), *Nonproliferation and US Foreign Policy*, pp. 410–13.

24. Betts, 'Paranoids, Pygmies, Pariahs and Nonproliferation', p. 177.
25. Betts, 'Preventing the Development of South African Nuclear Weapons', pp. 403, 405; Jaster, 'Politics and the "Afrikaner Bomb",' p. 850.
26. Adelman and Knight, 'Can South Africa go Nuclear?', p. 645; Donnelly and Raiford, *US Foreign Policy Toward South Africa*, p. v; Denis Venter, 'South Africa and the International Controversy surrounding its Nuclear Capability', *Politikon*, 5 (1978) 21.
27. Kapur, *International Nuclear Proliferation*, p. 262.
28. For a discussion of the West's dilemma in its nuclear relations with South Africa, see: Betts, 'Preventing the Development of South African Nuclear Weapons', pp. 401, 405–6. See also: Donnelly and Raiford, *US Foreign Policy Toward South Africa*, p. 29.
29. See Chapter 8.
30. Betts, 'Paranoids, Pygmies, Pariahs and Nonproliferation', p. 183.
31. Betts, 'Preventing the Development of South African Nuclear Weapons', p. 406.
32. Spence, 'Nuclear Weapons and South Africa', p. 424.
33. Barry Cohen and Mohamed A. El-Khawas (eds), *The Kissinger Study on Southern Africa* (Nottingham: Spokesman Books, 1975) p. 50.
34. Quoted in Betts, 'A Diplomatic Bomb for South Africa?', p. 113.
35. See Chapter 6 and: Venter, 'South Africa and the International Controversy surrounding its Nuclear Capability', pp. 21, 27.
36. Joseph A. Yager, *International Cooperation in Nuclear Energy* (Washington DC: The Brookings Institution, 1981) p. 113.
37. *Die Beeld*, 24 August 1977, quoted in Jaster, 'Politics and the "Afrikaner Bomb" ', p. 844.
38. Adelman and Knight, 'Can South Africa go Nuclear?', p. 646.

Appendix

1. Technical terms, such as *fissile* and *isotope*, are explained in Chapter 1.
2. See Figure 1.1.
3. Thus, for example, Glackin states that twenty-three processes were discussed in a 1972 report of the US Atomic Energy Commission, 'while others have appeared in unclassified literature in the form of patent abstracts, etc.' (James J. Glackin, 'The Dangerous Drift in Uranium Enrichment', *Bulletin of the Atomic Scientists*, 32 (February 1976) 22). For a brief description of some of the more esoteric techniques, see: Stockholm International Peace Research Institute, *Uranium Enrichment and Nuclear Weapon Proliferation* (London: Taylor & Francis, 1983) p. 187.
4. The high-speed moving parts are either the separation elements themselves, as in the case of the gas-centrifuge, or the compressors used to accelerate or compress the gaseous uranium hexafluoride, as in the case of the diffusion and aerodynamic technologies (see below).
5. Marian Radetzki, *Uranium: A Strategic Source of Energy* (London: Croom Helm, 1981) pp. 49–50, 85–7; P. Jelinek-Fink, 'The Impact of Enrichment Policies on the Uranium Market', in Mining Journal Books

(ed.), *Uranium Supply and Demand*, Proceedings of the Third International Symposium of the Uranium Institute (London: Mining Journal Books, 1978) pp. 49, 51; Jean-Paul Langlois, 'The Uranium Market and its Characteristics', in ibid., pp. 20, 24; The Uranium Institute, *The Uranium Equation: The Balance of Supply and Demand 1980–1995* (London: Mining Journal Books, 1981) pp. 16, 18; International Nuclear Fuel Cycle Evaluation, *Enrichment Availability*, Report of INFCE Working Group 2 (Vienna: IAEA, 1980) pp. 78–9, 82–3; Thomas L. Neff, *The International Uranium Market* (Cambridge, Mass.: Ballinger, 1984) p. 48.

6.　INFCE, *Enrichment Availability*, pp. 73, 78.

7.　J. Rotblat, 'Nuclear Energy and Nuclear Weapon Proliferation', in Stockholm International Peace Research Institute, *Nuclear Energy and Nuclear Weapons Proliferation* (London: Taylor & Francis, 1979) p. 404. Similar values can be computed from Table A.1.

8.　See Chapter 1, Table 1.1.

9.　This account is based on the following sources which provide a valuable critique of IAEA safeguarding arrangements, as they might be applied to enrichment plants: INFCE, *Enrichment Availability*, pp. 128–31, 136–9, 147; SIPRI, *Uranium Enrichment and Nuclear Weapon Proliferation*, pp. 44–52. (See Chapter 2 for a more general account of IAEA safeguards.)

10.　'The Present Status of IAEA Safeguards on Nuclear Fuel Cycle Facilities', *IAEA Bulletin*, 22 (August 1980) 35.

11.　INFCE, *Enrichment Availability*, p. 130. The International Nuclear Fuel Cycle Evaluation programme is discussed in Chapter 2.

12.　SIPRI, *Uranium Enrichment and Nuclear Weapon Proliferation*, p. 43; Sidney Moglewer, 'IAEA Safeguards and Non-proliferation', *Bulletin of the Atomic Scientists*, 37 (October 1981) 27.

13.　See below and Chapter 5 above.

14.　See: *Nucleonics Week*, 24 March 1983.

15　SIPRI, *Uranium Enrichment and Nuclear Weapon Proliferation*, pp. 197–8.

16.　Ibid., p. 214; Neff, *The International Uranium Market*, p. 21.

17.　Central Intelligence Agency, *Nuclear Energy*, ER 77–10468 (Washington DC: CIA, 1977) p. 37. See also: INFCE, *Enrichment Availability*, p. 71; Neff, *The International Uranium Market*, p. 45; Ole Pedersen, 'Developments in the Uranium Enrichment Industry', *IAEA Bulletin*, 19 (February 1977) 50.

18.　SIPRI, *Uranium Enrichment and Nuclear Weapon Proliferation*, p. 201; Neff, *The International Uranium Market*, p. 44; Michael J. Brenner, *Nuclear Power and Non-proliferation: The Remaking of US Policy* (Cambridge University Press, 1981) pp. 24–7, 52–3.

19.　SIPRI, *Uranium Enrichment and Nuclear Weapon Proliferation*, pp. 199–200, 220–1.

20.　For the domestic political background to this decision, see: Brenner, *Nuclear Power and Non-proliferation*, pp. 18–61.

21.　Ibid., pp. 34–9, 46n, 51–7.

22.　Ibid., pp. 107–9; Jelinek-Fink, 'The Impact of Enrichment Policies on the

Uranium Industry', pp. 53, 55; Pedersen, 'Developments in the Uranium Enrichment Industry', pp. 40, 47; Radetzki, *Uranium: A Strategic Source of Energy*, pp. 87–90. Because of doubts in America concerning the competitiveness of her centrifuge technology compared with laser technology discussed below, construction of the first plant at Portsmouth was later abandoned in 1985 (see p. 175 below).

23. Henry D. Jacoby, 'Uranium Dependence and the Proliferation Problem', *Technology Review*, June 1977, p. 21. See also: Brenner, *Nuclear Power and Non-proliferation*, pp. 14–15; Bertrand Goldschmidt, 'A Historical Survey of Nonproliferation Policies', *International Security*, 2 (1977) 208, 216.

24. Brenner, *Nuclear Power and Non-proliferation*, p. 16.

25. For details of Japanese plans to establish an enrichment capacity, see: SIPRI, *Uranium Enrichment and Nuclear Weapon Proliferation*, pp. 225–6; Ichiro Hori, 'Japan's Nuclear Energy Policy and the Problems Involved', in The Uranium Institute, *Uranium and Nuclear Energy: 1980*, Proceedings of the Fifth International Symposium of the Uranium Institute (Guildford: Westbury House, 1981) p. 56; Jean-Pierre Rougeau, 'The Enrichment Industry reaches Maturity', in ibid., p. 184; *The Energy Daily*, 31 August 1984.

26. Pierre Wyart, 'Guidelines for Long-term Natural Uranium Supply Contracts', in The Uranium Institute, *Uranium and Nuclear Energy: 1980*, p. 196; Steven J. Warnecke, *Uranium, Nonproliferation and Energy Security* (Paris: Atlantic Institute for International Affairs, 1979) p. 98.

27. Mason Willrich and Philip M. Marston, 'Prospects for a Uranium Cartel', *Orbis*, 19 (1975) 178, 181. According to Pedersen, in the early 1970s Japan 'explored the possibility of enrichment plants with Australia, Canada, South Africa, URENCO, and the USA' (Pedersen, 'Developments in the Uranium Enrichment Industry', p. 50).

28. INFCE, *Enrichment Availability*, pp. 21, 29, 125–6, 140–1; Rougeau, 'The Enrichment Industry reaches Maturity', pp. 185–7.

29. Thomas L. Neff and Henry D. Jacoby, 'Nonproliferation Strategy in a Changing Nuclear Fuel Market', *Foreign Affairs*, 57 (1979) 1134; Thomas L. Neff and Henry D. Jacoby, 'World Uranium: Softening Markets and Rising Security', *Technology Review*, January 1981, p. 29.

30. SIPRI, *Uranium Enrichment and Nuclear Weapon Proliferation*, pp. 122–4.

31. Ibid., p. 125; *Nuclear Engineering International*, February 1984, p. 8.

32. SIPRI, *Uranium Enrichment and Nuclear Weapon Proliferation*, pp. 127–8.

33. Theoretically, separative work varies with the fourth power of the rotational velocity. So a doubling of speed should increase the separation sixteen times (CIA, *Nuclear Energy*, p. 16).

34. INFCE, *Enrichment Availability*, p. 131.

35. The description of aerodynamic processes in this section is based on: Manson Benedict, Thomas H. Pigford and Hans Wolfgang-Levi, *Nuclear Chemical Engineering* (New York: McGraw Hill, 1981) pp. 634–5, 876, 888–95. According to a letter to *Science*, 25 July 1975, earlier work on

nozzle enrichment had been done in Britain and the United States during the Second World War.

36. Glackin, 'The Dangerous Drift in Uranium Enrichment', pp. 27–8.

37. See: Ted Greenwood, George W. Rathjens and Jack Ruina, *Nuclear Power and Weapons Proliferation*, Adelphi Papers no. 130 (London: International Institute for Strategic Studies, 1976) pp. 23, 25, 27; *Science*, 30 May 1975.

38. SIPRI, *Uranium Enrichment and Nuclear Weapon Proliferation*, pp. 142–3; *Nuclear Engineering International*, November 1983, pp. 33–4; David J. Myers, 'Brazil: Reluctant Pursuit of the Nuclear Option,' *Orbis*, 27 (1984) 892.

39. Stockholm International Peace Research Institute, *World Armaments and Disarmament, SIPRI Yearbook 1978* (London: Taylor & Francis, 1978) pp. 72–3; SIPRI, *Uranium Enrichment and Nuclear Weapon Proliferation*, p. 143.

40. Benedict *et al.*, *Nuclear Chemical Engineering*, p. 876. See also ibid., p. 889.

41. Ibid., pp. 888–9, 893–5. See also SIPRI, *Uranium Enrichment and Nuclear Weapon Proliferation*, pp. 143–4; INFCE, *Enrichment Availability*, p. 43.

42. Pedersen, 'Developments in the Uranium Enrichment Industry', p. 42; Greenwood *et al.*, *Nuclear Power and Weapons Proliferation*, p. 27.

43. INFCE, *Enrichment Availability*, p. 24; Glackin, 'The Dangerous Drift in Uranium Enrichment', p. 23.

44. Greenwood *et al.*, *Nuclear Power and Weapons Proliferation*, p. 22.

45. SIPRI, *Uranium Enrichment and Nuclear Weapon Proliferation*, pp. 14, 22, 178–9.

46. Ibid., pp. 146–57; INFCE, *Enrichment Availability*, pp. 73, 145.

47. William C. Potter, *Nuclear Power and Nonproliferation: An Interdisciplinary Perspective* (Cambridge, Mass.: Oelgeschlager, Gunn & Hain, 1982) pp. 73–4; SIPRI, *Uranium Enrichment and Nuclear Weapon Proliferation*, pp. 21, 173, 207; *New Scientist*, 27 May 1982, p. 554.

48. See: Allen Krass, 'Laser Enrichment of Plutonium', in Stockholm International Peace Research Institute, *World Armaments and Disarmament, SIPRI Yearbook 1982* (London: Taylor & Francis, 1982) pp. 281–9; SIPRI, *Uranium Enrichment and Nuclear Weapon Proliferation*, p. 173; George Palmer and Dan I. Bolef, 'Laser Isotope Separation: the Plutonium Connection', *Bulletin of the Atomic Scientists*, 40 (March 1984) 26–31.

49. Benedict *et al.*, *Nuclear Chemical Engineering*, pp. 635, 817; *New Scientist*, 6 August 1981, p. 328; 27 May 1982, p. 554; *Science*, 22 March 1974, pp. 1172–4; 21 May 1982, p. 830; 21 June 1985, pp. 1407–9; *Nuclear Fuel*, 19 December 1983; 27 February 1984; 12 March 1984; 17 June 1985; 9 September 1985.

Bibliography

Adams, James, *The Unnatural Alliance* (London: Quartet Books, 1984)

Adekanye, J'Bayo, 'Nigeria's Investment in Nuclear Power: A Research Note', *Arms Control*, 4 (May 1983)

Adelman, Kenneth L., 'The Strategy of Defiance: South Africa', *Comparative Strategy*, 1 (1978)

Adelman, Kenneth, 'The Club of Pariahs', *Africa Report*, 25 (November–December 1980)

Adelman, Kenneth and Knight, Albion, 'Can South Africa go Nuclear?', *Orbis*, 23 (Fall 1979)

Adeniran, Tunde, 'Nuclear Proliferation and Black Africa: The Coming Crisis of Choice', *Third World Quarterly*, 3 (October 1981)

Adeniran, Tunde, 'Black Africa Reacts', *Bulletin of the Atomic Scientists*, 38 (August/September 1982)

African National Congress of South Africa, *The Nuclear Conspiracy: FRG Collaborates to Strengthen Apartheid* (Bonn: ANC, 1975)

African National Congress of South Africa, *Conspiracy to Arm Apartheid Continues: FRG–SA Collaboration* (Bonn: ANC, 1977)

Anti-Apartheid Movement (AAB) in the Federal Republic of Germany and West Berlin, *Reply: Answer to a Denial of the Government of the Federal Republic of Germany concerning the Military–Nuclear Collaboration between the Federal Republic of Germany and South Africa* (Bonn: AAB, 1979)

Barnaby, Dr Frank, 'Nuclear South Africa', *New Scientist*, 80 (19 October 1978)

Barrett, John (ed.), *South Africa and the Future of World Energy Resources* (Braamfontein: South African Institute of International Affairs, 1975)

Beaton, Leonard and Maddox, John, *The Spread of Nuclear Weapons* (London: Chatto & Windus, 1962)

Bechhoefer, Bernhard, G., 'Negotiating the Statute of the International Atomic Energy Agency', *International Organization*, 13 (Winter 1959)

Benedict, Manson, Pigford, Thomas H. and Wolfgang-Levi, Hans, *Nuclear Chemical Engineering* (New York: McGraw-Hill, 1981)

Berridge, Geoff, *Economic Power in Anglo-South African Diplomacy: Simonstown, Sharpeville and After* (London: Macmillan, 1981)

Betts, Richard, K., 'Paranoids, Pygmies, Pariahs and Nonproliferation', *Foreign Policy*, no. 26 (Spring 1977)

Betts, Richard, K., 'A Diplomatic Bomb for South Africa?', *International Security*, 4 (Fall 1979)

Betts, Richard K., 'A Diplomatic Bomb? South Africa's Nuclear Potential', in Joseph A. Yager (ed.), *Nonproliferation and US Foreign Policy* (Washington DC: The Brookings Institution, 1980)

Betts, Richard K., 'Preventing the Development of South African Nuclear Weapons', in Joseph A. Yager (ed.), *Nonproliferation and US Foreign Policy* (Washington DC: The Brookings Institution, 1980)

Bissell, Richard E., *South Africa and the United States: The Erosion of an Influence Relationship* (New York: Praeger, 1982)

Bissell, Richard E. and Crocker, Chester A. (eds), *South Africa into the 1980s* (Boulder: Westview Press, 1979)

Boardman, Robert and Keeley, James E. (eds), *Nuclear Exports and World Politics* (New York: St Martin's Press, 1983)

Boskma, P., 'Jet Nozzle and Vortex Tube Enrichment Technologies', in Stockholm International Peace Research Institute, *Nuclear Energy and Nuclear Weapons Proliferation* (London: Taylor & Francis, 1979)

Bowman, Larry W., 'The Strategic Importance of South Africa to the United States: An Appraisal and Policy Analysis', *African Affairs*, 81 (April 1982)

Brenner, Michael, J., *Nuclear Power and Non-proliferation: The Remaking of US Policy* (Cambridge University Press, 1981)

Brito, Dagobert L., Intriligator, Michael D. and Wick, Adele E. (eds), *Strategies for Managing Nuclear Proliferation* (Lexington, Mass.: D. C. Heath & Co., 1983)

Bronowski, J., 'Nuclear Power – A Great Opportunity for Southern Africa', *Optima*, 4 (December 1954)

Bunce, Peter L., 'The Growth of South Africa's Defence Industry and its Israeli Connection', *Journal of the Royal United Services Institute for Defence Studies*, 129 (June 1984)

Bustin, Edouard, 'South Africa's Foreign Policy Alternatives and Deterrence Needs', in Onkar Marwah and Ann Schulz (eds), *Nuclear Proliferation and the Near-Nuclear Countries* (Cambridge, Mass.: Ballinger, 1975)

Cassuto, Aldo, 'Can Uranium Enrichment Enrich South Africa?', *The World Today*, 26 (October 1970)

Central Intelligence Agency, *Nuclear Energy*, ER 77-10468 (Washington DC: CIA, 1977)

Červenka, Zdenek and Rogers, Barbara, *The Nuclear Axis: Secret Collaboration between West Germany and South Africa* (London: Julian Friedmann, 1978)

Chari, P. R, 'South Africa's Nuclear Option', *India International Centre Quarterly*, 3 (1976)

Christie, Renfrew, *Electricity, Industry and Class in South Africa* (London: Macmillan, 1984)

Cohen, Barry and El-Khawas, Mohamed A. (eds), *The Kissinger Study on Southern Africa* (Nottingham: Spokesman Books, 1975)

Coker, Christopher, 'South Africa and the Western Alliance 1949-81: A History of Illusions', *Journal of the Royal United Services Institute for Defence Studies*, 127 (June 1982)

Commission to Study the Organization of Peace, *Organizing Peace in the Nuclear Age* (New York University Press, 1959)

Crocker, Chester A., 'Current and Projected Military Balances in Southern Africa', in Richard E. Bissell and Chester A. Crocker (eds), *South Africa into the 1980s* (Boulder: Westview Press, 1979)

Crocker, Chester A., *South Africa's Defense Posture: Coping with Vulnerability*, The Washington Papers, vol. 9, no. 8 (Beverly Hills: Sage Publications, 1981)

de St Jorre, John, *A House Divided: South Africa's Uncertain Future* (Washington DC: Carnegie Endowment for International Peace, 1977)

de Villiers, J. W. L., 'The Future of Nuclear Energy: South Africa in Relation to World Developments', in John Barrett (ed.), *South Africa and the Future of World Energy Resources* (Braamfontein: South African Institute of

International Affairs, 1975)

Dingeman, James, 'Covert Operations in Central and Southern Africa', in Western Massachusetts Association of Concerned African Scholars (ed.), *US Military Involvement in Southern Africa* (Boston: South End Press, 1978)

Donnelly, Warren H. and Raiford, William N., *US Foreign Policy Toward South Africa: The Case of Nuclear Cooperation*, Congressional Research Service Report no. 82–24S–F (Washington DC: The Library of Congress, 1981)

Dunn, Lewis A., 'Nuclear "Gray Marketeering"', *International Security*, 1 (Winter 1977)

Dunn, Lewis, A., 'Half past India's Bang', *Foreign Policy*, no. 36 (Fall 1979)

Dunn, Lewis A., *Controlling the Bomb: Nuclear Proliferation in the 1980s* (New Haven: Yale University Press, 1982)

Epstein, William, *The Last Chance: Nuclear Proliferation and Arms Control* (New York: Macmillan, 1976)

European Nuclear Energy Agency and International Atomic Energy Agency, *Uranium Production and Short Term Demand* (Paris: OECD, 1969)

Fact v. Fiction: Rebuttal of the Charges of Alleged Cooperation between the Federal Republic of Germany and South Africa in the Nuclear and Military Fields (Bonn: Press and Information Office of the Government of the Federal Republic of Germany, 1978)

Farinelli, U., 'A Preliminary Evaluation of the Technical Aspects of INFCE', in Stockholm International Peace Research Institute, *Nuclear Energy and Nuclear Weapons Proliferation* (London: Taylor & Francis, 1979)

Fischer, David, *International Safeguards 1979* (London: International Consultative Group on Nuclear Energy (Rockefeller Foundation/Royal Institute of International Affairs), 1979)

Fischer, David, *The Spread of Nuclear Weapons: Western Europe's Influence on South Africa*, CEPS Working Document no. 6 (Brussels: Centre for European Policy Studies, 1985)

Gann, L. H. and Duignan, Peter, *South Africa: War, Revolution, or Peace?* (Stanford: Hoover Institution Press, 1978)

Gillette, Robert, 'Uranium Enrichment: With Help, South Africa is Progressing', *Science*, 188 (13 June 1975)

Glackin, James J., 'The Dangerous Drift in Uranium Enrichment', *Bulletin of the Atomic Scientists*, 32 (February 1976)

Goldblat, J., 'Implementation of the Non-Proliferation Treaty', in Stockholm International Peace Research Institute, *Nuclear Energy and Nuclear Weapons Proliferation* (London: Taylor & Francis, 1979)

Goldblat, Jozef and Millan, Victor, 'Militarization and Arms Control in Latin America', in Stockholm International Peace Research Institute, *World Armaments and Disarmament, SIPRI Yearbook 1982* (London: Taylor & Francis, 1982)

Goldschmidt, Bertrand, 'A Historical Survey of Nonproliferation Policies', *International Security*, 2 (Summer 1977)

Goldschmidt, Bertrand, 'The Origins of the International Atomic Energy Agency', *IAEA Bulletin*, 19 (August 1977)

Goldschmidt, Bertrand, *The Atomic Complex: A Worldwide Political History of Nuclear Energy* (La Grange Park, Illinois: American Nuclear Society, 1982)

Gowing, Margaret, *Britain and Atomic Energy, 1939–1945* (London:

Macmillan, 1964)

Gowing, Margaret, *Independence and Deterrence: Britain and Atomic Energy, 1945–1952*, vol. 1, 'Policy-making' (London: Macmillan, 1974)

Graham, Thomas W., 'The Economics of Producing Nuclear Weapons in "Nth" Countries', in Dagobert L. Brito, Michael D. Intriligator and Adele E. Wick (eds), *Strategies for Managing Nuclear Proliferation* (Lexington, Mass.: D. C. Heath & Co., 1983)

Greenberg, D.S., 'South Africa: Booming Nation's Research and Industry Benefit from Close Ties with the United States', *Science*, 169 (10 July 1970)

Greenwood, Ted, Rathjens, George W. and Ruina, Jack, *Nuclear Power and Weapons Proliferation*, Adelphi Papers no. 130 (London: International Institute for Strategic Studies, 1976)

Gutteridge, William, *South Africa: Strategy for Survival?*, Conflict Studies no. 131 (London: Institute for the Study of Conflict, 1981)

Hammond, Allen L., 'Uranium: Will There Be a Shortage or an Embarrassment of Enrichment?', *Science*, 192 (28 May 1976)

Harkavy, Robert E., 'Pariah States and Nuclear Proliferation', *International Organization*, 35 (Winter 1981)

Haselkorn, Avigdor, 'Israel: From an Option to a Bomb in the Basement?' in Robert M. Lawrence and Joel Larus (eds), *Nuclear Proliferation PHASE II* (Lawrence: University Press of Kansas, 1974)

Henderson, Robert D'A., 'Nigeria: Future Nuclear Power?', *Orbis*, 25 (Summer 1981)

Herron, L. W., 'A Lawyer's View of Safeguards and Non-proliferation', *IAEA Bulletin*, 24 (September 1982)

Hopkins, J. C., 'Nuclear Weapon Technology', in Stockholm International Peace Research Institute, *Nuclear Proliferation Problems* (Cambridge, Mass.: The MIT Press, 1974)

Hori, Ichiro, 'Japan's Nuclear Energy Policy and the Problems Involved', in The Uranium Institute, *Uranium and Nuclear Energy: 1980* (Guildford: Westbury House, 1981)

International Institute for Strategic Studies, *The Military Balance 1985–1986* (London: IISS, 1985)

International Institute for Strategic Studies, *Strategic Survey 1974* to *Strategic Survey 1984–1985* inclusive (London: IISS, 1975 to 1985 inclusive)

International Nuclear Fuel Cycle Evaluation, *INFCE Summary Volume* (Vienna: IAEA, 1980)

International Nuclear Fuel Cycle Evaluation, *Enrichment Availability*, Report of INFCE Working Group 2 (Vienna: IAEA, 1980)

Jacoby, Henry D., 'Uranium Dependence and the Proliferation Problem', *Technology Review*, 80 (June 1977)

Jaster, Robert S., *South Africa's Narrowing Security Options*, Adelphi Papers no. 159 (London: International Institute for Strategic Studies, 1980)

Jaster, Robert S., 'Politics and the "Afrikaner Bomb"', *Orbis*, 27 (Winter 1984)

Jaster, Robert S., 'South Africa', in Jed C. Snyder and Samuel F. Wells, Jr (eds), *Limiting Nuclear Proliferation* (Cambridge, Mass.: Ballinger, 1985)

Jelinek-Fink, P., 'The Impact of Enrichment Policies on the Uranium Market', in Mining Journal Books Ltd (ed.), *Uranium Supply and Demand* (London: Mining Journal Books, 1978)

Kapur, Ashok, *International Nuclear Proliferation: Multilateral Diplomacy and Regional Aspects* (London: Praeger, 1979)

King, John Kerry (ed.), *International Political Effects of the Spread of Nuclear Weapons* (Washington DC: US Government Printing Office, 1979)

Kramish, Arnold, 'Nuclear Flashes in the Night', *The Washington Quarterly*, 3 (Summer 1980)

Kramish, Arnold, 'Four Decades of Living with the Genie: United States Nuclear Export Policy', in Robert Boardman and James F. Keeley (eds), *Nuclear Exports and World Politics* (New York: St Martin's Press, 1983)

Krass, Allen, 'Laser Enrichment of Plutonium', in Stockholm International Peace Research Institute, *World Armaments and Disarmament, SIPRI Yearbook 1982* (London: Taylor & Francis, 1982)

Krugmann, Hartmut, 'The German–Brazilian Nuclear Deal', *Bulletin of the Atomic Scientists*, 37 (February 1981)

Langlois, Jean-Paul, 'The Uranium Market and its Characteristics', in Mining Journal Books Ltd (ed.), *Uranium Supply and Demand* (London: Mining Journal Books, 1978)

Lawrence, Robert M. and Larus, Joel (eds), *Nuclear Proliferation PHASE II* (Lawrence: University Press of Kansas, 1974)

Legum, Colin (ed.), *Africa Contemporary Record*, Annual Survey and Documents, X to XVI, 1977–8 to 1983–4 inclusive (London and New York: Africana Publishing Co., 1979 to 1985 inclusive)

Lodgaard, Sverre, 'Nuclear Power and Nuclear Proliferation: Export Policies and Proliferation Resistance', in Stockholm International Peace Research Institute, *World Armaments and Disarmament, SIPRI Yearbook 1979* (London: Taylor & Francis, 1979)

Lodgaard, Sverre, 'Prospects for Non-proliferation', *Survival*, 22 (July/August 1980)

Maddox, John, *Prospects for Nuclear Proliferation*, Adelphi Papers no. 113 (London: International Institute for Strategic Studies, 1975)

Marwah, Onkar and Schulz, Ann (eds), *Nuclear Proliferation and the Near-Nuclear Countries* (Cambridge, Mass.: Ballinger, 1975)

Mazrui, Ali, 'Africa's Nuclear Future', *Survival*, 22 (March/April 1980)

Meyer, Stephen M., *The Dynamics of Nuclear Proliferation* (University of Chicago Press, 1984)

Mining Journal Books Ltd (ed.), *Uranium Supply and Demand*, Proceedings of the Third International Symposium of the Uranium Institute (London: Mining Journal Books, 1978)

Moglewer, Sidney, 'IAEA Safeguards and Non-proliferation', *Bulletin of the Atomic Scientists*, 37 (October 1981)

Mohan, C. Raja, 'Atomic Teeth to Apartheid: South Africa and Nuclear Weapons', in K. Subrahmanyam (ed.), *Nuclear Myths and Realities: India's Dilemma* (New Delhi: ABC Publishing House, 1981)

Mugomba, Agrippah T., 'The Militarization of the Indian Ocean and the Liberation of Southern Africa', *Journal of Southern African Affairs*, 4 (July 1979)

Muller, Mike, 'The Enriching Politics of South Africa's Uranium', *New Scientist*, 62 (2 May 1974)

Myers, David, J., 'Brazil: Reluctant Pursuit of the Nuclear Option', *Orbis*, 27 (Winter 1984)

Neff, Thomas L., *The International Uranium Market* (Cambridge, Mass.: Ballinger, 1984)

Neff, Thomas L. and Jacoby, Henry D., 'Nonproliferation Strategy in a Changing Nuclear Fuel Market', *Foreign Affairs*, 57 (Summer 1979)

Neff, Thomas L. and Jacoby, Henry D., 'World Uranium: Softening Markets and Rising Security', *Technology Review*, 83 (January 1981)

Newby-Fraser, A. R., *Chain Reaction: Twenty Years of Nuclear Research and Development in South Africa* (Pretoria: Atomic Energy Board, 1979)

Nieburg, H. L., *Nuclear Secrecy and Foreign Policy* (Washington DC: Public Affairs Press, 1964)

Nogee, Joseph L., 'Soviet Nuclear Proliferation Policy: Dilemmas and Contradictions', *Orbis*, 24 (Winter 1981)

OECD Nuclear Energy Agency and IAEA, *Uranium Resources, Production and Demand* (Paris: OECD, 1973, 1979, 1982, 1983)

Ogunbadejo, Oye, 'Africa's Nuclear Capability', *The Journal of Modern African Studies*, 22 (March 1984)

Ogunbadejo, Oye, 'Nuclear Capability and Nigeria's Foreign Policy', in Colin Legum (ed.), *Africa Contemporary Record*, Annual Survey and Documents, XVI, 1983–4 (New York: Africana Publishing Co., 1985)

Okolo, Julius Emeka, 'Nuclearization of Nigeria', *Comparative Strategy*, 5 (1985)

Palmer, George and Bolef, Dan I., 'Laser Isotope Separation: the Plutonium Connection', *Bulletin of the Atomic Scientists*, 40 (March 1984)

Pedersen, Ole, 'Developments in the Uranium Enrichment Industry', *IAEA Bulletin*, 19 (February 1977)

Perera, Judith, 'Argentina's Nuclear Red Herring', *New Scientist*, 100 (8 December 1983)

Perera, Judith, 'Brazil Struggles with Nuclear Power,' *New Scientist*, 102 (17 May 1984)

Perry, William and Kern, Sheila, 'The Brazilian Nuclear Program in A Foreign Policy Context', *Comparative Strategy*, 1 (1978)

Poneman, Daniel, 'Nuclear Proliferation Prospects for Argentina', *Orbis*, 27 (Winter 1984)

Potter, William C., *Nuclear Power and Nonproliferation: An Interdisciplinary Perspective* (Cambridge, Mass.: Oelgeschlager, Gunn and Hain, 1982)

Price, Robert M., 'Pretoria's Southern African Strategy', *African Affairs*, 83 (January 1984)

Pringle, Peter and Spigelman, James, *The Nuclear Barons* (New York: Holt, Rinehart & Winston, 1981)

Quester, George H., 'The Politics of Twenty Nuclear Powers', in Richard Rosecrance (ed.), *The Future of the International Strategic System* (San Francisco: Chandler, 1972)

Quester, George, *The Politics of Nuclear Proliferation* (Baltimore, Md.: Johns Hopkins University Press, 1973)

Radetzki, Marian, *Uranium: A Strategic Source of Energy* (London: Croom Helm, 1981)

Raiford, William N., *The European Role in Africa and US Interests*, Congressional Research Service Report no. 81–202F (Washington DC: The Library of Congress, 1981)

Rochlin, Gene I., 'The Development and Deployment of Nuclear Weapons

Systems in a Proliferating World', in John Kerry King (ed.), *International Political Effects of the Spread of Nuclear Weapons* (Washington DC: US Government Printing Office, 1979)

Rogers, Barbara, 'The Nuclear Threat from South Africa', *Africa*, no. 113 (January 1981)

Rosecrance, Richard (ed.), *The Future of the International Strategic System* (San Francisco: Chandler, 1972)

Rotberg, Robert I., *Suffer the Future: Policy Choices in Southern Africa* (Cambridge, Mass.: Harvard University Press, 1980)

Rotberg, Robert I. and Kriger, Norma, 'Uranium and the Nuclear Industry', in Robert I. Rotberg, *Suffer the Future: Policy Choices in Southern Africa* (Cambridge, Mass.: Harvard University Press, 1980)

Rotblat, J., 'Nuclear Energy and Nuclear Weapon Proliferation', in Stockholm International Peace Research Institute, *Nuclear Energy and Nuclear Weapons Proliferation* (London: Taylor & Francis, 1979)

Rougeau, Jean-Pierre, 'The Enrichment Industry Reaches Maturity', in The Uranium Institute, *Uranium and Nuclear Energy: 1980* (Guildford: Westbury House, 1981)

Roux, Dr A. J. A., 'South Africa's Position in the World Nuclear Energy Picture', paper presented at the Sectoral Industrial Congress of the Afrikaanse Handelsinstituut, Johannesburg on 1 May 1973, and reprinted in Ashok Kapur, *International Nuclear Proliferation: Multilateral Diplomacy and Regional Aspects* (London: Praeger, 1979)

Sanders, B., 'Nuclear Exporting Policies', in Stockholm International Peace Research Institute, *Nuclear Energy and Nuclear Weapons Proliferation* (London: Taylor & Francis, 1979)

Shaw, Timothy M. and Heard, Kenneth A. (eds), *Cooperation and Conflict in Southern Africa: Papers on a Regional Subsystem* (Washington DC: University Press of America, 1976)

Smith, Dan, *South Africa's Nuclear Capability* (London: World Campaign against Military and Nuclear Collaboration with South Africa, 1980)

Smith, Gerard and Rathjens, George, 'Reassessing Nuclear Nonproliferation Policy', *Foreign Affairs*, 59 (Spring 1981)

Snyder, Jed C. and Wells, Samuel F., Jr. (eds), *Limiting Nuclear Proliferation* (Cambridge, Mass.: Ballinger, 1985)

Spector, Leonard S., *Nuclear Proliferation Today* (Cambridge, Mass.: Ballinger, for the Carnegie Endowment for International Peace, 1984).

Spence, J. E., 'The Republic of South Africa: Proliferation and the Politics of "Outward Movement" ', in Robert M. Lawrence and Joel Larus (eds), *Nuclear Proliferation PHASE II* (Lawrence: University Press of Kansas, 1974)

Spence J. E., 'Nuclear Weapons and the Obstacles to World Order', *Optima*, 24 (1974)

Spence, J. E., 'South Africa's Nuclear Potential', in J. E. Spence, *The Political and Military Framework*, Study Project on External Investment in South Africa and Namibia (SW Africa) (London: Africa Publications Trust, 1975)

Spence, J. E., 'Nuclear Weapons and South Africa – The Incentives and Constraints on Policy', in Timothy M. Shaw and Kenneth A. Heard (eds), *Cooperation and Conflict in Southern Africa: Papers on a Regional Subsystem* (Washington DC: University Press of America, 1976)

Spence, J. E., *International Problems of Nuclear Proliferation and the South African Position*, SAIIA Occasional Paper (Braamfontein: South African Institute of International Affairs, 1980)

Spence, J. E., 'South Africa: The Nuclear Option', *African Affairs*, 80 (October 1981)

Stauffer, Nancy, 'Uranium Exporters: Who They Are and How They Work', *Technology Review*, 83 (January 1981)

Stephany, Manfred, 'Influence of Stockpiles on the Market for Natural Uranium', in The Uranium Institute, *Uranium and Nuclear Energy: 1981* (London: Butterworth, 1982)

Stockholm International Peace Research Institute, *World Armaments and Disarmament, SIPRI Yearbook 1972* (London: Paul Elek, 1972)

Stockholm International Peace Research Institute, *World Armaments and Disarmament, SIPRI Yearbook 1976* (London: The MIT Press, 1976)

Stockholm International Peace Research Institute, *World Armaments and Disarmament, SIPRI Yearbook 1977* (Cambridge, Mass.: The MIT Press, 1977)

Stockholm International Peace Research Institute, *World Armaments and Disarmament, SIPRI Yearbook 1978* to *SIPRI Yearbook 1985* inclusive (London: Taylor & Francis, 1978 to 1985 inclusive)

Stockholm International Peace Research Institute, *Nuclear Proliferation Problems* (Cambridge, Mass.: The MIT Press, 1974)

Stockholm International Peace Research Institute, *Southern Africa: The Escalation of a Conflict* (New York: Praeger, 1976)

Stockholm International Peace Research Institute, *Nuclear Energy and Nuclear Weapons Proliferation* (London: Taylor & Francis, 1979)

Stockholm International Peace Research Institute, *Uranium Enrichment and Nuclear Weapon Proliferation* (London: Taylor & Francis, 1983)

Stoessinger, John G., 'Atoms for Peace: The International Atomic Energy Agency', in Commission to Study the Organization of Peace, *Organizing Peace in the Nuclear Age* (New York University Press, 1959)

Subrahmanyam, K., 'The Nuclear Issue and International Security', *Bulletin of the Atomic Scientists*, 33 (February 1977)

Subrahmanyam, K. (ed.), *Nuclear Myths and Realities: India's Dilemma* (New Delhi: ABC Publishing House, 1981)

Taylor, June H. and Yokell, Michael D., *Yellowcake: The International Uranium Cartel* (Pergamon: New York, 1979)

UN Centre for Disarmament, Department of Political and Security Council Affairs, *South Africa's Plan and Capability in the Nuclear Field*, Report of the Secretary-General, Document A/35/402 (New York: United Nations, 1981)

Uranium Institute, The, *Uranium and Nuclear Energy: 1980*, Proceedings of the Fifth International Symposium of the Uranium Institute (Guildford: Westbury House, 1981)

Uranium Institute, The, *The Uranium Equation: The Balance of Supply and Demand 1980–1995* (London: Mining Journal Books, 1981)

Uranium Institute, The, *Uranium and Nuclear Energy: 1981*, Proceedings of the Sixth International Symposium of the Uranium Institute (London: Butterworth, 1982)

Uranium Institute, The, *Uranium Supply and Demand: Perspectives to 1995* (London: The Uranium Institute, 1984)

US Bureau of Mines, *The Mineral Industry of the Republic of South Africa*, preprint from the 1977 Bureau of Mines Minerals Yearbook (Washington DC: US Government Printing Office, 1981)

US Congress, House, Committee on International Relations, Subcommittee on International Resources, Food and Energy, *Resource Development in South Africa and US policy*, Hearings, 94th Congress (Washington DC: US Government Printing Office, 1976)

US Congress, House, Committee on International Relations, Subcommittee on Africa, *United States–South Africa Relations: Nuclear Cooperation*, Hearings, 95th Congress (Washington DC: US Government Printing Office, 1977)

Venter, Denis, 'South Africa and the International Controversy surrounding its Nuclear Capability', *Politikon*, 5 (June 1978)

von Kienlin, Dr A., 'Commercial Effects of Current Non-proliferation Policies', in Mining Journal Books Ltd (ed.), *Uranium Supply and Demand* (London: Mining Journal Books, 1978)

Walker, William and Lönnroth, Måns, *Nuclear Power Struggles: Industrial Competition and Proliferation Control* (London: George Allen & Unwin, 1983)

Walters, Ronald W., 'US Policy and Nuclear Proliferation in South Africa', in Western Massachusetts Association of Concerned African Scholars (ed.), *US Military Involvement in Southern Africa* (Boston: South End Press, 1978)

Waltz, Kenneth N., *The Spread of Nuclear Weapons: More May Be Better*, Adelphi Papers no. 171 (London: International Institute for Strategic Studies, 1981)

Warnecke, Steven J., *Uranium, Nonproliferation and Energy Security*, Atlantic Paper no. 37 (Paris: Atlantic Institute for International Affairs, 1979)

Western Massachusetts Association of Concerned African Scholars (ed.), *US Military Involvement in Southern Africa* (Boston: South End Press, 1978)

Wick, Dr Gerald, 'New Vistas for Isotope Separation', *New Scientist*, 51 (23 September 1971)

Willrich, Mason, 'A Workable International Nuclear Energy Regime', *The Washington Quarterly*, 2 (Spring 1979)

Willrich, Mason and Marston, Philip M., 'Prospects for a Uranium Cartel', *Orbis*, 19 (Spring 1975)

Wohlstetter, Albert, Brown, Thomas, Jones, Gregory, McGarvey, David, Rowan, Henry, Taylor, Vincent and Wohlstetter, Roberta, *Moving Towards Life in a Nuclear Armed Crowd?*, Final Report, ACDA/PAB–263 (Los Angeles: Pan Heuristics, 1976)

Wohlstetter, Albert, Brown, Thomas, Jones, Gregory, McGarvey, David, Rowan, Henry, Taylor, Vincent and Wohlstetter, Roberta, 'The Military Potential of Civilian Nuclear Energy: Moving Towards Life in a Nuclear Armed Crowd', *Minerva*, 15 (Autumn–Winter 1977)

World Campaign against Military and Nuclear Collaboration with South Africa (ed.), *Nuclear Collaboration with South Africa*, Report of a seminar organised by the United Nations Special Committee against Apartheid (London: World Campaign against Military and Nuclear Collaboration with South Africa, 1979)

Wyart, Pierre, 'Guidelines for Long-term Natural Uranium Supply Contracts', in The Uranium Institute, *Uranium and Nuclear Energy: 1980* (Guildford: Westbury House, 1981)

Yager, Joseph A. (ed.), *Nonproliferation and US Foreign Policy* (Washington DC: The Brookings Institution, 1980)

Yager, Joseph A., 'Influencing Incentives and Capabilities', in Joseph A. Yager (ed.), *Nonproliferation and US Foreign Policy* (Washington DC: The Brookings Institution, 1980)

Yager, Joseph A., *International Cooperation in Nuclear Energy* (Washington DC: The Brookings Institution, 1981)

Index

vortex tube enrichment, 27; *see also*
helikon enrichment technique

waste disposal, 4, 29, 31, 37, 96; *see
also* radioactive waste
weapons-grade material, 3–5, 7, 21,
25, 28, 45, 83, 99, 105, 120–2,
143, 148, 157, 160–1, 173, 174–
5; *see also* fissile material, high-
enriched uranium, plutonium-
239
weapons-testing, 7–8, 41, 114, 116–
17, 123–4; *see also* atmospheric
testing, peaceful nuclear
explosion
West Germany
imports of uranium from Namibia,
80
imports of uranium from South
Africa, 76, 89, 94, 136
nuclear relations with South
Africa, xvi, 87–90, 103, 113,

125, 136–7, 144, 146–7, 190n,
195n
Western Suppliers Group (policy), 12,
16–18, 20, 26, 28, 34, 77–8, 105,
108, 110
Westinghouse corporation, 75–6
white population of South Africa,
xiv–xv, 47, 50, 52, 56–7, 60–1,
64–6, 69, 98, 114, 129, 130–1,
140, 149, 200n; *see also* Afrikaner
population of South Africa

yellowcake, *see under* uranium
concentrate
Young, Andrew, 155

Zaire, 46, 59, 127; *see also* Belgian
Congo
Zambia, 48, 51, 58–9, 127
Zangger Committee, 27, 180n
Zimbabwe, 48, 49, 52, 55, 58–9, 127;
see also Rhodesia